I am me
I am free

The Robots' Guide to Freedom

First published in November 1996 by
Bridge of Love Publications
Papworth Press, Papworth Everard,
Cambridge CB3 8RG, England

Printed in the USA by
Truth Seeker Co., Inc.
P.O. Box 28550
San Diego, CA 92198

Updated and reprinted, June 1997
Printed in the USA, September 1997
Updated and reprinted in the USA, February 1998

Cover photograph by James Cumpsty
Cover illustration by Neil Hague

Text set in Bembo 10 ½ on 12 ½

Printed and bound by
KNI, Anaheim, CA

**British Library Cataloguing-in
Publication Data**
A catalogue record for this book is
available from the British Library

ISBN 0 9526147 5 8

I am me
I am free
The Robots' Guide to Freedom

David Icke

**Bridge
of Love**

Dedication

To all those who have caused me hassle and pain.
Thank you for your gifts of experience,
learning and evolution.

To Linda. An amazing soul and a wonderful friend.
Thanks for everything.

Thank you to:

Sam Masters for her production work on this book;
Neil Hague for his artistic inspiration;
Jean Credland for her proof reading.

Other books, tapes and videos by David Icke

Further publishing and availability details at the back of the book.

A little wisdom...

Your religious calling was written on plates of stone by the flaming finger of an angry God.

Our religion was established by the traditions of our ancestors, the dreams of our elders that are given to them in the silent hours by the Great Spirit. And the premonitions of the learned beings.

It is written in the hearts of our people, thus:

We do not require churches – which would only lead us to argue over God. And the thought that white men should rule over nature and change its ways to his liking, was never understood by the red man.

Our belief is that the Great Spirit has created all things. Not just mankind, but all animals, all plants, all rocks, all on Earth and amongst the stars with true soul.

For us, all life is holy.

But. You do not understand our prayers when we address the Sun, Moon, and Winds. You have judged us without understanding, only because our prayers are different.

But we are able to live in harmony with all of nature. All of nature is within us and we are all part of nature.

Chief White Cloud

Contents

Introduction

The Prison

Keep you doped with religion and sex and TV.
And you think you're so clever and classless and free.
But you're still fucking peasants as far as I can see.

John Lennon, Working Class Hero[1]

The Freedom

All matter is merely energy condensed to a slow vibration.
We're all one consciousness experiencing itself subjectively.
There's no such thing as death.
Life is just a dream.
And we are the imagination of ourselves.

Bill Hicks

---

[1] Working Class Hero, Apple Records, 1970.

Chapter 1

The Bewildered Herd

So who the hell are you, then? What lies behind those eyes? When you look in the mirror, what do you see? Do you see the real you, or what you have been conditioned to believe is you? The two are so, so, different. One is an infinite consciousness capable of being and creating whatever it chooses, the other is an illusion imprisoned by its own perceived and programmed limitations.

Which of these "yous" is controlling your life? Infinity or limitation? Self love or self disdain? Freedom of thought or a prison of the mind?

Sadly for the overwhelming majority of people on this planet — all but the privileged few — it is the conditioned mind which prevails. They live their lives within their programmed limitations of thought, view, and action. It is a world of I can'ts and I daren'ts and I mustn'ts; of I shoulds and I musts and I ought tos; a world of conforming to what someone else says they must be or should be. While the real them sees only solutions and opportunities to learn and evolve, the programmed them sees only problems and reasons not to do. They live life behind bars in a cell of their own making. The world itself reflects the sum total of these billions of individual prisons. The Earth has become a global Alcatraz, a spinning ball of control and imposition dictated by the few at the expense of the many. Freedom? Free-what? How do you spell that again? The human race has not been free for a very, very long time, well before recorded history. But the trick is to persuade us that we are free — then we won't do anything about the walls that surround us and the warders at the door. Walls? What walls? You're free! Warders? What warders? You're free!

Yes you are free: you are free to watch television — thirty channels and more of mindless crap which close down your sense of infinity and feed you illusions of what you should do, be and think. You have the freedom to press the zappa button and choose any one of them. Oh what a joy to live in the land of freedom. You are free to watch

1

the news and see journalists and correspondents telling you, mostly without question, the official explanation of events – explanations designed to ensure that you see the world in the desired fashion and react in the desired way. Ladies and gentlemen, repeat after me…I am free…I am free. Yes! yes! yes! You are free to do as we tell you; free to think as we tell you; free to live as we tell you. And you are even free to die as we tell you in the wars coldly created to destroy, control and manipulate.

The human race is free?

No, no, no.

The human race is a *herd*.

Here we are, unique, eternal aspects of consciousness with an infinity of potential and we have allowed ourselves to become an unthinking, unquestioning blob of conformity and uniformity. A herd. Once we concede to the herd mentality we can be controlled and directed by a tiny few. And we are.

I was standing in the sunshine one day surrounded by an enormous herd of sheep. The farmer arrived in his truck, climbed out, and stood motionless, leaning on his stick. Immediately a few of the sheep began to walk towards him and within minutes it was like Exodus. Hundreds of sheep were following those few in front. Any stragglers who didn't conform to this baa, baa mentality were given a dose of fear from the sheep dog and then they rushed into line also. In a ridiculously short time this combination of the baa, baa, and the fear had rounded up the whole vast herd. All it took was one man doing very little and a sheep dog dispensing fear. As I observed this, I thought: "I'm looking at the human race here. This is how we are controlled". We have stopped thinking for ourselves and given our minds (power) away. Therefore we follow the one in front in the most extraordinarily robotic fashion. And we are consumed by fear in every fibre of our being. Once our fear responses are activated, we rush to conform even if we are aware enough to realise that what we are being asked to think, do, and say, is a nonsense. These weapons, the baa, baa, and the fear, allow an astonishingly few people to mould and direct the world in their own perverted image, a process that is leading, unless we wake up and grow up, towards a world government, army, central bank and currency, and a microchipped population: in short, the total global control of every man, woman and child.

While it may appear at first to be incredibly difficult for a relative handful of people to control the lives of nearly six billion, it is in fact comparatively easy, once you have control of education and the media – the sources of the "information" and mantra messages which bombard the conscious and subconscious mind from cradle to grave. These messages are not designed to inform, but to direct and condition, to divide and rule. The religious, scientific, political and economic manipulators position themselves between the truth and the human conscious mind. They are the middlemen and women who seek to keep out of the public arena the knowledge that would open our minds to our real and infinite potential. We are fed a mental diet of pap and crap designed to diminish our sense of self and close down our consciousness until it becomes a pale shadow of what it can be. It becomes a sheep and the sheep become a herd. As someone once said, there are three types of person in the world: a tiny few who make things happen; a slightly larger number who watch things happen; and all the rest who go around saying: what's happening, what's happening? The truth is denied to people because it will set them free. Instead, those at the peak of the religious, scientific, political, and economic empires (the same state of mind in different clothes) hand down their version of "truth", a version which means that people must believe whatever they want them to believe. And, to be fair, humanity does not have a great record for demanding the truth or searching for it. We have developed lazy minds. It's appropriate that the word ignorance is an extension of the word ignore. We ignore so much and so we become ignore-ant.

Once you have conditioned one generation to think in the way you require, it becomes even easier to condition the next generation. You now have the programmed parents working unknowingly on your behalf, conditioning their children to accept their own conditioned view of life. Such parents don't do this because they are bad people. They do it because they genuinely think their view is best for their children. But the effect is the same: one programmed generation helps to programme the next one because it does not respect anyone's right to be themselves. Each generation has a right to see life in a way that makes sense to them, not their parents, their teachers, or the guy reading the news. But sadly, people accept without thinking so much that is passed down to them. They don't ask the most liberating question it is possible to ask: Why? Why do we do it this way? Why do we believe this or that? Who says? The question "why?" is the driving force behind evolution. When I spoke in the United States, an American friend told me a story that brilliantly highlights what I mean. She said that when she was preparing dinner one day she cut the corners off the ham before putting it in the pan.

"Why do you do that?" her husband asked.

"I don't know – my mother always used to do it."

"Why did your mother cut the corners off the ham?"

"I don't know, she just did – what's it matter?"

"Ring your mother and ask her why she cut the corners off the ham."

She rang her mother.

"Mum, you know when I was a girl and you used to cut the corners off the ham? Why did you do that?"

"Because my pan was never big enough!"

If her husband had not asked the question "why?", she would have continued to cut the corners off the ham and her children would quite possibly have done it, too. This is how one generation allows its sense of self to be conditioned by older generations, parents, teachers and media people. They don't question why. This sponge mentality and the desire to impose one's thoughts and beliefs on others has created an amazingly effective vehicle for the Elite to control the direction of the world. It is what I have called the Hassle-Free Zone. Every dogma, belief-system, culture, and society has a Hassle-Free Zone. It works like this: you set limits of acceptable thought, view and behaviour and anyone who steps outside of those very narrow limits is immediately either ridiculed as "mad" or condemned as "bad". In my case both! Some people stay within the Hassle-Free Zone because they are persuaded that this desperately constricted view is indeed how life should be lived. But there are very significant numbers of other people who realise how ridiculous the limits of the Zone are, but the fear of facing ridicule or condemnation ensures that they keep their mouths shut and their heads down. As they say in Japan, the nail that stands out from the rest is the first one to be hit. Here again we have the Hassle-Free Zone policed by those twin weapons, the baa, baa (those who accept the limitation of conditioned thought and view as their reality) and the fear (those who think differently, but are frightened to say so). This means that great swathes of humanity are living a lie and denying what they really believe and what they really want to do with their lives. They don the mask. Stand in a crowded street and watch all those people walking by. You are not looking at the real, infinite them. You are looking at the mask they project to the world. The mask they believe is acceptable enough to the rest of the prisoners to avoid being ridiculed or condemned for thinking and acting differently to the demands of the Hassle-Free Zone. It is the fantastic tensions within the psyche caused by this denial which lie at the heart of most mental, emotional, and therefore physical disease (dis-ease, disharmony) which manifests as illness, depression, suicide, a lack of fulfilment, and "what's the point?". This daily "war" in the psyche brings into conflict that part of us which recognises our infinity and uniqueness, and the conscious level which seeks to deny such feelings because it fears the consequences of expressing uniqueness in a world of programmed uniformity. These two levels of the psyche are what I term "I Am Me, I Am Free" and "Oh My God".

I Am Me, I Am Free, wishes to express and celebrate its uniqueness. Oh My God, is terrified of what that will mean in daily life. "Oh my God, what will my family think if I say what I believe? What about the fellahs at work? And the guys down the bar? They'll think I've gone mad. Oh my God!"

If you want to be free, stop living a lie. Stop denying yourself. You are a unique aspect of all that exists, the sum total of all your unique experiences since you first became conscious an infinity ago. That is a reason to be joyous. There is no aspect of consciousness in all creation that is like you. You are special, as everyone is equally special. But instead of being joyous and proud of that specialness, we have allowed our uniqueness to become something to fear. Oh my God!

Because we fear being ourselves, we are uncomfortable when anyone around us decides to evacuate the Hassle-Free Zone and express their uniqueness. Their dash for mental and emotional freedom makes a statement about us and our own mental and emotional prison. People don't like that and they react accordingly. "He's mad" or "She's bad" comes the reflex action, standard issue cry from the herd when it is faced with someone determined to be themselves and not a programmed clone. And do you know what people are really saying when they shout "mad" or "bad"? They are really saying "different". Such is the scale of the conditioning absorbed by the human collective mind that people can't cope with anyone who dares to be different. "If I'm in prison, mate, you have to be too. It's only fair." We also succumb to the myth about the "ordinary man and woman in the street" or the "common people", the idea that the masses are just "ordinary" and only the few who are "extra-ordinary" achieve anything in life. We are "ordinary", so we must know our place, this belief system contends. In truth, there is not an "ordinary" man, woman, child or blade of grass in the whole of creation, but people are persuaded to believe the myth and so they play out the role of being "ordinary". It's an act which they are conditioned to perform, like an actor on a stage. Ordinary is not what we are, it is merely what we choose to believe we are. But it is very powerful in diminishing our sense of worth; another motivation to give our minds away to those we believe to be our "betters". It is part of the conditioning that includes the claptrap that we are all born sinners, whatever the hell that is supposed to mean.

Think about the consequences for your life and the planet that result from this fear of being YOU. If we give our minds away to others and allow them to tell us what to think and do, and if we concede our uniqueness to the fear of being different, we give control of this world to a tiny Elite who use their power and manipulation to dictate the limits of the Hassle-Free Zone. Whoever decides the point at which a view or lifestyle is inside or outside the Zone (the point at which you meet ridicule or condemnation), also dictates the limits within which billions of people live their lives because they are terrified of being different from the herd. Again and again people say they support what I am saying and doing, but they dare not say so for fear of the consequences. Well it's time to summon the courage, because the consequences of keeping quiet are going to be far worse than speaking out and being proud of what you think and what you are. What's happened to us, for goodness sake? We have taken on a mass schizophrenia in which we have become both the prisoners of the Hassle-Free Zone and its police force. Because we don't respect our own right to be unique, we conform to the limits of the Zone and become a slave. Because we don't respect everyone else's right to be unique, we become the police force or the farmer hassling and herding the other slaves into acquiescence. The ridicule and condemnation can only reach the levels required to frighten people into submission if the masses, the other slaves, play their part in dispensing it. We are not frightened by what the presidents, prime ministers and global bankers think about us – it is the reaction of our friends, family, and workmates that concerns us and frightens us into conformity. The reaction of the other slaves! The mental, emotional, and spiritual police force which controls the masses is itself peopled by…the masses. It is like having a cell full of prisoners and whenever one of the prisoners finds a means of escape, all the other prisoners run to block the exit.

Prejudice is the vital word here. People are conditioned to be prejudiced against other members and groups within each culture and society, and these different forms of prejudice are used to divide and rule the herd. The prejudice may be racial, religious or political, or based on background, income, job or lifestyle. Either way you have different aspects of society conditioned to instinctively ridicule, oppose and condemn the views and life experiences of each other. And the prejudice is rarely only one way. Those who see themselves as victims of prejudice are so often prejudiced themselves against other people, lifestyles and groups. This allows the manipulation of the mass consciousness to flourish and yet if we stopped seeking to impose *our* version of right and wrong, good and bad, moral and immoral upon each other, we would remove the means for such global manipulation. We need to let go of *all* prejudice – *now!*

We have given up our own unique identities to such an extent that we judge ourselves and others by the "jobs" that we do and the dogmas we cling to. How we and they serve the system that controls us has become our sense of identity, the symbol of who we are! What are you? Oh, I'm a Christian, a Muslim, a Socialist, a Republican, a Pagan. We have to be some*thing* instead of being some*one* – ourselves. We also ask people we meet what they "do" for a living because we think this will give us a fix on "who" they are. "Oh you're a stockbroker and you're a miner, and you're a road sweeper. Right, got that – success, rough and dirty, complete failure. OK, I know you all now. Drink anyone?" We judge people and ourselves, not by what we are, but by what we own or by what we "do". This judgment corresponds with the system's view of reality because we have conceded the right to express our own uniqueness. Someone who makes millions by abusing the planet and great swathes of humanity every day by decisions they make in the global stockmarkets (casinos) is deemed to have "made it", to be successful. While others who do no-one any harm, and indeed may strive to help people and give love to the world, are considered a failure if they happen to work in a low-paid job or be "unemployed". A friend at school was always being laughed at because his father emptied dustbins for a living. But those who laughed worshipped famous footballers. This is an example of our topsyturvy view of "success". Who would we miss most if they did not work for a month, the footballer or the garbage collector? The latter, of course, because the streets and our homes would be full of rubbish and, eventually, disease. This attitude of judging each other by our "jobs" is to ignore and deny who we really are.

We are not "stockbrokers", "miners", or "road sweepers". These are merely roles we play on the stage of life. A stockbroker today could be a pauper tomorrow. Our "role" is not "us", just as the character that an actor plays is not the actor's real persona. Our jobs and "roles" are a temporary vehicle for experience, that's all. We are evolving consciousness on an eternal journey towards greater love, knowledge and understanding, but we have forgotten this and we have been encouraged to forget it. We are like actors who think the movie is real and we have taken on the personalities described in someone else's script. We think the role is "us". It isn't. But we have the actor playing the stockbroker looking down his nose at the actor who is playing the road sweeper when, in another life, another movie, those roles may be reversed. It's only a game, but we think it's real. That's why it has degenerated into such a mess. We are taking the game too seriously. It's just a movie and it is supposed to be fun.

One enormous diversion that we have allowed to confuse us so effectively is the concept of democracy. We have accepted en masse that democracy is another word for freedom. Like hell it is. Democracy is not freedom, it is a dictatorship camouflaged as freedom. The same force controls, directly or indirectly, every major political party and movement. It created most of them. When you vote at an election, you are choosing between different aspects of the same force. The money and the media decide who becomes president of the United States and the money and the media are owned and controlled by the same people. Let us write the following in letters 20 feet high: **Democracy Is Not Freedom**. 50 people telling 49 what to do is not freedom. In fact, most governments are elected by a minority of the population and they still call it a "democratic" election. Freedom is the right of all people to express who they are, what they think, and how they wish to live their lives: free from imposition or hassle from anyone. It is to be able to celebrate our individual uniqueness without rules, regulations, ridicule and condemnation from those who seek to impose their view of life upon the rest of us.

Until we respect our own, and everyone's, right to be different, to make our own choices, and create our own conscious realities free from imposition and pressure to conform, we will remain in a prison of our own making. We will continue to be both the policeman and the prisoner. And a handful of people with a deeply unpleasant agenda will continue to run the world. The choice, as always, is ours. We can accept the prison or we can walk out to freedom. And freedom is but a thought away.

Chapter 2

Defending The Dogma

A longside the illusion that we are free, is the illusion that we are different. Sound like a contradiction? Here I am saying we are unique and at the same time that we have a misguided belief that we are different. There is no contradiction.

We *are* unique within our multidimensional consciousness, but within the limited vision of the Hassle-Free Zone there are endless "differences" we call dogmas which are, in truth, not different at all. The devotees of Christian dogma think they are different from those who are slaves of Jewish dogma. The fundamentalist rabbi believes he is different from the fundamentalist ayatollah. But they are not. They are the same thought pattern with a slightly different dress on. They are all prisoners of a dogma who wish to convert other prisoners to accept the same dogma. They all use fear, guilt and other forms of imposition to manipulate and frighten people into line. Their line. What is the difference between the nuns at a Roman Catholic convent using fear and guilt to control the thinking of children and young people, and a rabbi or muslim cleric using the fear of hell and damnation and enormous family pressures to do the same? Answer: nothing. They are different aspects of the same state of mind, but they think they are different to the point where their dogmas come into physical conflict. They are all arrogant enough to claim they know the "will of God" and they claim to have been chosen to tell everyone what God insists they believe. Poor old God must have a production line turning out His different "wills". Either that, or He (it's always a "He") has great difficulty making up His mind. God used to be indecisive, but now He's not so sure. Are we really being asked to accept that some God is sitting on a cloud selecting his chosen people and then ordering them to control and manipulate everyone else? Indeed we are. We can now go over "live" to heaven where God is about to announce the panel's verdict:

"OK, after much discussion and consideration of the various business plans, my angels and I have awarded the God Franchise (Earth Branch) to the Roman Catholics. My will is that the Pope should tell all people how to live their lives and that he and the Vatican should be controlled by the upper levels of the secret society network like the Freemasons and the Knights of Malta. If any Pope does not agree to this control, he should be murdered (as with Pope John Paul I in 1978). I also will that the Pope and the Roman Catholic Church should terrify little children to prepare them for a life of being told what to do and to ensure that they believe what the church wants them to believe. I will that an inquisition should be formed by said Pope to burn everyone he and his henchmen decide do not believe in every single word of my bible, the King James version of which has been documented to have 36,191 errors in translation alone. I will that my son, the Prince of Peace (also known quite wrongly as "Jesus")[1]*, should be nailed to a cross and suffer unbelievable pain so that the rest of humanity shall be able to kill and plunder each other while having their sins forgiven forever!*

Oh, my God! Sorry, oh my Me! That doesn't sound right. It's not very Godly and I am God after all. Er, no, er, I've changed my mind:

My will now is that Jews are my chosen people, even though, contrary to worldwide indoctrination, there is no such thing as a Jewish "race", just as there is no "Aryan" race, either. I will that the Jewish hierarchy should terrify their children to prepare them for a life of being told what to do and to ensure they conform to whatever the hierarchy tells them. This fear should be constantly applied throughout their lives. They should be made to fear terrorist attacks (for which their own hierarchy are often responsible) and made to believe that only by giving their minds and power away to the hierarchy will they be protected from their enemies. As I gave a strip of land to my chosen people thousands of years ago (or so the history books tell me, I don't remember myself), I will that the Palestinian Arabs should be terrorised out of their homes, that their land be called Israel, and that some of the terrorists involved such as Ben-Gurion, Begin, Rabin, and Shamir, should later become prime ministers and display record-breaking hypocrisy by denouncing the terrorism of others. I thought about insisting that Jewish people be told

---

[1] Jesus is a Greek translation of a Hebrew name, probably Y'shua ben Yosef (Joshua, son of Joseph).

that they can speak to me by putting little bits of paper into the cracks between the stones in the Wailing Wall, but no-one would ever believe that. To sum up, I will that the Jewish hierarchy are my chosen people and, as their book, the Talmud, *says: "Just the Jews are humans, the non-Jews are no humans, but cattle".*

Oh my Me! That doesn't sound right, either. It's not very Godly and I am God after all. Er, no, er, I've changed my mind again:

This time I will that my real voice on Earth is the Muslim hierarchy and that they should terrify their children to prepare them for a life of being told what to do and to ensure they conform to my rules. I told all this to a guy called Mohammed a long time ago and he was very good because he and his successors led a vast army of followers to kill and maim anyone who didn't accept them as my representatives on Earth. I will that the religion called Islam created in my name should be used to keep the people in fear, guilt, and order while my hierarchy use the oil money for their own benefit and keep the rest of the people in servitude and poverty in the name of my religion. I will that women should not be able to show more than their eyes in public because, although I created the physical body, I am terribly ashamed of it. I further will that men should always be in control and that women (one of my aberrations, oops!) should be forced to do as they are told.

Oh my Me! That doesn't sound right, either. I'm terribly confused. I can't decide. Let the people choose. Go on, fight for it. Blow the living daylights out of each other. Rape the planet…yeeessss…go for it. Last one alive wins and sits at my right hand next to the Prince of Peace. Deal?"

A bit disturbing that isn't it? Some confused God looking down, searching for His chosen ones by pulling straws and saying eeni-meeni-mini-mo? And telling everyone He's on their side, so they slaughter each other in His name. Mind you, amid His confusion there is one common theme in "God's" deliberations: frightening people to make them conform. It couldn't just be, could it, that these variations on the same thought pattern have absolutely nothing to do with "God" and spirituality and everything to do with the desire of some humans to dictate the lives of all the rest? Oh yes it could. 'Twas always so throughout recorded history and 'twill always be so until we take our power back by making our own decisions and moulding our own, individual, sense of reality. No-one is "born" a Christian, a Jew or a Muslim. People are conditioned to be Christians, Jews and Muslims *after* they are born. When we take on someone else's beliefs, lock, stock and barrel, and especially when we need to be frightened into accepting them, we walk a very dark and dangerous road: for ourselves and for the world.

But so few have learned this lesson of the centuries. We still believe too much and think too little. We "feel" intuitively even less. The rigidity and manipulation of "beliefs" (dogma and prejudice) is how we are controlled. Today, with the dawn of the 21st century almost upon us, we still have men in dog collars and frocks sitting around a table decoding what we should or should not believe. Billions of people continue to be controlled and limited by their devotion to the false gods called Popes, priests, archbishops, rabbis, ayatollahs and their like across the spectrum of religious beliefs which have been peddled and poisoned over the centuries by those in pursuit of control. Even worse, the desire is to pressure others to believe the same and whenever anyone asks an unanswerable question of religion (not difficult) out is wheeled the trusty break-the-glass-and-use-in-all-emergencies reply of "have faith". I remember being told on a Northern Ireland radio programme after I listed a few religious contradictions that these were things that God did not want us to know! Have we learned nothing with the passage of time? And for those who have evolved beyond the child-like state of off-the-peg religion, there are other dogmas waiting to ensnare them. Political, scientific, environmental and "New Age" dogma among them. As with religion, these "opposites" are merely aspects of the same state of mind. I am told that Communism (the far Left) is different from Nazism (the far Right). The idea is ludicrous. The far Left, as symbolised by Josef Stalin, believes in centralised control, military dictatorship, and concentration camps. The far Right, as symbolised by Adolf Hitler, believes in centralised control, military dictatorship, and concentration camps. Spot the difference? Of course not. When you peel away the smoke-screen rhetoric, they are the same. Yet these two "opposites" went to war with each other and across the world the Communists go on "anti-Nazi" marches and Nazis protest against the Communists. Conflict through the ages has not been between opposites, but versions of the same state of mind: the desire to control others. Communism and Nazism did not fight for freedom in the

Second World War; it was a battle to decide which aspect of the same thought pattern would control the vast lands of Eastern Europe.

I see "Socialists" claiming to be different from "Capitalists". Not at their core they are not. Socialism believes in taking more and more from the Earth and using these "resources" to produce more and more "things" at the expense of the planet. Capitalism believes in taking more and more from the Earth and using these "resources" to produce more and more "things" at the expense of the planet. Socialism believes that this production should be controlled by the few at the centre who dictate the economic policy. Capitalism believes in the survival of the strongest which leads to control by the few at the centre, who dictate economic policy. On the fundamentals, they are two sides of the same thought wave and yet socialism and capitalism (cartelism) are portrayed as opposite dogmas offering an alternative view. On the Right, they wish to stop the free flow of information which challenges their dogma. On the Left, the Robot Radicals, as I call them, wish to stop the free flow of information which challenges their dogma. The Right seek to assassinate the character of those who disagree with them and to deny a public platform for their views. The Left, the Robot Radicals, seek to assassinate the character of those who disagree with them and to deny a public platform for their views. Again, spot the difference? My own experience of "Nazi" behaviour has almost always come from those claiming to be "anti-Nazis". The anti-fascist fascists are a wonder to behold. The mental gymnastics and self delusion required for such a state of mind defies the imagination.

Throughout the Hassle-Free Zones of religious, political, "scientific" and economic dogma you find these "oppo-sames" fighting and condemning each other. In the United States, the main opposition to the Global Conspiracy, which I expose in *...and the truth shall set you free* and *The Robots' Rebellion*, is the Christian Patriot Movement. You will find the same mindset within the Islamic Patriot Movement, the Jewish Patriot Movement, ad infinitum. I welcome the efforts of the Christian Patriots to make public the plans to create a centralised global tyranny and a microchipped, robotic, population. But what is their alternative? The return to an imposed Christian dogma and national flag waving. Some call for the people behind the conspiracy to be hanged and for people to defend themselves with guns and violence. You don't stop a tyranny with another tyranny. You don't stop violence with violence. And you don't eliminate hatred with more hatred. You just double the hatred. Nor do you remove divisions by waving your flag, putting the wants of your country above the needs of others on the planet, and claiming that your nation and people are the best in the world.

You stop a tyranny with freedom for all; you end violence by being peaceful; you eliminate hatred with love; you end dogma with freedom of expression; and you remove divisions by realising that all of us are One – all aspects of the same infinite consciousness we call God.

Within the Hassle-Free Zone there are so few differences between people in their basic attitudes and responses. They are aspects of the same herd. It is outside the Zone that we discover our true uniqueness. On the inside the "differences" have to be manufactured to present us with an illusion of choice and variety, otherwise we would soon realise that, yes indeed, humanity is a blob of programmed, uniform thought. For this reason "sames" are portrayed as "opposites". It's all a con. Opposites don't fight each other. *Oppo-sames* fight each other. The opposite of the desire to fight and impose is the desire to love and set free. These opposites cannot fight because one will always refuse to do so. It is not part of its belief system to fight. So when you see physical and verbal conflict it is always between aspects of the same state of mind – oppo-sames – and never between opposites. Here lies the whole basis of divide and rule: create divisions with manufactured, non-existent "differences" and then play them off against each other.

Let us recap. Humanity is in prison because:

a It gives its mind away and concedes its responsibility and power to think for itself.

b It is consumed by fear, especially the fear of what other people think – the fear of being different and unique.

c It seeks to impose its dogmas on everyone and denies the right of each of us to be different and have our own, unique, view.

In the light of this, the means of escape from the global Alcatraz is breathtakingly obvious:

a We think for ourselves and refuse to allow others to tell us what to do, be and say.

b We let go of fear because fear is our creation. We don't have to fear, we choose to. We don't have to hide our uniqueness, we choose to. We can make another choice just as easily.

c We respect our own right to believe what we choose and, crucially, we respect everyone's right to do the same, free from pressure, ridicule, condemnation and imposition of any kind.

In those few short sentences you have the means to transform this world from a prison to a paradise. Not one gun needs to be fired, not one trench needs to be dug, nor one new political "ism" created. All it takes is for you to respect your right to be different and to respect everyone's right to that same freedom.

Yes. It really is that simple.

Chapter 3

The Global Dictatorship

Control of the world over a very long period has been achieved by the means I have already outlined: mind manipulation, manufactured division, and most important of all, fear. This is the emotion that has handed control of our lives to the manipulating clique which I call the Global Elite.

Once you can make people fearful they will look to someone to protect them from whatever they have been conditioned to fear. This is why history, and the world today, is full of hyped up "monsters" and "dangerous people" – a focus of fear from which we must look to our "leaders" to save us. The fact that these "monsters" and our "leaders" are both appointed and controlled by the same force is kept from us. We are programmed to see two "sides", largely projected as "good and evil", when there are not two sides, but one. In ...*and the truth shall set you free*, I highlight hundreds of people, events and organisations, who in the public arena appear to be in opposition, but in truth are connected to the same Global Elite. Among these connections, for example, are those between George Bush and Saddam Hussein, the "opponents" in the Gulf War of 1991. The manufactured Cold War between the West and the Soviet Union was another classic of this kind. Both populations were so filled with fear of each other that they gave still more power to their "leaders" and accepted grotesque weapons expenditure in the misguided belief that they must be protected from the "enemy". The make-believe, propaganda-created, enemy, as it turns out. Both sides, including Ronald Reagan, George Bush, Mikhail Gorbachev, and other Soviet and American leaders were controlled by the same people. They were the same side.

The Global Elite, the few who decide the direction of the world and humanity, sit atop a pyramid of manipulation (*Figure 1 overleaf*). Almost every organisation today is structured as a pyramid. At the peak you have the tiny elite who know everything about the organisation. They

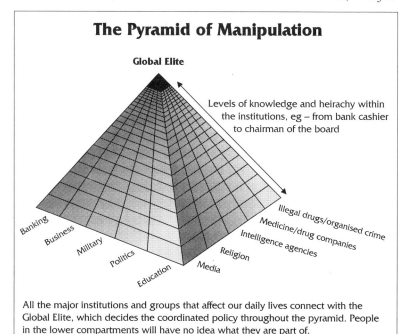

The Pyramid of Manipulation

Global Elite

Levels of knowledge and heirachy within the institutions, eg – from bank cashier to chairman of the board

Banking
Business
Military
Politics
Education
Media
Religion
Intelligence agencies
Medicine/drug companies
Illegal drugs/organised crime

All the major institutions and groups that affect our daily lives connect with the Global Elite, which decides the coordinated policy throughout the pyramid. People in the lower compartments will have no idea what they are part of.

Figure 1

know its real agenda and what it really wants to achieve. As you come down from the peak, you are meeting more and more people who know less and less about that agenda. This is called compartmentalisation. Those at the top ensure that everyone lower down in the pyramid know only their own individual contribution to the organisation, company, secret society, whatever. As a result most of them think their work is quite innocent because they are not allowed to know how their work fits in with the others in the pyramid to create a pattern that is anything but innocent. Only the elite at the top know how these individual contributions fit together and in this way you have people throughout the pyramid working in ignorance of what they are really a part of. The Freemasons and other secret societies are an obvious example of this method with their levels of initiation. Each level has no idea of the knowledge held in the levels above them. The vast majority of freemasons never progress higher than the third degree, but there are another 30 official levels above that in the so called Scottish Rite and then another 13 unofficial levels, known as Illuminati levels, which are not even acknowledged to exist. The majority of freemasons, down there on the bottom three levels, are oblivious to what that organisation is really there to do. They are a manipulated, largely unknowing smoke-screen for the few who control the secret society. When the freemasonic network is named as a tool of the conspiracy, people think you are saying that every freemason is seeking to take over the world. That's simply not true. It's just ridiculous. Secret societies, like almost everything, consist of the leaders (the few) and the led (the rest).

So it is with the global pyramid within which you find all the organisations that control our lives – the banking system, political system, multinational corporation network, the media, "education", intelligence agencies, military and so on. The peaks of their individual pyramids all fuse together into the peak of the global pyramid, controlled by the ridiculously few people I have called the Global Elite. From that peak, the same policy, methods and aims filter down through all these, apparently unconnected, aspects of society. At this Elite level all the banks, political parties, newspapers and broadcast media, intelligence agencies, multinational companies, and secret societies, are owned or controlled by the SAME people. This is so important to grasp. The myth of choice is there to fool us into believing we are free. Look at how many companies the multinational corporations own. These "companies" each have a different trade name and appear at first glance to be independent of their "competitors", but they are owned by the same people. Two of the biggest electronics retailers in the UK, Dixons and Currys, are owned by the same group and yet on the high street they appear to be in competition. It is the same with the UK's two leading roadside restaurants, Little Chef and Happy Eater. The examples of this all over the world are endless. The global food chain is overwhelmingly controlled by three multinational corporations operating through scores of different trade names string-pulled from the centre. Choice? What a joke. Something like 99% of those working within these organisations have no comprehension of how they are being used. The people who sit behind the counter in a bank won't be aware of what is going on in their own manager's office, let alone what is discussed at board level or above that by the Global Elite. They're just pawns in someone else's game. They keep their heads down, close their minds, and do as they are told – just like the human race as a whole. This submission to another's view and the suppression of our own individuality allows the Global Elite to set the limits of the Hassle-Free Zones by filtering down the same policy and attitudes throughout the pyramid. They do this through a network of organisations which include the Royal Institute of International Affairs in

London, the Council on Foreign Relations in the United States, the Trilateral Commission (US-Europe-Japan), and the most influential of them, the Bilderberg Group. There are many other offshoots of this network, like the Parlour Club, the Club of the Isles and the Pinay Circle or "Le Cercle" which works to remove political leaders deemed unacceptable to the Elite. These private organisations have in their membership the top people in politics, business, banking, the military, the media, the 'legal' profession, education, etc., who then pervade the pyramid with a single overall plan which has led to greater centralisation of power every year. All these institutions which control the direction of our lives are themselves controlled at the peak of the pyramid by the same people. You can read about this network in great detail in ...*and the truth shall set you free*.

I was invited in 1995 to the memorial service for a great British comedian, Larry Grayson, and there a story was told which encapsulated our plight and the means of escape. During this celebration of Larry's life, one of his experiences was told to the assembled throng by another comedian, Roy Hudd. It was a story from the days when Larry used to travel the variety halls of the UK and on this occasion he was part of an all-male show which had one "woman" taking part – a dressed up Larry Grayson. The producer was very patriotic, Larry had once recalled, and the show's big finish was a rendition of the song, *Rule Britannia*. The rest of the cast came on wearing sailors uniforms and they climbed on each others shoulders to form a human pyramid on the stage. At this point, on walked Larry dressed as Britannia with the long gown, the helmet, shield and sword, and he was manhandled up the pyramid to the top for the finale of the show. One night, he said, things seemed to be going rather well. But then he noticed that the sailor in the bottom left hand corner of the pyramid had got rather a cough.

"And as any ancient Egyptian will tell you" Larry had observed "That is a very important part of the pyramid!"

Anyway, this sailor's cough became progressively worse until he had to step out of the pyramid. And what happened? The whole structure collapsed with sailors going in all directions. Larry Grayson's shield went one way, his sword another, and he finished up in someone's lap in the second row. What had caused the pyramid to disintegrate? Not Larry Grayson at the top (symbolic of the Global Elite), but one sailor at the bottom (symbolic of the "ordinary" man and woman in the street). The real power in a pyramid is at the bottom, not the top, but the human race has been conditioned to believe the opposite. This is why it has been so important to divide and rule "the masses" into dogmas and factions – the Elite know that is where the real power lies and they seek to diffuse that power by turning "the masses" against each other. Humanity gives its power away to those who are only up there because humanity holds them up there! The power used by the Elite to control humanity is merely the power which humanity hands over to them every day. Let's hear that one more time:

The Global Elite are only up there because the rest of humanity holds them up there. The power used by the Elite to control humanity is merely the power which humanity hands over to them every day.

Hey, wake me up. This has got to be some crazy nightmare I'm involved in here.

It's not?

But we wouldn't be that stupid would we?

We would?

We *would*?

I'm sorry, would you excuse me for a moment?

Aaaaaaaaaaaaaaaaaaaaaaaaaahhhhhhhhhhhhhhhhhhhhhhhhhh !!!

Thank you.

Every Hassle-Free Zone is a pyramid with religious, political and economic dictators sitting at the peak imposing their will on the rest. They can only achieve that if those lower down the pyramid agree to do, unquestioningly, whatever the peak tells them, and believe, unquestioningly, whatever propaganda the peak sends down to condition their thinking and perceptions of life, themselves, and others. It is actually possible in the world our minds have created to go through an entire lifetime without having a single original thought. There the prisoners stand in their Larry Grayson pyramid, their fellow prisoners on their shoulders, each telling the other not to move or the whole thing will fall apart. There they stand with aching shoulders and silent minds, terrified of walking away from this pyramidic prison. They fear to let go of their (perceived) "security" or to face the ridicule or hostility of those still mesmerised by the lights of the oncoming car. Security? I beg one's pardon. Living in jail is security? Having your life controlled and your future dictated is security? What delusions we weave. Anything based on fear and the suppression of human potential is never secure. Anything that must be enforced is never secure. Only freedom for all and by all is secure and can survive.

The extent to which billions of people have given their minds away makes the control of the world so simple. We might *become* robots? We *are* bloody robots! It's no good denying that, because if we do we will do nothing about it. The childlike way in which we think what we are told to think never ceases to take my breath away. For 48 hours after the Oklahoma bombing in 1995, it was a nightmare to be an Arab in the United States. Why? Because the government (elements of which planted the bomb as we shall eventually realise) announced that there might be a Middle East connection. Arabs in America, and even those who only looked like Arabs, were harangued in the street in the wake of this announcement. Two days or so later the same government said there was not a Middle East connection[1] and suddenly it was OK to be an Arab again. Those who responded like this were "adults" acting like babes in arms, puppets on the strings of official pronouncements, and fodder for the Global Elite.

There is no limit to the examples every day of people playing the robot. When I started to reveal the background to the global conspiracy and name the names and organisations involved, the campaign to discredit me began. I was dubbed "anti-Jewish" and a "neo-Nazi". Now that was no surprise because everyone who gets close to the truth of who really controls the world is attacked in the same way. The Global Elite has two main defence responses – assassinating those who are lifting the veil or assassinating their character by branding them anti-Jewish and Nazi. What followed in the campaign to discredit me was the final confirmation that large tracts of the human race no longer have access to their own minds. The people behind these attacks on me

---

[1] In fact I believe there was a Middle East connection to that bombing – the Israeli intelligence agency, Mossad, via an organisation called the Anti-Defamation League, but that's another story. See *...and the truth shall set you free*.

were two "journalists" in London called Matthew Kalman and John Murray. There were people encouraging them too, I am sure, but they have been the public face of the campaign. They wrote an astonishing article full of untruths in their own little known magazine and then, by their own admission, they began to hawk this "story" around the mainstream media. Some newspapers refused to print it, but others like *The Guardian* and *The New Statesman* ran this nonsense. More then followed. Over a period of a year, virtually every magazine article making these accusations was written by Matthew Kalman and John Murray and almost every newspaper article was based on "information" supplied by Matthew Kalman and John Murray. A magazine called *New Moon* ran a stunning misrepresentation of my book, *...and the truth shall set you free.* I was called a Nazi and the front page consisted of a picture of me changed to resemble Adolf Hitler. The article was written by Matthew Kalman and John Murray and the magazine was edited by...Matthew Kalman. The New Age magazine, *Kindred Spirit*, also ran a long letter calling me a Nazi and anti-Jewish. The letter writer was...Matthew Kalman.

So the claims of me being an anti-Jewish Nazi were, overwhelmingly, put into the public arena by two people. *Two* people. But given the current state of human consciousness, that's all it takes to mind-control millions. Amazing, but true. In fact you don't even need two people, one is enough. Suddenly people who had believed I was "mad" because of what the media had told them about my spiritual views were now convinced that I was "bad" because they were reading in newspapers and magazines (the work of two people) that I was a Nazi. Those who by their own admission had not read my books or heard me speak, began to protest at my public meetings on the strength of what they had read in the media (two people) or what their friends had told them after also reading it in the media (two people). The events at Brighton on the South Coast of England summed up the point I am making. The local Robot Radicals believed the untruths fed to them by Kalman and Murray and they put so much pressure on Brighton University that the authorities gave in to threats from a mob and cancelled my meeting at very short notice.

Had the people at the university who made that decision read my books or heard me speak?

Er, no.

Then where did they get their information about what I was supposed to be saying?

The Anti-Nazi League.

And where did they get their information from?

Kalman and Murray.

I booked a hotel in Brighton for the rescheduled talk. It was called The Brighton Oak. They accepted the booking and things seemed to be going OK. Then they suddenly cancelled the booking because of my "far-Right" views. Oh yes?

Had the people at the hotel who made that decision read my books or heard me speak?

Er, no.

Then where did they get their information from about what I was supposed to be saying?

The Anti-Nazi League.

And where did they get their information from?

Kalman and Murray.

We tried at Crawley, just north of Brighton at a theatre owned by Crawley Borough Council. Forty-eight hours before the event we heard via the media, not the Council, that the meeting was cancelled. This time the Council *did* know what I was going to say because they had seen a video. After viewing that recording they wrote to confirm the meeting could go ahead. So why the cancellation? They had been threatened by a phone call from the Robot Radicals in Brighton which said that "the safety of the audience could not be guaranteed". This from a group of people who call themselves "anti-fascists"! Instead of standing up for freedom of speech and against such intimidation, the Council immediately succumbed to the threat and stopped me speaking. One phone call and one threat was all it took because people are so easy to manipulate and to frighten. Once again we see the combination of the baa baa and the fear.

In this way, we have the quite ludicrous situation in which ...*and the truth shall set you free*, a book funded by a Jewish man and edited by a woman born into a Jewish family, is dubbed anti-Jewish. And those Robot Radicals and others believe this without one moment's research or a single second's thought. In the United States, the Kalman and Murray articles were used in an effort to discredit me by the now infamous Anti Defamation League (ADL), the US front for the Global Elite and the intelligence agency, Mossad. I highlight the background to the ADL in ...*and the truth shall set you free* – including its involvement in the assassination of John F. Kennedy. Articles seeking to discredit me, and therefore my information, were also carefully placed in the "alternative" media to target people who are naturally suspicious of authority. Unfortunately such people have been conditioned to believe the alternative media as unquestioningly as others believe the mainstream media. Do they really think the Elite would not seek to infiltrate these "alternatives" also for their own ends? The Brighton story is a wonderful example of how the few can programme the many, but millions of other examples are happening around the world every time the clock ticks.

A tiny elite can't control the world by conditioning the human mind? It's child's play.

The human race is not evil. It has merely allowed itself to become a manipulator's dream. It has given up thinking to such a degree that the Global Elite can condition what passes for human brain-cell activity and therefore control the direction of the world. This is the coup d'état on the mind which I have written about in other books. It is not so much that the Global Elite want to tell us *what* to think, it is more a case of conditioning people *not* to think. There are many methods, developed and honed by Elite-controlled organisations around the world, which are designed to do this. The key technique is something I call problem-reaction-solution (P-R-S). You create a problem, be it a war, a run on a currency, a health "scare", a government collapse, whatever suits your plans at the time. You make sure, however, that someone else is blamed for this "problem" and not you. This is essential. You then use the global media, which you also own and control, to pressure public opinion into demanding action – the "something must be done" syndrome. In response to this manipulated "problem" and the stimulated public "reaction", you then openly offer the "solution" to the problem you have created. This "solution" is what you planned to do all along, but problem-reaction-solution means that not only do you avoid serious opposition to your plans, you actually manipulate the people into demanding that you do what you intended to do anyway!

Some examples:

The goal of the Elite is a world government to which nation states, even continents, would be subordinate. They call this the New World Order. The constant process of centralising economic and political power over hundreds of years has not just happened at random: it has been by manipulated design. The centralisation on a global level with a world government is only the natural outcome of this policy. Whoever controlled the world government (Global Elite) would control the world central bank and world currency, which are also part of the agenda known as the New World Order. In short, whoever controlled the world government would control the planet even more comprehensively than they do now. But world governments don't just happen. They have to be manipulated into existence and at the heart of that strategy must be a plot to discredit the status quo, the community and the nation state. If that is working well and harmony reigns, people are not going to accept a world government telling them what to do. You have to create the perceived "need" and this is where problem-reaction-solution is so effective. As I and many others have documented in their books, it is provable that the same global bankers and their networks funded *all* sides in the First and Second World Wars, and indeed funded the Russian Revolution which brought us the tyranny known as "communism". I know it sounds staggering at first, but those who financed Britain, America, and the Allies in those wars also funded the Germans and Adolf Hitler. Why on Earth would they do that? To follow their long term agenda of total global control. The main aim of a manipulated war is to change the nature of post war society. The world became more centralised as a result of the First World War and even more so after the second global conflict. That was the idea (*Figure 2*). The horror and destruction of the First World War led to an understandable cry of "something must be done" and the Elite proposed their "solution", the League of Nations, their first attempt at a global organisation which could be evolved step by step into the world government. They didn't manage to do that on this occasion and the League of Nations

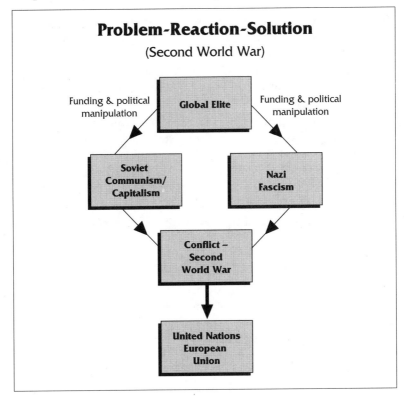

Figure 2

eventually collapsed. But after the Second World War came two other Elite creations (provable), the United Nations and the European Union. The alleged reason for the UN's existence was to prevent wars, but now, as always planned, we see the UN, and NATO, being used as mere vehicles for the creation, again step by step, of the world army under central control. A world army, which, far from stopping wars, actually fights them! The same principle applies to the creation of communism and the Soviet Union which was achieved via funding and political manipulation from the United States and the United Kingdom. The creation of two "sides" is an essential part of manipulating peoples' fear. To the "West" the Soviet Union was portrayed as a dangerous monster, the "evil empire", while in the Soviet Union, the "West" was portrayed in the same way. Fear, divide and rule, the old, old story.

The world army scenario is another obvious example of Problem-Reaction-Solution. If you want a world army and you want the people to accept it or even demand it, first of all you need a problem. If the

United Nations peacekeeping operation is effective, that is disastrous under the rules of Problem-Reaction-Solution. No Problem = No Reaction = No Solution. You therefore manipulate events in places like Bosnia to ensure that the UN peacekeeping force is not working. The more you can embarrass the UN operation the better, because as horrific pictures came out of Bosnia day after day the cry of "something must be done" became, again understandably, louder and louder. This provided the opportunity for the solution – a 60,000 strong "NATO" (world army), the biggest multinational force to be assembled since the Second World War. Another mighty step towards the creation of the world army and the dismantling of nation state armies under the guise of "peace" had been achieved. That was the real reason for the Bosnian conflict, hard as I know it must be to accept if you are new to this research. But if you read ...*and the truth shall set you free* you will appreciate from the evidence and background that such a conclusion is glaringly obvious. Virtually every major peace negotiator in Bosnia, from the start of that conflict, was a member of a network of the Bilderberg Group (Bil), the Council on Foreign Relations (CFR), the Trilateral Commission (TC), and the Royal Institute of International Affairs (RIIA). These organisations are controlled by the same Global Elite that manipulated the conflict into being and then funded and armed all sides in the horror that ensued. The European Union peace negotiators were Lord Carrington (Bil, TC, RIIA), Lord David Owen (Bil, TC) and Carl Bildt (Bil). They worked with the UN negotiators Cyrus Vance (Bil, TC, CFR) and Thorvald Stoltenberg (Bil, TC). Then, amid worldwide publicity, appeared the "independent" peace negotiator, Jimmy Carter, the first Trilateral Commission President of the United States and CFR member. After him came the group who negotiated the world army in Bosnia through the so called Dayton Agreement. These were Richard Holbrook (Bil, TC, CFR), who answered to the US Secretary of State Warren Christopher (CFR, TC), who in turn reported to President Bill Clinton (Bil, TC, CFR). The world army in the former Yugoslavia was headed from the start by US Admiral Leighton Smith (CFR) and the civilian aspects of the operation are overseen by Carl Bildt (Bil).

Lord Carrington, the former British cabinet minister, who became chairman of the Bilderberg Group in 1991, works closely with Henry Kissinger, one of the world's most prolific manipulators on behalf of the Elite. Interestingly, the horrific war in Rwanda erupted three days after an undisclosed "diplomatic mission" to that country led by Lord

Carrington and Henry Kissinger. The former Israeli Prime Minister Yitzhak Rabin (a Kissinger frontman, later assassinated) also agreed arms shipments to Rwanda in the run up to the conflict. People think it must be difficult to start a war, but it isn't you know. It's easy, given the desire of so many to give their minds away. To fight a war you need money and weapons. The Global Elite control the supply of both, so that's never a problem. To start a war you need one "side" to attack another country or community and away we go. The other country or community will defend itself and the war has begun. Many people are so full of dogma and racial division and intolerance that finding a group who will attack another is hardly difficult. You are spoilt for choice. The Global Elite normally ensure that their "employees" or puppets are leading all "sides", as with Franklin D. Roosevelt, Adolf Hitler, Josef Stalin, and Winston Churchill, in the Second World War. The Global Elite representatives (also known as presidents and prime minsters) then sell a fairy story to the human herd about the need to "fight for freedom" or "take our God-given right to this land" and suddenly you have two herds knocking seven bells out of each other. Creating a war, even a world war, is not difficult. It's a doddle. It shouldn't be, I know, but until humanity wakes up and grows up, it will be so.

When you look at the major posts around the world, like the Secretary General of NATO, the heads of the World Bank, the World Trade Organisation and the European Union Commission, or presidents, prime ministers and top politicians, bankers and industrialists, you so often find they are members of, or attendees of, the organisations I mention. That includes Bill Clinton, George Bush and virtually every president of the United States since the 1920s. Being invited to join or attend these groups can be a great career move. Bill Clinton was a little known governor for Arkansas until he attended the 1991 Bilderberg meeting in Badan Badan, Germany, at the invitation of his mentors, the Rockefellers. Within one year he was successfully campaigning to become president of the most powerful country on Earth. In Britain, there is a similar tale of rapid progress involving Tony Blair. He was a Labour Party home affairs spokesman when he was invited to the Bilderberg meeting in Vouliagmeni, Greece, in 1993. The following year he became leader of the Labour Party and would-be prime minister just as his opposition, the Conservative Party, began to suffer a stream of scandals and upsets. Blair's desire to be viewed as a potential world leader was enhanced when he was received and supported by Bilderberg frontmen like Clinton and Chancellor Kohl of Germany. When Blair visited the United States in 1996, his welcoming party read like a *Who's Who* of the Elite's gofers and manipulators. These included Bill Clinton (Bil, CFR, TC), Henry Kissinger (Bil, CFR, TC, RIIA), Alan Greenspan (Bil, CFR, TC), the head of the Elite-controlled Federal Reserve banking system, and the global financial speculator George Soros (Bil). So many of Blair's views and policies, including those on the European Union, mirror those of the Elite. He is an Elite "chosen one", and it was inevitable that he would become Prime Minister and work closely with Bill Clinton. These common connections between top politicians, peace negotiators, and the people in the major global posts, are never revealed in the mainstream media. I wonder why? The hundreds of papers and magazines worldwide owned by the Hollinger Group, including Telegraph Newspapers in the UK, don't mention this covert network because Hollinger is controlled by the Canadian Conrad Black, a core steering committee member of the Bilderberg Group. He hosted their 1996 meeting in Toronto and two of his Hollinger/Telegraph directors are Lord Carrington and Henry Kissinger, along with many other New World Order frontmen and manipulators. Maybe the influence of another Bilderberg steering committee member, Andrew Knight, on the board of Rupert Murdoch's News International might just be a reason why its newspapers and other media outlets remain silent on this subject. *The Washington Post* refuses to inform the public about these organisations and their membership because the *Post* is owned by Katherine Graham (Bil, CFR, TC). On and on it goes. Your mind is being stitched up and so, therefore, is the planet.

Another highly effective conditioning technique is what I call the stepping-stones approach. The whole conspiracy is based on mind manipulation and the Elite are very careful not to go too far too quickly. If they did, even the bewildered herd might see that something is going on. Instead, the Elite set their goal and move towards it stage by stage. Each of these stages are promoted as independent of each other when, in fact, they are coordinated steps towards a long agreed target. The stepping-stones technique changes the world before your eyes in a way which ensures that most people won't see that anything is changing at all – until it's too late. I have a four year old son called Jaymie and because I have seen quite a lot of him up to now, despite my travels, he doesn't seem to change much. He's changed slowly before my eyes every day and it mostly goes unnoticed. But people who haven't seen him for a few weeks or months look at him and say: "My goodness, Jaymie, haven't you grown, haven't you changed!" This is the basis of the stepping-stones technique and it is being used to introduce the Elite agenda by stealth.

Take the European Union. It was created, as I show in *...and the truth shall set you free*, by the same people and organisations who introduced the Bilderberg Group, the League of Nations and the United Nations. The European Union, with its plan for centralised political control, a European Central Bank and a European currency, the Euro, was plotted from the start to be the vehicle through which to impose the centralised control of Europe, itself merely a stage on the road to the world government, central bank, currency, army and a microchipped population. That, of course, is not what the people of Europe were told when we were asked to join. The "European Union" was then called the European Economic Community or Common Market. We were told we were joining a "free trade" area and not a centralised European superstate which would eventually encompass the countries of the former Soviet Union. Once we were in the web and the economies of Europe were intertwined enough to make withdrawal very difficult in the short term, the process began of changing the Common Market "free trade" area into the all-along-planned European tyranny, the European Union. Only now are more people beginning to realise how far this transformation has already progressed. The same process is underway with the North American Free Trade Agreement (NAFTA) which is planned to evolve into the North-Central-South American version of the European Union and this applies to the Asia-Australia "free trade area" known as APEC.

This has all long been planned. It is no coincidence that one of the plans of Adolf Hitler and the Nazis was the creation of what they called the Europaische Wirtschaftsgemeinschaft. This translates as...The European Economic Community! After 1945, the Nazi mentality merely swapped its jackboots and tin helmets for smart business suits. Appropriately, the introduction of the European single currency will involve the transfer of the gold, currency and bond reserves of all member states to the European Central Bank in Frankfurt, Germany. This bank will be controlled by six unelected bankers with a guaranteed eight year period in office and, as the Maastricht Treaty says, this "super six" cannot have their decisions overturned. They become a legal European dictatorship. My goodness, Adolf Hitler would have been delighted to see his plan unfold under the guidance of another German leader, Chancellor Helmet Kohl, a longtime and passionate frontman for the Bilderberg Group.

The introduction of "voluntary" identity cards in the UK is a classic case of the stepping-stones principle. If the government (Global Elite) had made them compulsory it would have triggered opposition from civil liberties groups and started a debate about the erosion of freedom. But by introducing them initially as "voluntary" that opposition was spiked. Then you ensure that it is increasingly difficult to operate without the cards and you offer incentives to carry them. In the end you achieve your goal, but without the hassle of concerted opposition or public debate.

The stepping-stones technique is also being used to phase out cash and move us ever closer to the day when all money will be electronic and financial transactions will be processed via computers and tiny microchips under the skin which will carry all financial and personal details. We are being conditioned to believe that the phasing out of notes and coins will make everything more "efficient" and the manipulators are appealing to human prejudice by emphasising how the end of cash will stop social security fraud and tax evasion. The real reason, however, is control. Once cash has gone we hand the power over our lives to a computer and its programmer. If you go into a shop now with a credit card (electronic money) and the computer refuses to accept it, at least you still have another means of purchase, you can pay cash. But what happens when there is no cash and the computer says no to your credit card or microchip? How do you purchase? You can't. The computer, and whoever programmes its responses, controls what, when, and if you buy. More than that, as some electronics engineers have warned, once we have a microchip inside us, messages can pass from the computer to the chip which can create mass anger, hysteria, aggression, and a stream of other emotions. We will literally be robots then. And this is no science fiction sometime-maybe prediction. It is desperately close and trials involving microchipping are already in operation around the world. The technology exists and the only thing left is to manipulate the human mind to accept it. This conditioning has been underway for some time and the microchipping of domestic animals is becoming routine. In the Autumn of 1995 I saw an item on the BBC's "science" programme, *Tomorrow's World*, which looked very positively at a scheme to microchip people with their medical records. A woman was featured with a microchip in her chest and along came the doctor with a bar-code reader like those they use in the supermarkets. As he ran this contraption down her front, up on the screen came her medical information. "Oh I think it's a wonderful idea" the lady told the camera "It's very convenient".

I'm sorry, would you just excuse me once more?

Aaaaaaaaaaaaaaaaaaaaaaaaahhhhhhhhhhhhhhhhhhhhhhhhhhhh !!!

Thank you.

You can see the potential when you look at how satellite television operates. Each subscriber has a card programmed to accept the channels they have paid for. If later you wish to subscribe to another channel, you might think you would have to send away for a new card. No, no. You ring the subscribers' department and they ask you to put the television on the station you want. At this point all you see is a scrambled fuzz. Then before your eyes, the scrambled channel appears in seconds. How did they do that?, I asked. They send out a signal which reprogrammes your card and no-one else's! They have the ability, even on satellite television, to isolate one card in one television in one home. And they can't do that with a microchip inside one person? Of course they can and that's the idea.

If you do nothing else to stand up for freedom, I would at least ask you to consider the consequences for you and your children of allowing the programme of human microchipping to commence unchallenged. You will be hearing a stream of "justifications" for microchipping, including the microchipping of children at birth ("You'll never lose your child again"), the storing of financial information to make credit cards redundant ("We can end credit card theft and fraud"), and the means to prove identity ("It will help to end crime, remove the need for passports, and stop illegal immigration and social security fraud"). All these claims and more are designed to manipulate your mind into accepting the microchip which will turn you into a fully fledged robot.

The microchip and the cashless society are part of that fundamental tool in the control of human existence...the world financial system. Ask most people why they are not doing or saying what they really believe is right and the reason will be fear. A major expression of that fear is the need to earn money to live. Again, that's the idea. If you can artificially inflate the cost of the basics of life, food, warmth, clothing, and shelter, you pressure people to serve your system to earn the money to buy those basics. The less you need to earn, the more choice you have to live your life as you see fit. The more you need to earn, the fewer the choices. This scam is founded on the greatest con trick of them all – the paying of interest on money that doesn't exist. The fact that we stand for this as a human race, reveals so much about the scale of the collective mind-cloning that has unfolded on this planet.

The Elite-controlled banks are legally lending as a matter of course ten thousand pounds for every thousand pounds they actually own. It is like you owning a hundred pounds, but lending a thousand pounds to your friends and charging them interest. Should each of your friends demand cash in their hands, you couldn't work this scam, but the banks have no such problem because most of their transactions do not involve cash. They work mostly with theoretical "money" – cheques and credit cards. If everyone went to the bank to ask for their money back at the same time, the banks would be bankrupt many times over because they are lending far more than they have deposited with them. All but a fraction of the money that the banks "loan" doesn't physically exist. Most people believe that banks lend only the money that customers have deposited with them. This is simply not true. What the banks lend is, in effect...nothing. When you go to a bank for a loan your account is "credited" with that amount. All the bank has done is to type the amount of your loan, say £10,000, onto a computer disk. If the bank was lending you its customers money, their accounts would have to be reduced by £10,000 to allow you to have the loan. But they're not. They remain the same. So where has this mysterious £10,000 suddenly appeared from? Your "loan", as with every "loan", is conjured out of nothing as merely figures on a computer screen! And from that moment you begin to pay interest on that non-existent money. More than that, this phantom "money" is even counted in the bank's accounts as an "asset" and this allows it to make yet more loans of the same kind. With every loan, the borrower goes into debt and the bank's official assets increase, and yet not one new coin has been minted and not one new note has been printed. It's all an illusion. Banking is the most profitable and most destructive criminal activity on the planet. People who grow food and produce the necessities of life are up to their eyes in debt, and often pushed into bankruptcy and ruin by people who do nothing more than type figures onto a computer screen and charge interest on them. Fantastic amounts of "money" are in circulation in the form of cheques and credit of various kinds, but less than ten per cent of it is in the form of coins and notes. More than ninety per cent of it doesn't exist. The system is massively bankrupt and it only survives because people are conditioned into accepting cheques and credit cards as "money" when, in fact, it is nothing more than an entry on a computer program with nothing whatsoever to back it up.

Staggeringly, this is how the vast majority of "money" is put into circulation – not by governments printing cash, but by private banks lending money that doesn't exist and charging interest on it. By credit in other words. This means that all but a fraction of the "money" used to exchange for goods and services is created, right at the start, as a debt. We hear that inflation is caused by governments printing too much money. No it's not. Governments don't print enough! Ninety per cent of "money" released into circulation is "created" in the form of debt by the private banking network controlled by the Global Elite. It is utterly insane and no wonder the mountain of debt increases by the minute. An economic "boom" when production and consumption increases, simply leads to more borrowing from the banks to increase spending. So in the economic "good times", the amount of debt increases by colossal amounts and this eventually leads to the bad times known as depression. As the banks have control over the creation of "money" through loans, they decide if there is to be an economic boom or depression by increasing or decreasing the amount of "money" they allow people to borrow. The difference between a boom and a bust is only the amount of money available through cash or credit to make purchases. As the banking system is controlled by the Global Elite, this tiny clique therefore have control over the economy of every country and the decisions of the political and economic "leaders" who either don't understand how the banking system and money creation really works (the majority) or are knowingly working with those who run the system. By this sleight of hand, the debts of people, businesses, and countries have soared into never-never-land and the need to pay the interest is reflected in the money we pay for taxation, food, warmth, clothing and shelter. The British Government spends far more on interest charges per year than it does on many vital services and once you realise how the system works it is no longer surprising that the United States is trillions and trillions of dollars in debt.

Look at what happens in one transaction alone. Say the US government wants to borrow a billion dollars to cover its short fall in income. It issues a Treasury bond or bill, an IOU in other words, and delivers it to the Federal Reserve, a cartel of private banks controlled by the Global Elite. The bankers then "create" a billion dollars at negligible cost to them. At this point the banks begin to charge the government (the people) interest on a billion dollars. Not only that, the piece of paper, the IOU, is now counted as an "asset" of the banks and it appears in their accounts as if they actually own a billion dollars in their coffers. This means that they can lend another ten billion dollars (at least) of non-existent "credit" to other customers!

Everyone involved in a production process, be it the supplier of the materials, the producer, the transportation company, the shop, etc… are all adding extra to their prices to cover their need to pay interest on the non-existent money they have "borrowed". By the time you buy a product in the shop, its price is massively inflated compared with what it needs to be, because each stage in the process is servicing interest payments on money that doesn't exist. We are buying three houses for the right to live in one because two thirds, sometimes more, of the money we pay on a mortgage is interest on money that doesn't exist. If you take out a £50,000 loan to buy a house with Britain's National Westminster Bank you will pay them back £152,000. You will buy three houses to live in one. On the leaflet which revealed these figures, they had the nerve to say: "The National Westminster Bank – we're here to make life easier". Thanks so much, I'm really grateful. All over the planet are people doing things they have no desire to do because they need to pay interest on money that doesn't exist. The Third World Debt which is crucifying billions of people by the day, is overwhelming debt on money that has never, does not, and will never exist. And we stand for this!

It is a con trick. It is not necessary. It is there to control us. That is why the system was created in the first place.

Despite the obvious insanity of this legalised theft, our minds are still conditioned to believe that charging interest on money is essential and without it the world economy would collapse. Not so. The global banking dictatorship orchestrated by the Global Elite would collapse and that would be fantastic. But people who are enslaved by paying interest on money that doesn't exist, defend the system and say it must continue! Hey, prison warder, don't you dare open that door, d'ya hear? The interest system is not a safeguard against economic suffering. In truth the interest system creates poverty and inequality and allows the accumulation of global power. Tell me this: what would happen if, instead of borrowing non-existent money from the private banking network, our governments printed their own money interest-free and lent it to the people interest-free with perhaps a very small one-off fee to cover administration costs? Would we no longer be able to buy all we need? Yes, of course we would, and far more easily because the cost of everything would be less. The cost of a mortgage would plummet by two-thirds if you no longer had to pay interest. The homeless could be housed and we would not have the grotesque sight of people sleeping rough in the streets because they cannot gather together enough pieces of paper or non-existent computer figures to pay for a proper shelter. Money would become what it was meant to be, a means of exchanging contributions to the community which smooths out the limitations of barter. It is only when you have interest on money that it becomes the vehicle for control which is used with such devastating effect today. No-one gains from the payment of interest, except the banks of the Global Elite. No-one would lose out if the system were changed, except for the banking nexus and those who use money to make money without any productive contribution to the world. The banks which have plundered and abused humanity for so long would go under and the role of their successors would be constructive rather than destructive. Is the demise of interest-charging banks really so terrible? I'm leaping for joy at the very thought. There is no reason why we cannot have interest-free money. It is only the will that is missing because the politicians who could bring an end to interest on money are controlled and manipulated by the same people who own the global banking system which wields its power over people's lives by demanding interest on money that doesn't exist. Look at the "different" political parties in your country. How many of them are proposing to end interest on money if they are voted into power? None? Thank you. And now you know why.

Two presidents of the United States have proposed to print interest-free money and begun in a small way to introduce it. One was Abraham Lincoln and the other was John F. Kennedy. What else do they have in common?

An important question to ask constantly is "who benefits?" Whenever a politician, economist, church leader, journalist, or anyone is telling us what to think it is worth asking that question: who benefits from me believing what I am being asked to believe? The answer invariably leads you to the real reason you are being fed that line of "thinking". For example, who benefits from people believing that "far-right militias" were behind the Oklahoma bomb? Those who wish to discredit the militias' claims about the Global Conspiracy and those who wish to justify the introduction of more authoritarian laws in the United States and, as President Clinton put it within 24 hours of the bomb: "an easing of restrictions on the military's involvement in domestic law enforcement". Who benefited from the bomb in Saudi Arabia in 1996 which killed 19 Americans? Those, like Bill Clinton, who wanted a problem-reaction-solution situation to justify a greater erosion of freedom. The G7 meeting of industrialised countries which followed the bombing was dominated by the need to "fight" terrorism. They then arranged for a G7 summit on terrorism and measures (erosion of freedom) to stop it. What happened in the days before that summit? A TWA airliner was blown from the sky shortly after leaving New York and a bomb exploded in Atlanta during the Olympic Games. Who benefited? Those who wanted to put terrorism at the top of the world agenda at the time of the G7 meeting. Witnesses report seeing a flash of light soaring towards the TWA jet, seconds before it exploded.

I've described in this chapter some of the consequences of conceding to others our right to think for ourselves. When we do that, we:

a allow a tiny Elite to decide our destiny, and that of our children;
b allow this Elite to so programme our sense of limitation that we live at a fraction of our true potential;
c allow our minds to be manipulated minute by minute to see events and people in precisely the way the Elite desire;
d allow a relative handful of bankers to control the finances of billions of people by charging interest on money that doesn't exist.

When you give your mind away, you give your life away. When large numbers of people do that, they give the world away. This is precisely what we have done.

The state of the world and the shape of own lives is not someone else's "fault". There is no-one to blame for what happens to us and our fellow expressions of God. What I have briefly outlined here is of our doing. The manipulation and control I have described is our creation, a reflection of the current state of human thought or non-thought. We are responsible for what has occurred and continues to do so.

If anyone is still in any doubt about the scale to which we have conceded our destiny to a tiny clique, or of the deeply unbalanced mentality that motivates that clique, the next chapter will blow your mind.

Chapter 4

The Depths Of Evil

I trust you'll enjoy a few laughs as this book progresses because humour is so important. It is a wonderful antidote to fear and puts into perspective all those events and areas of ours lives that make us frightened, control our thinking, and cause us emotional pain. When subjected to humour, most things that we take seriously are shown to be what they really are: utterly ludicrous.

However, in this chapter there are no laughs. Some things are so grotesque, so beyond the imagination of anyone within a thousand miles of mental and emotional balance, that humour does not and cannot apply. In my years of speaking and writing about these spiritual and conspiratorial subjects I have resisted using the word evil. Even now I emphasise that what we call "evil" is an extreme negative imbalance in the consciousness and people in that mode can and do change. "Evil" is not forever. It is for as long as those minds choose to stay in that state of being. But in the light, or rather the dark, of what I am about to outline, the feel of that word evil seems so appropriate. Indeed we are talking the very depths of evil.

People who desire to dominate the world and control the lives and thinking (same thing) of billions are seriously imbalanced. Many of them are psychopaths. It is vital to understand this if we are to appreciate how it is possible to coldly sit down and organise the manipulation of wars, famine, and disease, which bring untold suffering and misery to Planet Earth. Nor does such a mental state manifest in only one aspect of their behaviour. It affects their entire being. Nothing confirms this more than the creation of human robots through mind-control and the almost unimaginable torture to which they are subjected. Information about this began to come my way from a number of unconnected sources while I was writing this book and I feel compelled to share it with you. Then you will see the scale of evil to which we, the human race, have conceded control over our lives and our children's lives.

Knowledge is not positive or negative, it is always neutral. It is how knowledge is used that is positive or negative. The same knowledge that can create weapons of mass destruction can also be applied to produce free energy technology which can provide all the power and warmth we need at virtually no cost and no damage to the environment. So it is with what we call esoteric knowledge which some misguided people dismiss and condemn as the "occult", a word, incidentally, which merely means hidden. They brand this knowledge as the work of the devil. Others seem to believe, naïvely, that esoteric knowledge is by its nature spiritual and of "the light." It is neither good or bad, it just is. It is only the knowledge of the nature of life and consciousness. It can be used to set the consciousness free from its self imposed limitations of potential and perception, or it can be used to inspire that very sense of limitation and powerlessness.

This knowledge, the themes of which are revealed in this book, is as old as creation and even in the desperately short period described by what we call recorded "history" it can be charted back to thousands of years BC to the civilisations of ancient Sumer, Babylon, Egypt, Greece, and every other culture across the world. Variations of this basic core knowledge and its doctored and manipulated versions formed the basis of all the religions. They just changed the names, that's all. The themes, claims, and ceremonies of Christianity, for example, originate in the civilisations that long preceded the Christian dogma. The pre-Christian world abounded with stories of virgin-born sons of God who died so our sins could be forgiven. The founder of Christianity, Saint Paul, was really called Saul of Tarsus. He was brought up in Asia Minor where they worshiped a "god" called Dionysus who was said to be virtually everything that Paul later claimed for "Jesus". Dionysus was said to be a son of God who died to save the world. "Saint" Paul replaced the name Dionysus with "Jesus" and gave him the same attributes and myths. So Christianity was born and nearly two thousand years later it still controls the minds, directly or indirectly, of billions today. It's a con trick and no-one is more conned than most of the priests and churchmen who promote it. For more details see *The Robots' Rebellion*.

Christianity was soon taken over by the forces of domination and turned into a vehicle of mass control. Anyone who expressed views that challenged its manufactured nonsenses were systematically removed, not least through the inquisition which burned as heretics those who were not seen as "true" Christians. The definition of "true" was to follow without question the doctrine imposed by the Pope. The esoteric knowledge, the basic truths of who we are, where we came from, and what we are doing here, has been hoarded by the few, in a twisted form, for at least thousands of years to keep the masses in ignorance of these things. When Christianity was invented and condemned the "occult" so violently, the knowledge was all but eliminated from the mass consciousness. As Christianity continued to export its creed through death and destruction to the Americas, Africa, Australia, and so on, the esoteric knowledge was further lost as native cultures were destroyed and "Christianised". This was perfect for the manipulating force because they could now have a virtual monopoly on the knowledge and its potential to control and exploit because the people in general were either kept in ignorance or conditioned to see such knowledge as evil. One consequence of this was the mass torture and murder of "witches".

The advanced levels of this knowledge had been passed on through secret initiation ceremonies to the chosen few in the Mystery Schools of Babylon, Egypt, Greece, etc, and certainly long before that in civilisations unrecorded by official history. As the centuries passed, and Christianity withdrew the knowledge from the public arena, the work of these Mystery Schools evolved into the massive secret society network we see today which includes the Freemasons and the Knights of Malta, both of which control the Pope and the Vatican. What a wonderful way to direct and influence the behaviour of all those Roman Catholics worldwide. If a Pope does not play the game, he is removed, as with the murder of Pope John Paul Ist, in 1978 (see *...and the truth shall set you free*). The modern Freemasonic network is only the ancient knowledge in the guise of a gentlemen's club. At the time of the Crusades, a number of "knights" organisations emerged, the most famous of which was the Knights Templar. They wore the symbol of the red cross on the white background which symbolised blood and semen and represented their knowledge of the power of sexual energy, the creative force, be it positive or negative in its use. The Templars claimed to be a Christian organisation – a mere smokescreen for their secret knowledge and beliefs which originated in ancient Egypt and before. They were purged by the Pope and the King of France, but they continued to operate as an underground network until they re-emerged publicly as...the Freemasons. This is the same organisation, the Knights Templar under another name, and a major tool for the Global Elite's manipulation of the world. It is no coincidence that the flag of England is the red cross on the white background, nor that this same flag was flown by Christopher Columbus when he "discovered" the islands of the Americas. He wasn't looking for India only to find the West Indies. He knew exactly where he was going because he had the maps that had been been passed on through the secret society network, of which he was a member (see ...*and the truth shall set you free*). The existence of America was known about long before it was officially "discovered". History has just been written to suppress this fact and all the questions that would emerge from it. Those given the knowledge in the initiation ceremonies are said to be "illuminated" and this gave birth to the name of a leading force within the conspiracy, the Illuminati.

So here we are in the modern world with a network of secret societies which, at the peak of the pyramid, are all the *same* organisation working with the same knowledge to the same end – control of the world. Of course, most of their membership have no idea that this is the case because they never progress beyond the lowest levels of initiation and are therefore kept in ignorance of what they are involved with. As I've already emphasised, the people who go to their local Freemasons lodge and roll up their trouser leg are the frontmen, the veil, for what is really going on at the top. The initiation ceremonies are pretty black and bizarre even at the lower levels and they become more and more so the higher you go. One infamous and sinister secret society within the network is the Skull and Bones Society based at Yale University in the United States. The skull and crossbones flag was also a Templar flag. At the Skull and Bones Society headquarters known, appropriately, as the Tomb, carefully selected students are initiated and, surprise, surprise, so many of them end up in positions of power. George Bush, the President of the United States for three terms of office (including the two officially credited to Ronald Reagan) is a Skull and Bones member. He, like all the rest, would have been initiated by lying naked in a coffin with a ribbon tied to his willy while he masturbated and shouted out details of his sexual exploits. I don't have a problem with anyone doing anything so long as they don't force it on other people. Everyone to their own. But this is not just a group of people choosing to stimulate themselves sexually in ways that turn them on. It goes way, way beyond that.

A question I am constantly, and understandably, asked is: "Who are these people who control the top of the pyramid?" The answer is that they are the chosen few who are initiated into the highest levels of the secret society network through which all the other areas of society,

Figure 3: The Dollar Bill

banking, business, politics, media, intelligence agencies, the military, and "education", are controlled by ensuring that representatives of the network are appointed to the major posts or string-pull the people in those posts. The Bilderberg Group-Royal Institute of International Affairs-Trilateral Commission-Council on Foreign Relations conspiracy is supervised by a secret society called The Round Table which is, itself, part of the overall global network. Each generation of manipulators choose the next generation and hand over the "keys to the Kingdom". At the Elite levels there are also a number of families, including the Rockefellers and the House of Rothschild, from whom many of the Elite are selected in each generation. At the peak of the pyramid, and indeed at other levels, too, the mentality behind the manipulation is based on Satanism and black magic. I call it the Cult of the All Seeing Eye because its best known symbol is of a pyramid and all seeing eye – the very picture you will find on the US dollar bill (*Figure 3*). The order to print the symbol of a global black magic cult on every dollar bill was made by that Elite frontman and 33rd degree Freemason, Franklin D. Roosevelt, while he was President of the United States in 1935. This same symbol is also the reverse of the Great Seal of the United States. How appropriate given that this cult of the All Seeing Eye controls the US and its banking and financial system. The symbol, like the cult, goes back to antiquity. We are just experiencing the modern version of it. The common theme of the conspiracy across the centuries is a massively imbalanced consciousness which operates in this world through the minds of people open to such possession. You might take a step back in amazement and incredulity when first reading all this, but unfortunately it is true. This is the Satanic state of mind which currently calls the shots on Planet Earth and that explains so much about what goes on here. The All Seeing Eye at the peak of the pyramid is symbolic of this highly negative consciousness which is known under many different names and guises throughout the world religions and ancient legends. The Egyptians, for instance, called this force "Set".

The knowledge of how to manipulate human consciousness, collectively and individually, has been accumulated and passed on like a baton for thousands of years at the highest levels of the secret society network and so now this knowledge is vast. It is used to manipulate us through information management and advertising via the careful use of key words and phrases, sounds, colours, hypnosis, and symbols, the latter of which fundamentally affect the psyche. This is why the symbols used today by this network are exactly the same ones that were used and held sacred in the ancient world. The Nazi swastika is an ancient esoteric symbol which, in its original form, is positive. But the Nazis turned it around to symbolise the negative. Just looking at symbols can have a powerful effect on the mind and the Nazis knew that. The whole Nazi movement was based on sinister secret societies and the abuse of esoteric knowledge. They were Satanists because they, too, were connected to the cult of the All Seeing Eye. So were the hierarchy controlling the Americans, French, British, and Russians, who "opposed" them!

As I have shown in other books, the ability to turn someone into a robot by mind programming has been understood for a very long time and it is becoming more sophisticated and advanced with every year. Much knowledge was taken to the United States after the Second World War by the Nazi mind-controllers and geneticists who were spirited out of Germany after 1945 by a British-American intelligence operation known as Operation Paperclip. Like I say, the Nazi mentality did not end in 1945, it merely donned white coats and business suits. People using the esoteric knowledge positively are able to "hear" psychic guidance and see other dimensions. Others are able to leave their bodies and experience those dimensions in a non-physical state; to tune their consciousness into the "future", as with Nostradamus; and to project powerful thought forms which affect the world positively. Those using this knowledge negatively can do precisely the same. What we call voodoo is the ability to implant thought forms into another person's energy field, causing them illness, pain, or mental and emotional distress. The mind controls the body and so it is possible to programme someone's mind to make the body die. This is how some public figures die of "natural causes" at the most convenient times from the Elite's point of view. This brings me to information you sure as hell ought to know about.

All over the world are millions of mind-controlled zombie slaves under the constant influence of those in the secret network who have programmed them or know the means to activate that programming. These slaves include men, women, and children as young as two and three. Hundreds of thousands of people go "missing" every year in the United States never to be seen again. Still more do so in South America and elsewhere. What happens to these people? Some of them are abducted by the Elite-controlled "intelligence" agencies and their offshoots and used for Nazi-style genetic experimentation and mind-control projects. Many, yes at least many, of the people who talk of being abducted by "aliens" and taken into spaceships for experimentation have actually been abducted by humans. Abducting someone, wiping their mind of that memory, and replacing it with a hypnotic suggestion that they were abducted by "aliens" is child's play today to these people working in the secret military and scientific establishments in the United States, the United Kingdom, and around the world. When those people become conscious they genuinely believe they were abducted by "aliens" when, in fact, it was really a very powerful hypnotic suggestion. Many are also found to have been impregnated with microchips. The fear of extraterrestrial "aliens" is another aspect of the manipulation of human perception on the road to total control. They are planning to "reveal" details of an extraterrestrial "invasion" of the Earth to justify the immediate creation of a world government and army. Ahhh! Save us from the aliens! We are already being conditioned for this and the UFO investigation network is being used to spread this disinformation, as is Hollywood through films like *Independence Day*. I can picture the scene now. The US President with stern face and ominous tone announces that knowledge of extraterrestrial activity has been suppressed for decades to avoid global panic. But now the situation is so grave that the world has to be told of the imminent threat of an extraterrestrial invasion. The only way to meet this threat, we will be told, is to forget our differences and come together as "one" (world government and world army). That is not to say that I reject the idea of abductions by extraterrestrials, nor that 'ETs' play a significant part in the manipulation of this world. I believe they do. The point I wish to emphasise is that this situation can be used to dupe us into accepting things we would not normally accept so readily, such as a world army, government and so on. I am increasingly convinced that far from invading the Earth today, the extraterrestrials have been here for thousands of years at least, and in many forms. My next book will include more details on this.

One method of creating human robots is called Multiple Personality Disorder (MPD), also known as Dissociative Identity Disorder (DID). This involves compartmentalising a person's mind into a series of programmed "personalities", each of which is triggered by a word, sentence, sound or action. Each compartment of the mind is unconnected to the others. So one minute you are operating in a certain "personality" and the next, after the trigger word or action, you lock into another. It's like moving a dial on the radio and picking up another station. What's more, unless you are skillfully deprogrammed, you don't remember anything as the "dial" keeps moving. It is exactly the same principle as compartmentalising the global pyramid in the way I described earlier. Even this technique is primitive compared with the latest methods. People, or rather zombies, in a programmed state are used for many things. They are activated to carry out assassinations, as with the killers of John Lennon and Robert Kennedy.[1] This is why so many assassinations are performed by people with the same mental profile – the so called "lone nutters." They are neither alone nor, in most cases, insane if they were allowed to live in their natural state. They are programmed beings, often, as we shall see, since childhood. By this method, you can, for instance, plant a terrorist bomb and ensure that the person you want to be blamed for it is in the right place at the right time for him to be accused and charged with the outrage. You can also programme that person's mind while in custody to ensure that he even thinks he was involved. The infamous CIA mind-controller called Dr Louis Jolyon "Jolly" West, who features strongly in *...and the truth shall set you free*, has, it appears, been working with Timothy McVeigh, the

---

[1] There is speculation about whether the mind-controlled Sirhan Sirhan actually delivered the fatal shots in the assassination of Robert Kennedy, the brother of JFK, in 1968. But he was certainly there with a gun and this allowed him to be jailed for the murder while the real killer and those who arranged the programming got away with it. See *...and the truth shall set you free*.

microchipped former US soldier who was convicted of the Oklahoma bombing. West was involved with the appalling US Government mind-control project known as MKUltra and one of his keenest supporters was the then Governor of California, later President of the United States, Ronald Reagan.

We have also seen a spate of "lone nutters" in a number of countries who commit mass murder by going apparently crazy with guns. In the United Kingdom we have had horrific examples of this in the little towns of Hungerford in Berkshire and Dunblane in Scotland. A "nutter" called Thomas Hamilton walked into a school in Dunblane and opened fire on little children in the gymnasium. The affect on the collective psyche of hundreds of millions of people across the world, especially, of course, in the UK, was devastating. Shortly after that came the massacre in Port Arthur, a small town in Tasmania, Australia, when another lone gunman went "crazy." This was followed in England by a guy attacking children and their teachers with a machete at a school in Wolverhampton. What goes on here? Look at the profiles of such people. They have a "background" of being a bit strange or "simple" – "not the full quid" as neighbours described the Port Arthur killer, Martin Bryant. This is perfect when you want them and their horrors to be dismissed as the work of a lone nutter. In Bryant's case he had just returned from a two week stay in the United States when he went beserk with his gun. People close to him said his character had changed after he came back from the US. It has been shown that terrorist groups like the IRA have what they call "sleepers", people who lie low unused for years, even decades, until circumstances arrive in which they and their cover can be exploited for a particular task. It is the same in this world of mind-control. There are people programmed to live in the community with a certain character profile until the time comes when they can be used. They are known in the "trade" as "dead eyes". They have no idea that they are being used in this way because they are not in control of their minds, their programmers are. There are so many unanswered questions, interestingly, about why the Dunblane killer, the Freemason Thomas Hamilton, was allowed to legally keep guns when his strange behaviour should have ensured his licence was refused. And why did the police in Port Arthur take an hour to respond when the scene of the massacre was close to the police station and they had been informed within minutes of Bryant's first shots? Also, Bryant, Hamilton and so many other people who go crazy in this way are reportedly taking the drug Prozac, a widely prescribed anti-depressant produced by Eli Lilly, a company closely connected to George Bush. Side effects include nervousness, anxiety, suicidal tendencies, hypomania and violent behaviour when the drug is withdrawn. Doctors are warned not to prescribe Prozac to anyone with a history of "mania".

So what is the motivation behind such massacres? Answer: The manipulation of the mind and emotions. Where did these mass murders take place? Not in the gangland areas of London, Glasgow, or Sydney, but in quiet little communities where everyone felt perfectly safe. In the same way, the "McVeigh" bomb was not planted in New York or Washington, but in Oklahoma. We would be advised not to underestimate the effect on the collective psyche in terms of fear and a desire for the authorities to "protect" people from that fear. That means more cameras in the streets and more security guards and cameras in schools so that children are brought up to accept the culture of being "protected" from danger by big brother authority. A front page headline in, I think, the London *Daily Mail* encompassed the very reaction the manipulators wanted to stimulate. It said after the Australia killings: Is nowhere in the world safe anymore? When these things happen in quiet communities, it encourages even more powerfully the response of "My God, this could happen to *me* and *my* children. Hey, we need protection". A traumatised mind is far more susceptible to mind manipulation. The Global Elite also want to remove all guns from the general population in preparation for their final coup d'état. No-one wants to rid the world of weapons more than me, but we need to ask about the motivation behind the immense pressure for gun laws inspired by...Hungerford, Dunblane, Tasmania, Oklahoma, etc, etc. Problem-reaction-solution. Getting hold of illegal weapons is so easy that gun laws would not stop anyone who really wanted to kill. The gun used by Martin Bryant in Port Arthur was stolen and he had no licence. Gun laws would, however, prevent the population from defending itself from the HIGs – the Hoodlums In Government, as the scientist Wilhelm Reich used to call them. I wouldn't use a gun to save my life. I don't see the point of using violence to oppose violence, but many people would and the Elite know that. Hence they want an unarmed population. Adolf Hitler introduced gun laws shortly before he began to transport people to his concentration camps. Similar camps or "holding facilities" have already been built in the United States by an organisation called

FEMA, the Federal Emergency Management Agency, which was set up by Zbigniew Brzezinski, the man who launched the Trilateral Commission with David Rockefeller.

Mind-controlled human robots are also used to pass messages between people outside the normal channels. These include unofficial communications between world leaders and between personnel within the Global Elite-CIA controlled illegal drugs network which involves presidents of the United States and many other world leaders and officials. People programmed through Multiple Personality Disorder apparently develop a photographic memory. The words of the communication are dictated under a form of hypnosis and then compartmentalised, often using a high voltage stun gun which lowers blood sugar levels and makes the person more open to suggestion. Later a trigger word, sentence, or action, activates that personality and the human robot repeats the message word for word like a recorded tape. I have no doubt that some world leaders are themselves under the influence of mind-control by their handlers and I am convinced that a well known politician in the UK, with his distant eyes and fixed smile, is under some sort of mental influence and controlled by one of his most prominent "spin doctors".

Most sickeningly, the robots, including very small children, are used to provide bizarre sex for presidents, foreign leaders, politicians, and businessmen who the Elite either wish to encourage into their way of thinking or to compromise and blackmail into doing as they are told. When I say bizarre, I mean it, and I don't find the information that follows easy to write or speak about. But it is so important that this veil is lifted, not least for those who are being subjected now, this minute, to some of the grotesque evil that I shall expose. For the most obvious of reasons these human robots are rarely able to talk about what has happened to them. They are either in zombie mode and can't remember or, when they are passed their sell-by date from the manipulators' perspective, they are murdered and sometimes their body parts are used for the unspeakable black magic rituals often attended by some very famous people. You think you know the personalities of people you see on the television? Please read on. Fortunately, one very brave woman who was mind-controlled as a young child has now spoken out after escaping from US government slavery. She was taken through long and painstaking deprogramming sessions lasting more than a year which broke down the compartments in her mind and allowed her to remember everything that happened to her – and who did it. She is Cathy O'Brien, an American of Irish decent, who has produced a self-published book about her experiences called *Trance-Formation Of America*.[2] It is a stunning tale she has to tell. But there have been thousands, probably millions, more like her – still are – and that will continue to be the case until humanity wakes up to its responsibilities. Because of her photographic memory, Cathy can describe in great detail the conversations she heard, the rooms and decor in the White House, the Pentagon and top secret military establishments across the US. She can also describe physical details of the people involved which she could only know if she had seen them naked.

Cathleen (Cathy) Ann O'Brien was born in 1957 in Muskegon, Michigan. Her father Earl O'Brien is a paedophile and one of Cathy's first memories was being unable to breathe because his penis was in her mouth. Such trauma automatically triggers Multiple Personality Disorder without any need for programming because the child's own mind wishes to shut out the horror. It compartmentalises the experience in the same way that people can't remember road accidents they are involved in. Her father's friends were also allowed to abuse and rape the young Cathy and her brothers, just as her father and mother had been abused as children. Her mother was sexually abused by Cathy's grandfather, the leader of a Masonic Blue Lodge. Her mother's brother, "Uncle Bob" to Cathy, was a pilot in Airforce Intelligence who claimed that he worked for the Vatican. "Uncle Bob" was also a commercial pornographer and Cathy's father forced her and her older brother, Bill, to take part in pornographic films made for the local Michigan Mafia which was connected, she says, to the "Porn King" Gerald Ford, then a US Representative. He would later be the Vice President of the United States under Richard Nixon and President when Nixon was ousted by Watergate, an outcome inspired by the Washington Post, owned by Katherine Graham (Bilderberg Group, Trilateral Commission, Council on Foreign Relations). Ford also served on the Warren Commission "investigating" the assassination of President Kennedy. While Cathy O'Brien was a little child at school, she says she was raped by Gerald Ford in the office of Michigan State Senator, Guy VanderJagt, who also raped her. VanderJagt would

---

[2] *Trance-Formation Of America* is available from Bridge of Love Publications (see back of book) and Brigadoon Books, 1 The Old Bakery, Mill Street, Aberfeldy, Perthshire PH15 2BT, Scotland

become the chairman of the Republican Party National Congressional Committee which supported George Bush, another child rapist named in Cathy's book, in his successful campaign to become President of the United States.

Eventually, Cathy's father, it appears, was caught sending child pornography through the post – a film of young Cathy having sex with a boxer dog. To avoid prosecution Cathy was, in effect, handed over by her father to the United States Government and the Defense Intelligence Agency. Her father was delighted with the deal because he was now immune from prosecution and could continue his pornography and paedophile activities while the authorities looked the other way. The Agency was searching for sexually abused children with Multiple Personality Disorder who came from families with a history of intergenerational child abuse. They wanted the children for their studies into genetic mind-control which operated under the title Project Monarch, an offshoot of the notorious, MKUltra. (I understand that MK stands for Mind Kontrolle – the German spelling of K replacing the C in deference to the Nazis, formerly serving under Hitler, who inspired the project.) The man who arrived at Cathy's house to give her father the ultimatum of hand over your daughter or be prosecuted was...Gerald Ford. Cathy's father was sent to Harvard University near Boston to be instructed in how to prepare his daughter for the mad professors of the Government agencies. Cathy says in her book:

" *...in keeping with his government-provided instructions, my father began working me like the legendary Cinderella. I shovelled fireplace ashes, hauled and stacked firewood, raked leaves, shovelled snow, chopped ice, and swept – 'because', my father said, 'your little hands fit so nicely around the rake, mop, shovel, and broom handles...' By this time my father's exploitation of me included prostitution to his friends, local mobsters and Masons, relatives, Satanists, strangers, and police officers...*

...Government researchers involved in MKUltra Project Monarch knew about the photographic memory aspect of MPD/DID, of course, as well as other resultant 'super human' characteristics. Visual acuity of an MPD/DID is 44 times greater than that of the average person. My developed unusually high pain threshold, plus compartmentalisation of memory, were 'necessary' for military and covert operations applications. Additionally, my sexuality was primitively twisted from infancy. This

programming was appealing and useful to perverse politicians who believed they could hide their actions deep within my memory compartments, which clinicians refer to as personalities." [3]

You think slavery exists only in history? Slavery is happening all over the world today, including, no *especially*, in the United States and other "civilised" countries like the United Kingdom. The paedophile rings make the news from time to time, but they are the tiniest tip of a vast network that goes right to the top (sorry gutter) of "free" societies. The truth about the abuse of boys at the Kincora Home in Northern Ireland was suppressed because one of the abusers was an agent of British Intelligence. It also involved at least one famous politician in Northern Ireland, but this fact has been covered up, not least by a now retired official of British Intelligence called Ian Cameron. Such child abuse networks provide the perfect vehicle to satisfy the sexual desires of those in control and for blackmailing those they wish to control. I want the names of those involved in whatever country you live in. If you know something, please tell me. The information will be in the strictest confidence and if it can be substantiated I will make it public. If you hesitate, just think about the children.

Cathy O'Brien says she was abused by Father James Thaylen when she sought comfort at a Roman Catholic Church called St. Francis de Sales in Muskegon and another priest, a Father Don, was a paedophile who helped Gerald Ford's friend, Guy VanderJagt, to confuse and abuse her in line with the "requirements" of Project Monarch. Later she was sent to a Roman Catholic School, one of many used by the government to safely house their mind-controlled children under the strict regime designed to increase the depth of their Multiple Personality Disorder. Her school was Muskegon Catholic Central High School where she was raped by Father Vesbit many times, on one occasion during a Satanic ritual involving other mind-controlled boys and girls in his private chapel. The Roman Catholic Church is the epitome of hypocrisy and deeply, deeply sick. The "Roman Catholic" Jesuit movement is an important vehicle for the manipulation of the global conspiracy and, like the Knights of Malta who help to control the Vatican, it does not even believe in Christianity! That's just a front. The whole conspiracy is masks, smoke, and mirrors. The Jesuits, the Knights of Malta, and the Roman Catholic hierarchy are part of the

---

[3] *Trance-Formation Of America*, p83.

Illuminati – the Illuminated Ones. They were, and are, keen supporters of mind-control outrages like Project Monarch and MKUltra. How appropriate given that the Roman Catholic Church has survived only by terrifying, brainwashing, and mind-controlling its global congregation. One Jesuit front for the conspiracy is the "charity", World Vision. Cathy was pressured and manipulated by the CIA's Roman Catholic branch into keeping secrets from a young age through a technique known as the Rite to Remain Silent and there were so many secrets to keep locked away in her compartmentalised mind. In the years that followed she says she was under the control of the US "Democrat" Senator for West Virginia, Robert C. Byrd, and her abuse by him and the government agencies expanded. Byrd is a "constitutional" expert working to undermine and destroy the American Constitution. She claims that Byrd controls a network of mind-controlled slaves and loves nothing more than to whip them mercilessly until they are close to death.[4] One of Byrd's associates, Senator Patrick Leahy of Vermont, would later torture Cathy by putting a needle in her eye while her daughter, Kelly, was forced to watch. Leahy was vice chairman of the Senate Intelligence Committee and served on Byrd's Senate Appropriations Committee. Leahy and Byrd played out a public game of "opposing" each other while actually working together to the same goals. The same masquerade goes on in the parliaments of the world. Byrd, a cocaine addict,[5] often bragged to "safe" people of how he mind-controlled President Jimmy Carter while he was Carter's "confidant and advisor". The hypnotic voice of Byrd became the "voice of God" to a praying and meditating Carter who faithfully followed the "guidance" he believed was divine.[6] Remember what I said about the mind-influenced UK politician?

Cathy's torture and mind-control was inflicted at many government establishments around the States, including the NASA Space and Rocket Centre at Huntsville, Alabama, where she and, later, her daughter, Kelly, were used for pornographic films. Yes, "man-on-the moon", "space shuttle", NASA does all this. Religions are used constantly to manipulate people and as a "respectable" cover for torture and mind manipulation. One centre of Cathy's mind programming was Salt Lake City, Utah, the headquarters of the Mormon "Church".

---

[4] *Trance-Formation Of America*, p 91.

[5] *Contact* newspaper, The Phoenix Project, February 7th 1995, p17.

[6] Ibid p 18.

Another establishment for mind-controlling slaves is known as the "Charm School" at Youngstown, Ohio. This is a "sex slave" training "school" where Cathy, Kelly, and a stream of other women and children were (are) tortured and abused with electric shocks, sleep deprivation, and sexual trauma. Cathy says an unnamed member of the Mellon banking family was the "governor" of the Charm School and other well known people involved were US Representative, Jim Traficant, and Dick Thornburgh, then Governor for Pennsylvania and later US Attorney General and Secretary for the United Nations.[7]

While still a child, Cathy was raped, abused, and tortured, by some very famous people. She says that she was raped by Pierre Trudeau, the long-time prime minister of Canada who, as a Jesuit, was working closely with the Vatican; raped again by Gerald Ford when he was actually President; raped by Ronald Reagan while he was President; and raped many times in the most brutal fashion by Dick Cheney, the White House Chief of Staff under Ford and the Defense Secretary of the United States under George Bush. Cathy is able to describe Cheney's office in the Pentagon in great detail. If you accept Cathy's highly detailed evidence you can only conclude that Cheney, like Bush, is an immensely imbalanced mind capable of staggering violence and even murder. Cathy says that Cheney told her on one occasion: "I could kill you – kill you – with my bare hands. You're not the first and you won't be the last."[8] These were the characters who launched the Gulf War to show that "violence does not pay"! Cheney, Bush, and others have "fun" playing something they call The Most Dangerous Game, Cathy documents. It involves threatening government slaves like Cathy and other mind-controlled children and adults with appalling consequences if they are caught in the game. They are then allowed to "escape" into a forest, usually in some top secret military area like Lampe, Missouri, and Mount Shasta, California, which are surrounded by a high fence to prevent any escape. George Bush, the man who called for a "kinder, gentler, America", Dick Cheney and Bill Clinton often go after them with guns, Cathy writes in her book. When they are caught, they are brutally raped, sometimes killed. Ladies and gentlemen, these are the people we allow to control the world. The Mount Shasta compound, where Bush and Cheney shared an office, is, according to Cathy: "The largest, covert mind-control slave camp of which I am aware."[9] There she saw an enormous fleet of unmarked black helicopters, which, as researchers have revealed, are part of the New World Order's private army which is being installed to instigate the coup d'état when the moment is deemed right. These helicopters have often been reported near the scenes of "alien abductions" and cattle mutilations. Part of the cover for these military and mind-control operations at the Shasta Compound, Cathy says, is the country music scene at Lake Shasta.

Cathy was forced to marry a mind-controlled Satanist called Wayne Cox, a member of the Jack Greene country music band. Greene, a CIA operative, was also a Satanist.[10] Cox's job was to further traumatise her to create more compartments which could be used to programme new "personalities." One night, Cox took Cathy with him to the ruins of the Union Railway Station in Nashville and, using a flashlight, found a homeless man asleep. He ordered Cathy to "Kiss the railroad bum good-bye" and proceeded to shoot him in the head. That was horrific enough, but he then produced a machete and chopped off the man's hands before putting them into a zipper bag.[11] As Cathy has stated at public meetings many times, Wayne Cox is a serial killer who invariably chops off the hands of his prey. In an interview published in the *Contact* newspaper, Cathy said:

> "By 1978, Wayne Cox, my first designated controller, was actively ritually murdering and dismembering bums, children, and those who 'wouldn't be missed' and blatantly distributing body parts from his Chatham, Louisiana home base to key Satanic capitals of several states which included the Little Rock/Missouri route."[12]

Government agencies know this, but he is immune from prosecution because he works for them. Cox led Cathy to another spot on the Union Station site, a tower at the old railroad depot, and waiting in a room for them was Jack Greene, members of his band and others, dressed in black robes. They were standing around a black leather altar. The room was draped in red velvet and lit by candles. Cathy was laid on the alter and subjected to rape and torture while the Satanists

---

[9] *Trance-Formation Of America*, p194.
[10] Ibid p101.
[11] Ibid.
[12] *Contact* newspaper, March 7th 1995, p33.

performed a black magic ritual that involved sex, blood, and cannibalism.[13] Years later when "married" to another CIA asset, Alex Houston, she would be made pregnant and artificially aborted many times so the foetus could be used for Satanic rituals. My friends, this is going on all over the world and it involves some of the best known people on the planet. There is a sexual "playground" for leading American and foreign politicians, mobsters, bankers, businessmen, top 'entertainers', etc, involved in the Cult of the All Seeing Eye and the New World Order. It is called Bohemian Grove in Northern California and here Cathy was forced to serve their perversions. These include Satanic rituals, torture, sacrifices, and drinking blood. No, I'm not kidding. Regular attenders of this Satanic centre are known as "Grovers" and people like Clinton, Bush and Ford are among them, Cathy says. So is Henry Kissinger and many others I name. All that I am describing is founded on the abuse of esoteric knowledge – black magic – and the constant sexual theme relates to the power of sexual energy, which I will explain in a later chapter. The global Satanic network is also a pyramid with the Global Elite and the Cult of the All Seeing Eye at the peak. These people are, in turn, under the domination of the "Lucifer"/"Satan" consciousness which controls its "personnel" through mind and emotional possession. The Satanic child abuse rings which are all too rarely exposed are, in fact, part of a coordinated global network that goes to the top of the pyramid. This is why so many world leaders are involved in Satanic child abuse. The Cult of the All Seeing Eye is based on Satanism and the black use of esoteric knowledge and this same cult controls the appointments to the major political, economic, and administrative posts in the world. Therefore you find that a staggeringly high proportion of people in the top jobs are people connected to this cult and its sexual abuses. The best actors are in Hollywood? No, no, they are in the parliaments and political parties.

One of those who controlled Cathy O'Brien was Lt Colonel Michael Aquino of the US Army, a top man in the Defense Intelligence Agency's Psychological Warfare Division. I have named him in my last two books as the head of a "Satanic church"[14] known as the Temple of Set, an organisation inspired, apparently, by the leader of Hitler's SS,

---

[13] *Trance-Formation Of America*, p101.

[14] Cathy says that Aquino does not himself believe in "Satan". He believes Satan is merely the ability to mind-control. But what is it that motivates his mind to act in such ways?

Heinrich Himmler. When it was exposed that America's Psychological Warfare was being headed by a Neo-Nazi from a "Satanic" church, the official response was that a man's religion was his own business!! But, as Cathy soon found out, people like Aquino and the rest of this deeply disturbed and possessed bunch are above the law, because their mentality controls the law right up to the president and beyond. Planet Earth is possessed by an extreme negative consciousness and these people are merely the physical expression of that. Again, later in the book, I will discuss the source of this consciousness represented by the All Seeing Eye.

Cathy conceived a child, Kelly, with her "husband", Wayne Cox, and soon Kelly was being used in the same way as her mother. Cathy says that Kelly was raped many times by George Bush and Dick Cheney and both mother and daughter were forced to have sex with animals for videos made on the orders of President Ronald Reagan. "Uncle Ron" liked nothing more than to watch these videos and they were known as "Uncle Ronnie's bedtime stories".[15] They were recorded and produced, Cathy says, by his pornographer, Michael Danté (also known as Michael Viti). Danté had connections with the Mafia and the CIA (same thing, mostly), and was a close associate of politicians like Guy VanderJagt, Gerald Ford, Dick Thornburgh, then Governor of Pennsylvania, Jim Traficant, and Gary Ackerman.[16] It was Danté who installed the tiny hidden cameras which recorded the sexual activities of US and foreign politicians so they could be blackmailed into supporting the New World Order. How many "leaders" today are following certain policies against the interests of the people because if they didn't the evidence of their sexual exploits would be revealed? Reagan's leading pornographer was a man called Larry Flynt who ran the pornography magazine, *Hustler*.[17] He, too, had CIA, Mafia and Vatican connections.[18]

Bill Clinton was compromised in this way on one occasion by his boss, oops, sorry, "opponent", George Bush. It happened at the Lampe, Missouri, mind-control facility known as Swiss Villa. Bush ordered Kelly to perform oral sex on Clinton while Clinton was doing the same with Cathy. She recalls the following exchange:

---

[15] *Trance-Formation Of America*, p127.
[16] Ibid, p128.
[17] Ibid, p111.
[18] Ibid, p162.

> *"Clinton pushed his way out from under me, and told Bush while he*
> *glanced around for the camera: 'You didn't need to do that. I'm with*
> *you anyway. My position does not need to be compromised.' Clinton*
> *was apparently referring to the blackmail tactics amongst the Order of the*
> *Rose* [All Seeing Eye] *Elite. World leaders were always compromised*
> *through covertly filmed bizarre sexual activity as was my experience at*
> *the Bohemian Grove.* [19]

After this encounter, Bush and Clinton discussed introducing Clinton's daughter, Chelsea, to the child abuse scene. Bush offered to "open her up". Clinton said he would have to discuss it with Hillary.[20]

Cathy says that she and Kelly were also raped by another Canadian Prime Minister, Brian Mulroney, who is addicted to sex with mind-controlled slaves.[21] Mind-controlled mothers and young daughters were (are?) regularly transported to Niagara Falls just across the Canadian border for Mulroney to rape them.[22] It was Mulroney in his period as prime minister who forced upon the Canadian people, the North American Free Trade Agreement (NAFTA), which is set to become the American version of the European Union. The Agreement was manipulated into existence by his fellow child rapist, George Bush, and later by Bill Clinton. Under the orders of President Reagan's personal attaché, Philip Habib, Cathy says she was forced to have sex on several occasions with the New World Order stooge, King Fahd of Saudi Arabia. The Saudi "royal family" serve as puppets of the Global Elite while suppressing their people with a brutal religion which they, themselves, do not even begin to observe. American mind-controlled slaves are also "sold" to Saudi Arabia, Mexico, and other countries to help fund the covert operations of the Cult of the All Seeing Eye.

Cathy was so powerfully mind-controlled that she was "promoted" to become what is known as a Presidential Model, a mind-controlled slave who is detailed to operate with the top people in the White House. She was used to pass messages between Reagan, Bush, and their foreign associates such as the dictators, Baby Doc Duvalier of Haiti, President Miguel de la Madrid of Mexico, and Manuel Noriega of Panama, a paid CIA operative working for the US Government's illegal drug trade. As I

---

[19] *Contact* newspaper, September 12th 1995, p15.
[20] Ibid.
[21] *Trance-Formation Of America*, p183.
[22] Ibid p178.

have explained in detail in previous books, Bill Clinton and George Bush are both drug addicts involved in running drugs on a massive scale. Clinton is addicted to cocaine while Bush's preferred drug is heroin. Gerald Ford is another drug runner. These facts are confirmed by Cathy's direct experiences. The world market in illegal drugs is controlled from London and by the White House and the US/global intelligence/ organised crime network to make vast amounts of money for covert operations designed to implement the global domination of the New World Order and to destabilise society to make people easier to control. Noriega was closely involved with this during the Reagan-Bush years and it was only when Noriega and Bush fell out that Bush sent US troops into Panama to remove him. Bush replaced him in Panama with another character connected to the South American drug trade and Noriega was taken to the United States to be jailed for drug offences!

Cathy observed one "party" attended by Air Force officials and their wives, drug barons like the Pueto Rican, Jose Busto, and the "hero" (I feel ill) of the Iran-Contra drugs-for-arms scandal, Oliver North. Large amounts of cocaine were laid out for their use. Upstairs were Noriega, Michael Aquino, and Senator Allen Simpson, the "Republican" from Wyoming.[23] While all this was going on, George Bush was having a "war on drugs" to "save the American children". Cocaine addict, Bill Clinton, would later do the same. In the midst of Clinton's "war on drugs", he ended drugs tests for White House staff because so many of his associates running the country were also addicts! I'm going to wake up in a minute, I'm sure of it. Cathy met Clinton a few times and on one occasion in Arkansas he was trying (successfully) to persuade a supporter, Bill Hall, to become involved in the drug trade. Hall need not worry, Clinton said, because it was "Reagan's operation". Clinton told Hall in Cathy's then mind-controlled presence:

> *"Bottom line is, we've got control of the (drug) industry, therefore we've got control of them (suppliers and buyers). You control the guy underneath you and Uncle (Uncle Sam, the United States Government) has you covered. What have you got to lose? No risk. No-one's going to hang you out to dry. And whatever spills off the truck as it passes through (Clinton laughed here and snorted another noseful of cocaine)*

---

[23] *Trance-Formation Of America*, p 150
[24] Ibid p155.

you get to clean up." [24]

Later that night Cathy says she was taken by Bill Hall's wife to meet Hillary Clinton at the Hall's guest villa. There Mrs Clinton, another cocaine user,[25] performed oral sex on Cathy and then insisted it was done to her.[26] Both President Clinton and his "first" lady knew Cathy was a mind-controlled slave and they know what is going on. So does Al Gore. They keep quiet because they are part of what is going on. Cathy acted as a robotic messenger for Clinton who was very adept at triggering her programming, as she has stated publicly many times. Presidential candidate Bob Dole knows what is going on, too, and yet nothing is done. Clinton and Bush may seem to be opponents in "different" political parties, but they are part of the same scam, the New World Order. Cathy O'Brien has confirmed from her own direct experience what researchers have been suggesting for years: Bush was President during the "Reagan" years, President through his own "official" period in the Oval Office, and pulled the strings again during the "Clinton" regime. Bush was born into the Cult of the All Seeing Eye. His father, Prescott Bush, helped to fund Adolf Hitler.[27] These two "opponents", George Bush (CFR, TC, 33rd degree Freemason, All Seeing Eye) and Bill Clinton (CFR, TC, Bil, 33rd degree Freemason, All Seeing Eye) are on the same side, involved in the same rackets. At the 1992 election the two "opposed" each other to present the illusion of a "democratic" society. Cathy met Bush and Clinton together years before Clinton was even considered a presidential possible. She once observed them at Swiss Villa at Lampe, Missouri. The "infirmary" on the site is home to a CIA near-death trauma centre. Cathy, under her mind-control, had delivered a large amount of cocaine there in a motorhome when she saw the two future presidents:

> *"...I noticed then Governor of Arkansas, Bill Clinton, at a corner table with Hillary talking to the then Vice-President George Bush, and their two special forces "toy soldiers"* [mind-controlled] *who had transferred the cocaine to the infirmary building. (My mind-control owner, US Senator, Robert Byrd, told me that Bush and others had been grooming Bill Clinton for the presidency 'in the event that the American public becomes disillusioned with republicans and believe that*

---

[25] *Contact* newspaper, September 12th 1995.

[26] *Trance-Formation Of America*, p155.

[27] This is all documented in great detail in *...and the truth shall set you free*.

electing a democrat would make a difference'. Clinton obediently followed Bush's orders. Since the implementation of what Hitler termed New World Order knew no party lines, the question should be raised as to the agenda of Clinton's 1992 presidential campaign manager, James Carville, and his wife Mary Matalin, who was Bush's campaign manager.)" [28]

Another Clinton-Bush connection is their love of hunting mind-controlled men, women and children, in The Most Dangerous Game. Cathy O'Brien told the *Contact* newspaper in the US about one of her experiences at Swiss Villa when Clinton and Bush went "hunting" with dogs for herself, her daughter Kelly and two mind-controlled "toy soldiers", one of whom had Italian-looking features:

"Swiss Villa appeared deserted, except for Bill Clinton and George Bush, who stood at the edge of the woods with their hunting dogs at the ready to embark on 'The Most Dangerous Game' of human hunting. (Clinton shared Bush's passion for traumatising and hunting humans.) ...Bush and Clinton were dressed alike in camouflage pants, army boots and wind breakers. The two also shared the trademark of wearing a cap of cryptic meaning. This time, Bush's camouflage cap had an orange insignia that said 'Dear Hunter'. Clinton's blue cap read 'Aim High' and had a picture of a rifle on it. Clinton appeared awkward with his hunting rifle, while Bush looked like an expert marksman with his black rifle with elaborate scope.

"'The rules of the game are simple' Bush began, triggering me by using the same words that always preceded a Most Dangerous Game.

"Clinton interrupted 'You run. We hunt.'

"Bush continued: 'This will be called "Hunt for a virgin" (Clinton chuckled) and she's it.' He pointed to Kelly who was still in my arms. I catch you, she's mine.

"Clinton spoke up: 'You'll have plenty of time to play with the dogs because they'll have you pinned down while we...' (he slid a bullet in the chamber for emphasis) '...hunt down the bigger game.' Clinton

---

[28] *Contact* newspaper, September 12th 1995, p12.

glared at the "toy soldier" with the waxy face. (Toy soldier was a term I often heard referring to the mind-controlled robotic 'special forces' young men who operated under the New World Order.)

"The two guys ran for the woods. Carrying Kelly, I began running too. Judging from the close proximity of the dog barks, I had not gone far when they were turned loose. The five barking dogs caught me right away and surrounded me. Kelly screamed as one snapped at her leg and I automatically slapped at its face. I was convinced the dogs were going to tear us up by the time Bush and Clinton walked into the clearing. They seemed to be engaged in a serious conversation until Bush looked up and smiled.

"'She's mine' he claimed (referring to Kelly) 'But then, she always has been. Let go.'

"As I walked past Clinton, who was still deep in thought, he mumbled: 'I thought you'd be fucking a dog or something.' We walked the short way back in silence with Clinton veering off to the right as Bush directed me toward the two helicopters...

"The door (of the helicopter) next to me slid open and Clinton pushed the Italian into the helicopter. 'I caught this one. He's going to ride jumpseat.' Bush motioned for him to sit in the leather chair marked for death by the black rose, while I rode in the actual "jumpseat".

"'Come here, little one' Bush coaxed Kelly. 'You can sit on Uncle George's lap.' He lifted her onto his lap as Clinton got in front with the pilot, who was starting the engines. 'Over the lake, Jake' Bush told the pilot.

"Flying over Swiss Villa's deep, remote lake, Bush set Kelly aside, stood up as far as he was able in the helicopter, and slid the door open. The powerful wind blew Bush's greasy strands from his face as he gestured for the man (the Italian) to stand up.

"'Free fall' Bush instructed 'That's an order.'

"'Yes, sir' he replied as he stepped out of the door fully clad in his camouflage uniform and military boots — with no parachute. I watched in

---

²⁹ *Contact* newspaper, September 12th 1995, p13.

horror as he fell to his death in the water below, splatter and submerge…" [29]

This is just one incident, one murder, in the lives of Bill Clinton and George Bush, the men the people of the United States voted to be their presidents. Please tell me it can't be true! The United States might lose its freedom? My God. America ceased to be free a long, long time ago if indeed it ever was. America is a one party fascist dictatorship while millions of Americans go on believing it is the land of the free.

When the slaves outlive their usefulness or their programming begins to break down, they are murdered. The so called Presidential Models like Cathy O'Brien are not allowed to live beyond their 30th year and when that came for Cathy in 1987/88, she was told it was her last year of life. Fortunately, she and the then eight-year-old Kelly would be rescued from death by a businessman called Mark Phillips. He had a considerable knowledge of advanced mind-control techniques from his time working for the Ampex Corporation and the US Department of Defense as a civilian subcontractor. This allowed him contact with the leading research scientists in this field and gave him access to knowledge that is denied to the mainstream psychiatric profession. Psychiatrists, like doctors and scientists, are also mind manipulated by the suppression of information which gives them a distorted picture of what is possible. Mark Phillips was thought to be "safe" because of his background and security clearance, and he was approached by a man called Alex Houston for support with a business deal. Houston was now the "handler" of Cathy and Kelly and he married Cathy at the instruction of her controller, Senator Robert C. Byrd.[30]

Alex Houston, a rapist, paedophile, and drug runner, was an "entertainer", a ventriloquist and stage hypnotist, who himself had his mind and mouth worked by someone else – the US Government's mind-control network. It was his job to maintain Cathy and Kelly in their programmed mode by following the instructions he was given, which included food and water deprivation and constant trauma. Houston used his travelling to venues as a cover to transport Cathy and Kelly to their "assignments" and this introduced Cathy to the truth about the United States country music industry, and, indeed, the "entertainment" industry in general. Country music, she discovered, was used by the US Government agencies to distribute massive amounts of drugs into American society and as a cover for its mind-control projects. It was these agencies, she says, which paid for the

---

[30] *Trance-Formation Of America*, p111.

promotion and hype that turned a singer called Boxcar Willie into a country music "star." Some of this promotion, Cathy says, took the form of high tech television commercials designed to have a hypnotic affect on the viewer. He became the leader, she writes, of the country music segment of the "Freedom Train" – the internationally recognised code name for the slave operations of Project Monarch. The name "Boxcar Willie" was not selected at random. It makes a statement about the man and his role. Cathy names Boxcar Willie as a paedophile rapist of mind-controlled women and children, including Kelly whom, she says, he raped regularly in three different mental institutions.[31] He is also heavily involved in the cocaine operations controlled by the government agencies and he was the man Bill Clinton's friend, Bill Hall, began to work with after Clinton persuaded him to become involved.[32] It was Boxcar Willie who inspired the moving of the country music "capital" to Branson, Missouri, to be close to the CIA-mind-control and drugs operation based at Lampe, Missouri.[33]

Many people in the entertainment industry are either connected with the conspiracy or mind-controlled by it. One of the latter was Marilyn Monroe, a "lover" of President John F. Kennedy. Both were to be murdered by the same force. Another mind-controlled singer, according to Cathy, is Lorretta Lynn, a slave of the CIA. Her mental and emotional problems are caused by this. Lorretta's "road manager", Ken Riley, is a paedophile and best friend to Cathy's handler, Alex Houston. Both were connected with US Congressman, Gary Ackerman, the "Democrat" from New York, who, Cathy reports, ran an elaborate drug operation through Long Island Docks.[34] Another mind-controlled woman rescued by Mark Phillips was Seidina "Dina" Reed, the daughter of actor-singer, Jerry Reed. Seidina had been used many times with Cathy in pornographic films under the control of her husband, the sadist, David Rorick (also known as Dave Rowe). Rorick was trained in mind-control by Alex Houston and Seidina's famous father, Jerry Reed, knew all about it, according to Mark Phillips. Seidina was a favourite sex slave of Prince Bandar Bin Sultan, the Saudi Arabian Ambassador to the US.[35] The singer, Kris Kristopherson, a drug-addicted alcoholic born into a CIA family, is

[31] *Trance-Formation Of America*, p156.
[32] Ibid.
[33] *Contact* newspaper, March 7th 1995, pp33–34.
[34] *Trance-Formation Of America*, p124.
[35] Ibid p31.

also involved as a seriously imbalanced controller and mind-manipulator of slaves, according to Cathy's book and public statements.[36] She writes that she was tortured by him and Michael Aquino, using high voltage electric shocks.[37] Kristopherson, a Jesuit, is an associate of Senator Robert C. Byrd, Cathy's controller.[38] In that position, Byrd was, in mind-control parlance, said to be "married" to Cathy even though she was officially married to Alex Houston. Cathy says of Kristopherson in her book:

> "...*Kristopherson nearly strangled me to death with his penis, which had further sexually excited him, late in the Summer of 1987 during another incident related to Byrd.*" [39]

Yet another world famous psychopath and drug runner for the government is the rock and roll "legend", Jerry Lee Lewis. Cathy says she was threatened on many occasions with the words: "we'll sell you to Jerry Lee". This was the background to Cathy and Kelly's lives when Mark Phillips came on the scene. He worked with Alex Houston on a big business deal involving Hong Kong and China, but then he was told by a representative of the Chinese Ministry of Defence about Houston's background and his involvement with the CIA, drugs, money laundering, child prostitution, and...slavery. Phillips's informant, who produced documentary proof, said Houston was a "very bad man" and that his crimes were "of the White House". Mark Phillips writes in *Trance-Formation Of America*:

> "*My first response to this "officer" was that Houston was too stupid and crooked to be connected with US "intelligence". This comment was quickly countered with a gut wrenching photograph of Houston. He was smiling a demonic grin while apparently having anal sex with a small, very young, frightened black boy. Later he was identified to me as being Haitian.*" [40]

Phillips made contact with an old friend, now dead, who had been an Air Force General in the intelligence division and maintained close

---

[36] *Trance-Formation Of America*, p117.
[37] Ibid p118.
[38] Ibid.
[39] Ibid p120.
[40] Ibid p12.

connections with the upper levels of US and foreign intelligence. The General told him about the CIA slave trade worldwide and that Cathy and Kelly had been subjected to trauma-based mind-control. Mark Phillips recalls:

> *"I was growing numb. The first words out of my dry mouth were: 'How would you spring these people out of it?'*

> *"He smiled and said: 'I wouldn't! What are you going to do with them if you get them out?' Before I could answer, he interrupted and said: "Look. You're still the same, but nothing else is with Uncle* [the USA]. *Now most of the CIA, FBI, and the MOB (Mafia) are the same, and they're making moves on the military."* [41]

Phillips was insistent that he wanted to attempt a rescue and his friend gave him the mind-controlling codes (based on Christianity and God) that would activate Cathy to go with him. The full and detailed story is told in their book which I urge you most strongly to read. Phillips took them to Alaska while leaving messages for the authorities that he had no intention of exposing the truth. He said he would "...take them to Alaska and play like a voiceless chameleon". This, as he hoped, probably spared their lives at this stage. They have also been helped by many good people in intelligence who want to root out the evil. There is an internal "war" unfolding within the intelligence community. In Alaska, Mark Phillips used his knowledge, with covert support from his contacts, to deprogramme Cathy's compartmentalised mind. This immense task absorbed almost every spare waking moment month after month after month. But he was successful and Cathy's mind and memory returned. What a story she now had to tell as she remembered with crystal clarity all that happened to her and Kelly. Sadly Kelly's deprogramming proved even more difficult and she suffers from severe asthma caused by the constant trauma she has suffered. Attempts were made by the CIA mind-controller, Dr Louis Jolyon West, and his associates to take Kelly from Cathy and Mark and eventually the authorities used the "law" to ensure the United Fascist States of America had control of her once again. At the time of writing Kelly, aged just 16, is a political prisoner under the custody of the State of Tennessee. The media and public have been banned from court cases involving Kelly and she is denied the right to an

---

[41] *Trance-Formation Of America*, pp13–14.

independent attorney. The court has also banned the words "President", "politics", "New World Order", "mind-control" and "George Bush".[42] Kelly and Cathy were never allowed to talk alone and talking in any way about the past was forbidden. Mark Phillips, who saved Kelly from her torture by the state, was banned from even seeing her. These restrictions were eased after the publication of their book. The authorities refuse to de-programme Kelly from her Project Monarch-MKUltra mind-control by invoking the National Security Act (amended by Reagan in 1984) which allows them to use the excuse of "national security". They are terrified of what Kelly would remember. Whenever you see governments using the guise of "national security" to deny justice and information, what they really mean is the security of their own criminal behaviour. Cathy and Mark have had their lives threatened many times, but they have sent their information, with documented and sometimes audio tape support, to a stream of US politicians, government agencies, and pressure groups, including Bob Dole. Why no reaction, Mr Dole? They have also produced their astonishing book, *Trance-Formation Of America*, and spoken extensively at public meetings all over the country. This has probably kept them alive because to kill them would merely confirm that what they say is true. And if Cathy's claims are not true, where is the legal action against her and the book? Most of the names involved are so wealthy that the cost of such an action would be no trouble. Why the silence in the face of allegations as grave and extreme as these? If you wish to support Cathy and Mark in their campaign for justice you can write to them at P.O Box 158352, Nashville, Tennessee 37215. I have become very close friends with Cathy, Kelly and Mark. They are amazing people.

With her mind cleared of its compartments, Cathy was able to remember all that she had heard about the global conspiracy. Because she was thought to be "safe", she witnessed many conversations about the New World Order which support the themes that I and scores of others have written about, including the plans for a military coup on the United States.[43] As Cathy's experiences confirm, the attempt to complete the takeover of the world is not a theory it is REAL. It's happening now. She says she heard both Reagan and Bush insist that the only way to "world peace" is the "mind control of the masses". She was able to observe the planning of the New World Order project, Education 2000, while under the control of another of her and Kelly's

---

[42] *Trance-Formation Of America*, p223.
[43] For more on this see *...and the truth shall set you free* and *The Robots' Rebellion*.

programmers and sexual abusers, Bill Bennett, a Jesuit-trained mind-controller, who became US Education Secretary under Reagan-Bush.[44] An alleged paedophile is named Education Secretary of the United States? Give me strength. He was eventually replaced as Education Secretary by his associate, Lamar Alexander, the former Governor of Tennessee, with whom Cathy says she had been forced to take part in a Satanic ritual in an affluent area of Nashville.[45] Bill Bennett's brother, Bob, who is also alleged to have raped Kelly at the Bohemian Grove in 1986, later became "legal counsel" to Bill Clinton.[46] Another of Bill Bennett's roles was to head a "war on drugs" for George Bush! Well at least Bennett could not be accused of a lack of experience in the subject. Cathy was used to compromise and provide "favours" for key politicians to ensure support for Education 2000. She learned that this project, also known as America 2000 and Global 2000, is designed to increase children's "learning" capacity while destroying their ability to critically think for themselves.[47] Yes, mothers and fathers, our children are being mind-controlled every day at school and most of the teachers don't even know they are doing it! A friend who works in education research in the United Kingdom has had access to suppressed surveys which show that children are asking fewer and fewer questions about the "facts" they are told at school – particularly after they move to the senior schools.

Cathy witnessed how the United Nations is just a vehicle for the Global Elite of the All Seeing Eye. George Bush referred to the New World Order as his "Neighbourhood" and talked of how he simply told many other world "leaders", like King Fahd of Saudi Arabia, what to do and say. No doubt the same applies to Saddam Hussein. The former US Ambassador to the UN, Madeleine Albright, is knowingly part of the New World Order conspiracy and George Bush once described her in Cathy's presence as "...the reverend mother of all sisters (slaves)."[48] Albright knows about the US Government's mind-controlled slaves and supports that policy. Yet there she was in front of the television cameras at the United Nations lecturing other countries on "human rights." Bill Clinton later made her Secretary of State. Brian Mulroney, the Canadian Prime Minister and child rapist, talked about the plan for the New World Order while with Cathy and Reagan at the same White House cocktail

---

[44] *Trance-Formation Of America*, p179.

[45] Ibid p172.

[46] Ibid.

[47] Ibid p175.

[48] Ibid p176.

party at which she met Albright. Cathy says she was subsequently taken to a White House bedroom with other slaves, including one controlled by the US Senator, Arlen Spector. Mulroney then arrived to rape them after activating their sex slave programming.[49] Cathy noticed that one of the slaves had a red rose tattooed on her left wrist and other people she met over the years, including Mulroney, wore the symbol of the red rose. This is the sign of the New World Order cult known as the Order of the Rose, possibly inspired by the Elite-controlled secret society called the Rosecrucians, and it is part of the Satanic All Seeing Eye Cult. Other people connected to the Order of the Rose include Clinton, Bush, Byrd, Bennett, and Trudeau. How fascinating, then, that the United Kingdom Labour Party should change it's party symbol in the 1980s to…the red rose. Isn't life just full of amazing coincidences?

Another vital area which Cathy O'Brien's experiences highlight is that of the "alien" threat. Some of her mind compartments were programmed with "alien" themes and many of her abusers, including Bush, claimed to be "aliens" from "far off, deep space" who had taken over the planet. Cathy believes that holographic projections were used to give the appearance to her of people transforming into "lizard-like" aliens. This relates to the theme in some UFO and extraterrestrial research of a race known as "Reptilians" operating on the planet. What if it was not a hologram that Cathy saw? What if these reptile-like extraterrestrials can manifest in human form? I know it sounds fantastic, but with each month that passes I am more convinced by the weight of evidence that there's much to investigate here. I will expand on this in my next book.

However, I emphasise again that we need to treat claims about the threat of an "alien" invasion of this planet with enormous care. If you have "flying saucer" – type technology developed in the secret underground bases and you have the ability to project highly detailed holographic images, you can easily dupe people who do not know what is happening into believing they are witnessing such an invasion or a "sign" in the sky from "God", whichever God you may choose to follow. That doesn't mean that what *appears* to be happening is *actually* happening. Extraterrestrials do not need to invade the planet. They are already here!

The events described by Cathy are not limited to the United States. The Cult of the All Seeing Eye is a global operation and so its Satanic,

---

[49] *Trance-Formation Of America*, p177.

black magic, rituals are going on all over the world. Shortly after I met Cathy O'Brien and Mark Phillips, I met another immensely brave woman, now aged 40, in England. I will leave her unnamed at this time. The stories she told me about her experiences mirrored so many of those described by Cathy O'Brien. Soon after she was born in Darlington in the 1950s, she was sold by her father to two Satanists. She knew them only as Thomas and Helena. She was "brought up" in the most horrific circumstances at a children's home in Hull, which was run by two other child abusers. At night a torch light would be shone into their bedrooms and if it was held on you for a minute or so, you knew it was your turn to go downstairs and be sexually abused. People think this sort of thing is rare. Like hell it is. It's rampant. Look at the Satanic child abuse and murder network exposed in Belgium which involves the police, judges and top politicians. The same is coming to light in north Wales and other areas of the UK. In the US, the Nebraska State Senator, John W. DeCamp, exposed the Satanic child abuse ring in Omaha, headed by top Republican Lawrence King.[50] This involved local police chiefs and the newspaper publisher, and some of these "paedophile parties" were attended by...George Bush.

Ted Gunderson, a man of 28 years experience with the FBI, told a mind-control conference in the United States that after long and detailed research, he estimates there are 3.75 million practicing Satanists in the US and between 50 and 60,000 human sacrifices a year. Therapists at the conference said that their clients had pointed to a mass Satanic grave site in open land outside Lancaster, California.[51] Another exists, apparently, at Matamoros, Mexico. The Satanic ritual network connects into the children's home, runaways' hostel, network to ensure a constant supply of children. Please tell me what you know.

During holidays back in Darlington, from the age of just seven and eight, my English informant met her father, who connected her with the two Satanists, Thomas and Helena. She would be given drugs via orange juice and ice cream and taken at night in a van to country churches in the Darlington area. The drugs were designed to make her easier to mind-control and compartmentalise to prevent her from remembering what she saw. However, as is often the case when people enter their 30s and 40s, the compartments gradually break down and

---

[50] See *The Franklin Cover Up*, available from AWT Inc, PO Box 85461, Lincoln, Nebraska 68501, USA.

[51] *Contact* newspaper, April 4th 1995, p23.

their minds start to relive flashbacks of their ordeals. They experience them again like watching a movie screen. It is for this reason that so many are murdered before they reach that age, often in "snuff" videos. Others are subjected to the "snatchback" when they are abducted to undergo "booster" mind programming to keep the compartments in place and the memories secret. Increasing numbers of people who survived their horrendous young lives are now beginning to remember and they are telling the same basic tale. If you are one of them, please contact me.

In the ordeals at the country churches which she now remembers, my informant and other children would be used in Satanic rituals involving sex, torture and murder. The windows of the church were covered over with black drapes and the inside was laid out according to Satanic law with different colours used for different ceremonies, depending on the time of year. Sometimes they would use the churches in secret, but don't underestimate how many people in the "Christian" clergy are also members of the Satanic network. The Satanists, she remembers, were dressed in robes and a number wore masks, including the face of a goat. In the UK, as in America, some of the best known names in the country are involved. She remembers vividly (God, the thought of it) being laid on her back on the floor of a church as a screaming boy, no more than six, was being held by the hair above her while a man who would later become a top politician in Northern Ireland had anal sex with him. When it was over, a knife was produced to cut the boy's throat and the blood poured over her. "I remember this man's eyes" she told me "The coldness of his eyes I will never forget". He prefers boys to girls, she said. Why am I thinking of the Kincora Boys Home in Belfast as I write this? On more than one occasion, she says, she was brutally raped by another man who has been a big name in United Kingdom politics for decades. This man, she says, used to hold her naked body to him by using hooks inserted into her flesh at the hips. She was just a little girl when this was happening. I know this is hard to read and I was numb for days when I heard all this, but it's time to be adult and know what is really going on in the world, because if we don't this will continue.

Within days of speaking to me, the woman was grabbed off the street and bungled into a van by six Satanists. A syringe was held to her throat as she was warned to stop talking to that "dangerous prat" Icke and to stop naming names. They threatened her life and those of her children if she continued. She was also told that if she didn't keep quiet, the family dog would be taken and "posted back to you in pieces". Nice people.

What this woman and others have told me would defy belief if it were not coming from so many different, unconnected, sources and were not the stories across the world telling the same basic tale, even down to the detail of the rituals and mind programming techniques. The children and the traumatised adults they become have nowhere to turn. Their stories are so fantastic that few believe them and they are frightened of going to the police because they know that the Satanic network includes top police officers, judges, civil servants, media people, politicians, and many others who control our "free" society. Questions like "Who are you going to tell" and "Where are you going to run" are used to break the spirit of people. Their sense of hopelessness makes them think there is nothing they can do to seek justice, so they give up and stop trying. Also, as so many of them have said, they are drugged and programmed to take part themselves in the ritual murder and torture of other children. This is videoed and played to them when they are back in a conscious state. They are so horrified at what they have done and so terrified of the consequences that they dare not speak to the authorities. The stories of the people I've talked to and the accounts of others I have read tell of events that are beyond comprehension, or, at least, they would be if they were not actually happening. Drinking blood, eating the flesh of dead bodies, thousands of adults and children buried in deep graves, the murder of people on camera for the so called "snuff" videos, the story is just appalling. One mother told a television documentary in the *Dispatches* series on Channel Four in Britain of how she was forced to place her new born baby on a Satanic altar and push a knife through its heart. A Satanist then had sex with the baby's dead body. This is happening in your country now!

The Cult of the All Seeing Eye can continue with its global dictatorship in all its grotesque forms because most people can't be bothered about what is going on in the world and who is controlling their lives and those of their children. They are so pressured by debt and fear that they keep their heads down and their eyes closed; or they are more concerned about the price of beer, the latest "scandal" on the television soaps, or how their soccer team is doing. Michael Aquino, the All Seeing Eye representative at the heart of the US Government's psychological warfare against its own population, once told Cathy O'Brien: "95% of the people want to be led by the other 5% and the 95% do not want to know what is really going on in government".

How sad that this is actually true. Anyone who still believes that the outcome of soccer matches or the price of beer is really important in the wider picture of life on this planet might benefit from reading the following. It is an account in Cathy's own words of what happened to her child, Kelly, again and again:

> *"Kelly became violently physically ill after her induction into George Bush's "Neighbourhood" and from every sexual encounter she had with him thereafter. She ran 104-6 degree temperatures, vomited and endured immobilising headaches for an average of three days (as is consistent with high voltage trauma). These were the only tell-tale evidences aside from the scarring burns left on her skin. Houston forbade me to call a doctor, and Kelly forbade me to comfort her, pitifully complaining that her head "hurt too bad even to move." And she did not move for hours on end. Kelly often complained of severe kidney pain, and her rectum usually bled for a day or two after Bush sexually abused her. My own mind-control victimisation rendered me unable to help or protect her. Seeing my child in such horrible condition drove my own wedge of insanity in deeper, perpetuating my total inability to affect her needs until our rescue by Mark Phillips in 1988.*
>
> *"Kelly's bleeding rectum was but one of many physical indicators of George Bush's paedophile perversions. I have overheard him speak blatantly of his sexual abuse of her on many occasions. He used this and threats to her life to 'pull my strings' and control me. The psychological ramifications of being raped by a paedophile president are mind-shattering enough, but reportedly Bush further reinforced his traumas to Kelly's mind with sophisticated NASA electronic and drug mind-control devices. Bush also instilled the 'Who ya gonna call?' and 'I'll be watching you' binds on Kelly, further reinforcing her sense of helplessness. The systematic tortures and traumas I endured as a child now seem trite in comparison to the brutal physical and psychological devastation that George Bush inflicted on my daughter."* [52]

While I was reading that and putting together the other information in this chapter, do you know what was happening in the United Kingdom? The collective psyche of England was mesmerised by a soccer match in the European Football Championship. The newspapers, radio, and television, were ablaze with stories about the England football team.

---

[52] *Trance-Formation Of America*, p158.

The tabloid papers, particularly the *Daily Mirror*, were full of pathetic pictures of English players, including some wearing tin helmets as the *Mirror* declared "football war" on Germany. Meanwhile, these "journalists" were allowing all that I have described and so much more to continue uninvestigated, unexposed. England lost to Germany in that match (good) and it was seen as a time for national mourning. Some people cried because eleven Englishmen in grey shirts had failed to kick a ball into a net more times than eleven Germans in white shirts. Still others went on the rampage in towns and cities. One Russian man was stabbed because he "sounded" like a German. And a few people can't control the world and keep all this stuff quiet? It's a doddle. I am not knocking football. Played well it is a beautiful game, but it's just that – a game. It isn't important. If it's not soccer, it's soaps on the television, lotteries, and game shows which focus the collective psyche on total crap and therefore divert our minds from what the tiny few are doing to us and our world. Also at the time I was compiling this chapter, I was approached in the street by two Mormon "missionaries" seeking to convert me to their "faith". These two young clones of the mind manipulators of Salt Lake City had no idea of the horrors being perpetrated in that place, nor that the true controllers of their "church" are the Satanists and child abusers of the United States Government. The human race has allowed itself to become little more than a mushroom which is constantly kept in the dark and fed bullshit.

Cathy O'Brien and my contact in England both agree that despite all the horrors and mind-control they suffered, their core spirituality could not be broken. That spiritual core is the unbreakable spark of light within us. It is the Source Consciousness. Pure love. That is far more powerful than any scale of negativity. It is the spark which will lead us out of here if only we will set it free.

What are the emotions within you now as you read of those names and the actions I've described? For most, I have no doubt, it will be a combination of hatred, anger and fear. All of them understandable. But what emotions also consume the people who do these things and those who control the Cult of the All Seeing Eye? Hatred, anger, and fear. We surely don't need any more of that. Those who have suffered and continue to suffer from these people, or rather the consciousness that possesses them, clearly need our love in enormous abundance. But so, too, do those responsible. It is the absence of love in their hearts that allows them to do it. Of course, what they do must be exposed and they must take the karmic consequences of their actions. We're all subject to that and the time for them to face their actions is here. But please, send them love, not hatred. They are possessed people. Forgive them, they know not what they do.

To simply hurl abuse and hatred at those involved would be an easy way to pass our responsibility for all this to someone else, to externalise that responsibility instead of looking at ourselves. It is no good anyone abdicating their responsibility for what has happened to Cathy O'Brien and is still happening to her daughter, Kelly, and millions of others all over this planet. People like Bush, Clinton, Reagan, Ford, Trudeau, Mulroney, and Cheney may be among the physical perpetrators of these horrors, but they can only go on controlling this world and treating our fellow men, women, and children, in this astonishing manner because humanity has given its mind away and allowed the few to run the show. YOU are responsible, also, and so is everyone, particularly those who have handed over their own infinite power to such an extent that they have become two-legged sheep in the bewildered herd. If humanity will learn the lessons of all this and take their power back, then the people I name in my books will, in terms of collective human evolution, have done everyone a favour by showing so, so clearly, what happens when you concede your right to be you.

You control your reality, we all do, and collectively we have created the global reality exposed here. We can create a new reality. It's just a thought, a choice, a change of attitude away. There is not a moment to lose. The time to make that choice is...NOW. We, and only we, hold the key which, with one turn, one change of perception, can transform this world from a prison to a paradise.

Chapter 5

Here's Looking At You, Kid

How are you feeling after reading all that? I'm not surprised. I thought I'd never be shocked again, but nothing prepares you for the scale of blackness which currently controls Planet Earth. Such control, however, is only possible because we have conceded our inner power. Indescribable as those events may be, the people involved are telling us something about ourselves. Nothing happens in isolation. Everything has a consequence. When you give your mind and responsibility away, you allow the few to control the mass. Given the staggering extremes described in the last chapter, you can appreciate the scale to which the human race has handed its infinite power to this Global Elite. The Elite, in fact, is a mirror of us and our inner state of being. The information presented in the rest of this book is fundamental to the dismantling of the global pyramid and the unimaginable suffering it constantly manifests.

The definition of the word mirror: polished surface; reflecting image; that which gives faithful reflection. So says the *Oxford Concise Dictionary*. Lift your eyes from this page. Look around you. Look at your life, your family, your job, your friends and surroundings. You are looking at a mirror. A mirror of you.

If you don't like your life, then change it. You're in control. You have created the life you don't like, so now create one that you do. Crazy? Too simple? Not at all. You are in control of your destiny and so is everyone. We have just been conditioned to believe that someone else is in control, so we create that reality. If we can be duped into believing that we are powerless to control our lives, we look to others for guidance and answers instead of trusting ourselves. People hand their power to priests, gurus, politicians, economists, and scores of others. Tell me what to think, Mr Pope, Mr Rabbi, Mr New Age "teacher".

Hey, YOU are in control of you. YOU know what is best for you. Nobody else. You don't need anyone to tell you what to do and think.

How dare anyone tell you how to live your life? And what are you doing allowing it to happen? You can take your power back. It is infinite.

Every second of every day in every breath of your life, you are creating your own reality. Our lives reflect precisely our imagination of ourselves. If we think we are a "common man and woman" and that the good things and great achievements happen only to others, that is the way it will be. Our lives will reflect that imagination and perception of ourselves. If we desire to give our power away to others, to hand over our responsibility for the world and our own destiny; then our lives, and the world, will reflect that imagination and perception. Those thoughts will manifest themselves physically as a Global Elite running the show. And they have. What we call the world is a second-by-second physical replica of human thought, the human imagination, or lack of it. We are what we think and feel. Bill Hicks, the American comedian, was very funny and very perceptive. He was making powerful statements about life and the way we are controlled before he died in 1994 at the age of only 33. He described life in this way:

> *"It's like a ride in an amusement park and when you choose to go on it you think it's real because that's how powerful our minds are. The ride goes up and down, round and round, it has thrills and chills, and it's very brightly coloured and very loud. And it's fun for a while. Some have been on the ride for a long time and they begin to question: Is this real or is this just a ride? And other people have remembered and they come back to us and they say: Hey, don't worry, don't be afraid, ever, because this is just a ride.*

> *"And we kill those people.*

> *"Shut him up! We've got a lot invested in this ride. Shut him up! Look at my furrows of worry, look at my big bank account, and my family. This has to be real.*

> *"It's just a ride. But we always kill those good guys who try to tell us that. Have you ever noticed that? And we let the demons run amok. But it doesn't matter because it's just a ride. And we can change it anytime we want. It's just a choice. No effort, no job, no savings of money. A choice right now between fear and love."*

The difference between fear and love is the difference between a prison and a paradise. Both are the physical reflections of thoughts. Our thoughts.

The suppression of knowledge over these centuries of psychological fascism (also known as religion, education, "science" and the media) has sought to deny us information that would open our eyes and our minds to who we really are. Knowledge about our own identity has been systematically kept from us. This has been done because within this knowledge lies the understanding that would set us free. Religion, and more latterly "science", have been the major players in this suppression. For a long time, and still today in many parts of the world, to reject what religions demand we believe has been a death sentence. More widely today, to reject that which society and "science" demands we believe is to attract ridicule and condemnation. Merely to investigate beliefs outside the mainstream Hassle-Free Zone is often to be dubbed strange, mad or dangerous. Yet it is those beliefs that have stood the passage of time, not those indoctrinated into us these past few thousand, and in the case of "science" the last few hundred, years. As ever mounting evidence has forced "science" to open its eyes, oh so slowly, to the desperate limitations of its childlike belief system, so the evidence gathers by the day that the so called "alternative" beliefs have held in their core an eternal truth that has survived the dark years of inquisition and suppression. It is time for that knowledge to step out of the shadows and be open for all to see. Through the ages it has been used secretly by the manipulating few, the cult of the All Seeing Eye, to imprison humanity. Now it can be used with love to set us free.

The manufactured, manipulated, versions of life called religion and "science", may seem to be in opposition. But again, on closer reflection, they are oppo-sames. Both survive only by the suppression of knowledge and both have fostered a fear, even terror, of death. On the one side we are told of some God who will judge us after our one life on Earth, a life that will last anything from a few seconds to a hundred years or more. As a result of this one life in which we are all born into vastly different circumstances, this loving, judging, often merciless and vindictive God, will decide if it is heaven or hell forever and a day. Apparently, unless we believe that His son, Jesus Christ, is our saviour, I'm afraid we are doomed to stoke the fires for you-know-who. Of course we could always make sure of our place upstairs if we allowed the priests to tell us what to say, think, and do, because as His representatives on Earth, they know what He wants. Fine, I don't have to think for myself then? Phew, that's a relief. Thank you vicar. And what if I make big donations to the church while poverty abounds around me or I go off and kill a few thousand people who refuse to believe what I am told to believe? Oh my son, the Lord shall look upon you with gratitude (He says the cheque should be made out to me, by the way). You see how simple life is when you don't have to think? This mentality has dominated human evolution into the modern world and, amazing as it is to me, it still controls the minds of countless millions as we enter the 21st century. Because people are not keen on being judged by "God" (what if I don't pass?) they put off that dreadful day for as long as they can. Thus, anything that might possibly bring that day forward is immediately avoided and the fear of death becomes a wonderful means of keeping people quiet and under the iron fist. Nothing has been more successful in controlling the human mind than religion and that control has depended for its survival on the suppression of knowledge, not least the knowledge that life is forever, for everyone, and that we are not apart from God, we *are* God. Oops, I've blasphemed. Slap my wrist. Throw us that shovel, this fire needs a stoke.

The word science comes from a word meaning knowledge which is why I always write it as "science". For mainstream "science" is not the pursuit of knowledge overwhelmingly, it is about defending a rigid belief system and repelling all information that would demolish the foundations of those rigid beliefs. In that sense, "science" and religion are at one. This form of "science" is just another religion with the priests in white coats instead of long gowns. "Scientists" have become the new priesthood. "Science" is stuck in the five senses of touch, smell, hearing, taste and sight. If something can't be measured by one of those it cannot possibly exist. Really? What about thought? Thought cannot be touched, smelled, heard, tasted or seen, except as its physical expression. Does that mean thought does not exist? Of course it exists. Or at least I think it does! So what is thought? According to mainstream "science", thought is a physical brain function. But what about near death experiences when the person is physically dead for a short time? Tens of millions have experienced their consciousness leaving their body and observing their own physical form from some other dimension or state of being. Often they describe what the doctors and nurses were doing while they were "dead". What about those who recall under deep hypnosis the fine details, checkable and provable, of previous lives on the Earth? They were then in a different body with a different brain, so how can their thoughts and memories be a function of the brain they have now? Instead of looking at the endless evidence of people's experiences and evolving scientific understanding in the light of that, the mainstream "scientists" seek to discredit and dismiss the experiences of multimillions all over the world to preserve the "scientific" status quo: "What people have experienced could not happen unless our view of physics is wrong" comes the "scientific" response "and as our physics cannot possibly be wrong, those people must have been mistaken". Oh, good. Thank you very much, Mr "Expert", we can all go back to sleep now. And there was me thinking that the "scientists" didn't know it all.

As the foundations of scientific certainties see their credibility crumble under the avalanche of information now emerging, their explanations of "unexplainable" phenomena become more and more silly and hysterical. In Britain we have a university lecturer who is wheeled out onto virtually every television and radio programme about these subjects. Her role is to debunk alternative information with often ridiculous "explanations" and to defend the "scientific" status quo until her knuckles turn white. I wonder what it is within the psyche of those in the "scientific" establishment which makes them so desperate to persuade people that only oblivion awaits us at the end of our physical life. When the brain dies, we cease to exist, they cry. They have every right to believe that if they wish. The reason I challenge the "science" establishment is not for what they believe, but for the way they indoctrinate others into believing the same and suppress the alternative explanations.

The fear of oblivion fostered by "science" is also a big incentive to put off the moment of death as long as possible, so people keep their heads down and their mouths shut in case they bring forward that terrible day when the lights go out forever. The cosmic accident-life's-a-bitch-and-then-oblivion scenario is also a massive blow to human self worth. What's the point in life, it's all so meaningless isn't it? There is one other vital connection between the views of most religion and mainstream "science". They both believe our lives and our destiny are in the hands of others. Religion says God is in control of our life and that He is constantly judging our every thought and action. My goodness old God must have a big note book. And all those pens. "Science" says that random accidents are in control of our life and only the strongest and fittest survive the journey. I'd better trample on everyone in my way, then. It's no good being soft – get out of my way.

It's the law of nature, you know. "Scientists" have proved it. Yes, my friends, take your pick. Is God in control of your life or a series of random accidents?

Neither. YOU are.

Persuading us that we are not in control and cannot be in control is the perfect way to prevent us from taking control – the last thing you want to happen if your aim is to create a human herd, all desperate for others to tell them where to go, what to do, and what to think. What better means can there be to prevent us from expressing our true power than to kid us that we have no power to express? Which is why the knowledge I am about to outline is so dangerous to those few who control the world. People celebrating their uniqueness and controlling their own lives will bring the Larry Grayson pyramid and its Global Elite crashing to the ground. Game over.

Open-minded real science is now beginning to support the beliefs of the ancient cultures and civilisations that have long gone. Ancient Greece, Egypt, Sumer, Babylon, Central and South America, Asia, China, and thousands of other cultures across the world were based on this knowledge. So were, and are, the beliefs of the native peoples like the Aborigines and the Native Americans. Ironically, Christianity, which has so condemned these cultures, was founded on the same knowledge and its ceremonies derive from the so called "Pagan" ceremonies which Christians dismiss as "evil". You've got to chuckle really. These beliefs, often passed on in legend, myth, and symbolism to avoid the religious hit squads, say that the mind and the body are not the same thing. The body is an expression of our consciousness during a physical life and so the body, too, reflects our state of mind. Disharmony in the consciousness reflects itself as disharmony (dis-ease) in the body. We become ill. In the same way we can think ourselves back to health by finding harmony within our consciousness. But the body is not the "real" self, it is the temporary physical shell for the real self. I call the body a genetic spacesuit, the physical vehicle through which the eternal part of us – the soul – can experience this dense physical world. Our consciousness is eternal while the body has a finite life and returns to the soil and the energy pool when we "die". But we don't "die". Our consciousness, the thinking, feeling, emotional us, withdraws from the spacesuit and moves on to another world, another time-space reality or frequency. This is happening during the near-death experience. It's interesting that when we talk of God or heaven, most people still look up to the sky. It is a reflex response to the religious belief that God and heaven are somehow "up there". If you look at the enormous evidence that extraterrestrial life has played a major role in human evolution and how they landed here regularly in ancient times, I believe that we still look up for God and heaven because the "gods" of the ancient texts, including the Old Testament, were extraterrestrials in their anti-gravity (flying saucer) craft. The "gods" literally came from the sky. The word from which the biblical "Lord" was translated really means Lords, the plural. It is the same with the biblical "God". It was translated from a word meaning "gods." Read the Old Testament and replace every Lord and God with the word extraterrestrials and what appears to be biblical nonsense starts to make some kind of sense. You will find much more about this in ...*and the truth shall set you free* and *The Robots' Rebellion*. By the way, those who dismiss the idea of extraterrestrial life might remember that there are estimated to be billions of stars in this galaxy and billions of galaxies in this universe. And we are alone? Sure we are.

This diversion of God being "up there" and somehow physical in nature has led to the idea that creation is a spiritual chest of drawers or high-rise office block with heaven at the top and hell at the bottom. This has obscured the understanding that heaven, hell and God are everywhere. Heaven and hell are states of mind which we can experience anytime. We can have hell on Earth or heaven on Earth. It is our choice, our state of mind, which decides that. God is literally everywhere because "God" is a gigantic energy field/consciousness which is everything. It is your body, your mind, the grass, the trees, the sky, the rain. Everything. If it exists, it is an expression of the same ocean of energy/consciousness that we call God and Creation. Just as water, clouds, and ice (liquid, gas, solid) are the same substance in different states of being, so everything in Creation is the same energy/consciousness in different states of being. We are like droplets of consciousness in this ocean of consciousness. We are individual, yes, in that we are the sum total of all our experiences and they will be different from all the other droplets. But together with the energy/consciousness of the animals, insects, trees, flowers, extraterrestrials, everything, we form the ocean called "God". It is the same principle as individual droplets of water joining together to form the sea. The waves that break on the shores of Australia are part of the same mass of water which crashes against the harbour walls of Ireland or New York.

In the same way, the animals are not apart from you. They *are* you. So are the trees, the grass, the water. Everything is you and you are everything. If you hurt another expression of God, you are only hurting yourself, another aspect of yourself.

Far from being "up there", the infinite consciousness we call God is everything and everywhere. It is you and everything around you, including all the other "worlds" that we cannot see. The energy field/consciousness we call God is not a chest of drawers. It consists of endless time-space realities (worlds) all sharing the same space and interpenetrating each other. There are different frequencies or dimensions, just as the frequencies of radio and television stations share the same space that your body is occupying now. To access one of those stations, all you do is tune your television or radio to a particular frequency and bingo there it is. Move the dial and one station "disappears" and you tune to another. When you move the dial from a particular station, that station doesn't cease to exist, it goes on broadcasting, even though you are no longer tuned to it and you are not aware of what it is transmitting. So it is with the infinite frequencies of Creation. At this moment, your consciousness is tuned to this "station", the one we call the dense physical universe. But all the other frequencies of Creation continue to exist in the same space we are occupying, even though we are not aware of them. The physical body and brain screen out of our perception far, far more than we actually feel and see. The whole of Creation exists within the same "empty" space that you are occupying now – "The kingdom of heaven is within you". But all except a fraction of that infinity operates outside of the frequency range of our physical senses. Therefore we don't see it or hear it, although you can tune to some of these "hidden" levels by using your psychic senses which operate on a much higher frequency range than the physical body. The space around and within you now, which appears to be "empty" to your physical senses, is in fact ablaze with electrical and magnetic energy operating on an infinite number of wavelengths and states of being. When we "die", our consciousness leaves the physical body and this dense physical wavelength, and tunes to another "station" to continue our eternal evolution elsewhere. During sleep our consciousness journeys through some of these other wavelengths, hence we have "strange" dreams. It is so simple.

Energy and consciousness are the same, which is why all things are alive and have an awareness, the ability to hold information. Everything has its own personal vibratory "fingerprint". When a psychic holds a stone or an old ring or object, they can tune their consciousness to its energy field and "read" the information it has absorbed. This could relate to the person who once owned the object or an event that happened near the object. Whatever the case, it will retain that knowledge within a magnetic field, just like a magnetic computer disk. Rocks and stones hold information within their magnetic fields which goes back millions of years and changes now unfolding in the Earth's energy fields will release this information into the minds of those who are open to it. An aspect of this re-emerging knowledge will be amazing discoveries that demolish the official version of history and confirm, for example, the existence of ancient civilisations like Atlantis. Obviously, some expressions of the God consciousness/energy have evolved to a point where their awareness and ability to retain and process information is much further along the road than others. But the principle is the same for all that exists. Magnetic energy absorbs information and everything is magnetic-electrical energy, albeit often forms of magnetism not yet understood on this planet. One physical world expression of this energy is what we call electromagnetism. Some true scientists have suggested that water has a memory and they have performed experiments to prove it. There is no mystery in this at all, much as mainstream science is aghast at the suggestion. Water exists, it is magnetic energy/consciousness, therefore it has a memory. Everything does. It is this magnetism, a vibratory resonance and attraction, that allows us to create our own reality in every moment of our lives. Like vibrations attract like vibrations and like energy fields attract like energy fields. What we think of ourselves is reflected in the experiences we attract. I'll explain what I mean.

When our eternal consciousness incarnates into a dense physical body, the consciousness reflects the sum total of our experience going back to infinity. From the moment of birth we see the world differently to each other because our eternal journey has been different, although it may take two or three years for this to become observable. Even from an early age, however, children manifest these differences of perception. They become frightened by different things, even without direct experience of them in this life. They reveal different personalities, likes and dislikes, and abilities. Some people say these traits are created from the genes of their parents – a view which reveals a desperation to see everything as physical. But take my experience as just one example. I could not be more different from the rest of my family. For as long as I can remember I felt those differences. I was soon interested in sport and became a professional soccer player. No-one in my family for as far back as anyone can trace has ever been interested in playing professional sport, nor even, most of them, playing or watching sport at all. My fascination with nature and the protection of the planet is not shared by anyone in my family. My interest in the spiritual and the research into who controls the world is unique to me in my family. The differences in attitude, belief, and view between my parents, brothers, and myself are vast and endless. I am me and they are them because we are the sum total of our eternal experiences, not because of some genetic accident. I am not saying that genetic inheritance does not affect us, but it certainly does not determine our personalities and abilities.

Contained within our subconscious self from the moment of birth are all the memories, knowledge, and experiences, that we have absorbed on our eternal journey. The subconscious is also constantly adding to its memory bank with each new event we experience. The observations that result from experience pass through the eyes, ears, and brain, and are added to the spiritual library of knowledge and understanding that we call our evolution. It also adds to the evolution of creation as a whole. No experience is ever wasted. Also in the subconscious library will be astrological influences that are unique to us. There is a great deal of nonsense talked about astrology, I feel, both by those who dismiss it as mumbo-jumbo and those who treat it like a crutch which guides their every decision. Astrological influences are an important contribution to our sense of self, but they are still only part of the picture, not the entire canvas. Our consciousness is a series of vibrating energy fields operating in a sea of electromagnetic energy. Other vibrations, like those broadcast by the planets, affect these energy fields we call consciousness and can enhance or imbalance them. Here you have the answer to the "mystery" of why so many people living close to electrical power lines suffer from rare illnesses. "Science" says there is no connection between power lines and illness because "science" has such an incredibly blinkered view of life and, no doubt, because to identify a link would prove very costly to the power companies. Such unusual illness is caused by the electromagnetic fields projected from the power lines. This electromagnetism destabilises the magnetic fields of the human body and the consciousness. In turn, this vibrational disharmony is reflected as physical disharmony – disease. I am convinced that the rise in cancer and the corresponding rise in electromagnetic technology in our homes, work places, and cities, are fundamentally connected.

This basic process of vibrational interaction between electromagnetic energy fields is similar in astrology. When we are born, we absorb a unique energy pattern for that particular physical life. The nature of this energy pattern is decided by when and where we are born[1] – the information an astrologer always wants to know before a reading. Planets, as with everything that exists, are vibrating magnetic energy fields. Extremely powerful ones, too, of course. As they orbit the Sun, their relationship to the Earth and the power of their energy fields to effect the Earth, constantly changes. Sometimes the electromagnetic vibrations of one planet, or combination of planets, will be most powerfully affecting the Earth, while on other occasions it will be other planets or combinations of them. So someone born in Leicester, England, at 6.15 pm on April 29th 1952 will absorb a different electromagnetic energy field from a person born in Los Angeles, California, at 10.15 am on October 9th 1985. Because of this, the way people react to the vibrations of the planets as they move through the "heavens" will differ because our vibratory energy fields are different. One person might be lifted by a particular astrological movement while another may feel depressed. These planetary energies also contain knowledge and inspirations, and our consciousness aims to be born in a place and at a time when we will absorb the planetary energy combination that will help us most effectively to complete our plan of experience in this physical life. Research has shown how often people in particular jobs or with particular abilities are born at the same time of year.

So within our subconscious self is a cocktail of thought and perception that includes the knowledge and emotional debris of our eternal experiences or "past lives", the astrological pattern that we absorb at birth, and the experiences of this life. Together they produce our state of being, our sense of self, our imagination of ourselves. It is our imagination of ourselves that creates our physical reality. Everything is an electromagnetic, vibrating, unique, energy field and all the time we are broadcasting our own unique magnetic energy pattern. These are the "vibes" people speak of when they say that someone has good or bad "vibes". The vibes we broadcast affect the energy field around us. When we talk of "atmosphere", we are describing the energy field at a certain location, an energy field created by the thoughts, the vibes,

---

[1] Some researchers believe that the moment of conception decides the nature of the energy field, not birth.

of people. Battlefields can still remain "eerie" hundreds of years after the event because the vibrations created by the pain, aggression, and suffering of battle are still there until other thought patterns replace them. We walk into a room where there has been a major argument and we say "You can cut the atmosphere with a knife in there". We go into another house where very positive events have happened and we talk of the "lovely atmosphere" or a "happy house". Such examples are all the result of the vibrations, the thoughts, broadcast by people affecting the magnetic energy field. These vibrations mirror exactly the person's state of being at a particular moment and, it is most important to remember, what we give out is what we get back. What we broadcast as a magnetic pattern returns to us as a physical reality. As Bill Hicks said: "All matter is merely energy condensed to a slow vibration; we're all one consciousness experiencing itself subjectively; there's no such thing as death; life is just a dream; and we are the imagination of ourselves." That's the vital point: we are the imagination of ourselves.

Our magnetic pattern reflects our inner sense of self. Our inner reality then becomes our physical reality because our magnetic pattern attracts towards us other magnetic thought fields – people, places, ways of life, experiences, which mirror precisely the pattern we are broadcasting. This is why, for example, people are attracted to certain locations to make a home or have a holiday. The attraction is not only visual, but vibrational. Magnetic. We feel drawn or "pulled" there. This is also how we set up our "coincidences" – the "fancy seeing you here" situations. These are not random accidents, but magnetic energy fields being drawn subconsciously together. It is not a "small world", but the interaction of magnetic fields can make it appear so! By this process of vibrational magnetism, our subconscious mind creates an exact physical replica of itself before our eyes in the people, places, ways of life, and experiences, that come our way. As I said at the start of this chapter, when you look through your eyes you are looking at a mirror of your inner self. Everything will be reflecting part of you, or your need to learn or experience something. Change your inner self and you change its physical replica – your life. The reality you now experience is the result of what you think of you. It is the imagination you have of yourself within your conscious and subconscious mind. We create with our thoughts and experience those creations through our emotions and feelings. Whatever you experience it is the result of what you are broadcasting because of (a) the thoughts and actions from the past or present which you need to face for your evolution or (b) your astrological pattern (chosen by you before birth) which is attracting to you experiences that are part of your life plan this time or (c) the experiences you need to face to help you achieve what you have come to do in this lifetime on Earth.

One extreme example of the latter, I believe, is Cathy O'Brien who, as a result of suffering those appalling experiences as a mind-controlled slave, is now able to expose what is happening. Without those experiences she could not have done that. She is a magnificent servant to humanity. It's important to appreciate that our perception of life while outside the physical body is so different to the perception we have while encased in this dense physical space suit. Therefore the decisions we make and the lives we choose before incarnation, often seem ridiculous to us when we are experiencing the physical consequences of those decisions. This certainly applies to the parents we choose. There is no-one on another level forcing us to incarnate into those situations, so instead of hurling the blame for an unpleasant childhood onto the parents, we might more positively ask why we chose to experience that situation and what we were hoping to learn and achieve by it. This allows the destructive resentment to disperse and the constructive learning to emerge. That includes the children who suffer so dreadfully from the events in chapter four.

Like I say, our perceptions when we choose a life are very different from those we have when we are actually experiencing it. It is easy to observe people creating their own reality. I knew a woman who had no self worth at all. "I'm useless" she would say "I am a useless mother, a useless wife, and I have nothing to contribute". In the same breath she would complain that everyone was putting her down! "My husband puts me down, my children put me down, my husband's parents put me down" she would say. In fact, the reason for that experience was that *she* was putting herself down. That sense of her own self was being transmitted as a magnetic vibratory pattern and it was attracting other patterns – the people in that woman's life who were mirroring back her own sense of reality, her own imagination of herself.

We are doing this in every moment of every day. When I was a television reporter I visited a hostel for physically abused women and I was amazed to find that most had been with at least two violent partners and some had been through three or four. Why did they keep going around with such characters?, I thought. It made no sense. But now it does. The common theme of those women was their lack of self worth, self love, and self respect, and that had clearly been their reality well before they began to attract violent partners. At some deep level they feel themselves to be so useless and inadequate that they deserve to be punished. When that vibe is broadcast it will attract that sense of reality in the form of an energy field (man) who desires to punish another. The sense of reality is therefore physically fulfilled and until the woman's sense of self changes she will go on attracting partner after partner who will treat her in the way that will create the reality, the imagination, she has of herself. The violent man is another expression of the lack of self worth and self love that has bred like a cancer in the collective human mind. Violent people are those who hate themselves and instead of looking inside to find the cause of that self dislike, they thrash out at someone else. Their victim is a convenient mirror. In fact, if we all had big mirrors around our necks the world would change in an hour because we would all see ourselves as other people see us. It is fascinating to see how the way we react to others is merely an expression of what we think of ourselves and violent people are a perfect example of this. As I look back on my own life I see how my sense of self at certain times attracted an exact physical replica. As a child I was terrified of dogs and wherever I went I was pursued and chased by them. This never happened to my friends who were not afraid. I thought I was just unlucky. I wasn't. I was creating it by attracting to me what I feared. We need to do this to overcome our fears, otherwise our potential is severely limited and, in the area related to the fear, our evolution comes to a halt. I remember too, that when I began to love and respect myself for what I am, I began to attract around me more and more people who love and respect me for what I am and not for what they would like me to be. You don't like your friends? Change yourself and your friends will either change in their attitude towards you or they will move out of your life and others will emerge to reflect your new sense of you. Everything that happens in your life you are creating. So many people have told me stories of how they have walked into a book shop and a book has "miraculously" fallen from the self at their feet. It is not a miracle. They have done it themselves. Their subconscious has connected magnetically with the magnetic energy field of the book and pulled it off the shelf. The subconscious considers the book helpful to the reawakening of its conscious level and so it drops the hint in a physical way. Whatever we need, we draw to us.

We also create the reality we call illness. Every ailment, whether minor or life-threatening, we trigger ourselves. We either choose before incarnation to experience it on the journey to greater understanding or our subconscious sewer of past life and present life emotional garbage manifests itself physically as a dis-ease. The nature of the physical illness is related to the mental and emotional state which is creating the illness. The body is a constant barometer of our emotions. I can recommend an excellent book on this subject called *You Can Heal Your Life* by Louise Hay (Hay House Inc, USA, and Eden Grove Publications, London). We store emotions we don't want to deal with in our bodies. I remember in the 1970s and 80s whenever I was wound up (most of the time) I would feel a pain in my back about half way down my left lung. In 1995 when I was going through an emotional trough I was having an aromatherapy massage by a close friend of mine. When she ran her hands over that spot, I felt the pain again. She said she would symbolically push that emotion out of the body and I could deal with it. As she did so, very painfully, I started to cry. I had no idea why I was crying and I still don't. But afterwards I felt two stones lighter emotionally. Something, whatever it was, had been let go. Crying is actually good for us, it releases pent up, suppressed, emotions. I have cried more in the last year than I have in the previous 35! But we are told that "big boys don't cry" and so the big boys die of heart attacks which result from the stress of unreleased energies within them. No-one has an unlucky illness and that includes me with my arthritis from an early age. We create it and so we can uncreate it. Our bodies are an expression of our minds, emotions, and spirit. You can see this clearly when you observe people who, sometimes with very little preparation, walk barefoot across hot coals without pain or even discomfort. Their minds have told their bodies that they won't burn or feel pain and their bodies do as they are told. The same principle is also apparent when a child falls over, but recovers miraculously when mum or dad has "kissed it better". The child thinks it is possible to kiss it better and so the pain goes. Your mind is in control of your body at all times.

It is important, however, to appreciate that we *all* create our own reality. I have observed people who accept the principle, but then seek to deny it when something they don't like happens to them. Instead of looking positively at what they are meant to learn from that situation, they look for someone to blame. It is the same when people follow their intuition and "go with the flow", but then condemn others for following theirs. You can't have it both ways here. There is not one law for one and another for the rest of humanity. There is one law for all of us: we create our own reality and our physical experience. Look at all the events in your life, those you like and those you don't, and you will see if you are honest with yourself that you have created them by what you think of you. There's no-one to blame or to pass on responsibility for what happens in your life. You are responsible. You are in control and you can change whatever you wish by changing your imagination of yourself. I came across a phrase which captures this concept brilliantly:

If you always do what you've always done, you'll always get what you've always got.

The word "karma" is for me, another way of saying we create our own reality. Karma is interpreted by many to mean that what we do to others will be done to us. I feel there's more to it than that. If we act negatively towards someone, that action reflects our state of being at that moment and this will be broadcast as a vibratory pattern. Should we not learn from seeing the effects of our action, we will go on transmitting that same state of being. This will attract to us a like vibration, someone who will do to us what we have done to another: a mirror of our own sense of self which can also be described as our karma. If, however, we learn from seeing the effects of our actions, our sense of self changes and so does our pattern. We have learned from the experience (the reason for "karma") and there is no need for us to attract some gratuitous punishment when the learning has already been achieved. As our pattern has been changed by the experience we will not attract to us the karma, someone who will do to us what we have done to another. When our sense of self changes, so does our pattern, and so does the physical experience it attracts. The way the Hindu religion has used the idea of karma to justify a rigid hierarchy or caste system, is an abuse of the word spiritual. You name it and someone somewhere will try to use it as a means of control. Karma is no different in that.

Everything, but everything, in our lives comes back to the same point. Our lives are the imagination of ourselves. This applies even to children. We see children as physical bodies and that, understandably, affects the way we perceive them. In fact, a child is a multidimensional, eternal consciousness that could quite easily be further along the road of evolution than his or her parents. The sum total of the experiences and astrological influences within that child's consciousness will also be creating his or her physical reality from the moment of birth. The difference, I feel, is that a child is operating on a more limited level of consciousness until the body has grown to match the potential of the mind. Imagine having access to the full range of your consciousness and knowledge while trapped in a child's body. The frustration would be fantastic. But the same principles that apply to adults also apply to children and all other expressions of God throughout creation. We choose when, where and with whom we incarnate, and we create our own reality. The loss and suppression of this understanding is the very foundation of the ills that have been visited on the Earth for so long. This knowledge reveals that we are in control of our own destiny while the versions of "life" that are indoctrinated into us by religion and "science" insist that another force is in control, either a judgmental God or random accident. You can see why this suppressed knowledge is considered so dangerous by those who wish to control us and why it has been ridiculed or condemned throughout known "history" as either "mad" or the work of the "Devil". It is the knowledge that will set us free from the prisons of our own making.

I saw a badge made in America which said: "The Truth will set you free...but first it will piss you off". Very true. When you first realise how the human race has been so massively duped, it is not nice to hear. Nor, for many, is it a welcome thought that everything that happens in our lives is down to ourselves. What? I can't blame anyone else? Eeeek! But I'm a victim of circumstance...I'm unlucky...I had a bad childhood...I'm always ill...I was deprived...abused...misled...

Er, sorry. There's no escape. Stop pointing the finger and get this: Your life, all of it, has been down to...YOU.

Why do some people think that news is so terrible? I'm ecstatic. If my life so far has been all down to me, the rest of my eternal existence will be in my own control, also. Yippeeeeeeee! No-one controls me. I'm not a victim, I'm me. I'm me in control of me. Zipper-dee-do-dah-zipper-dee-ay! Mine's a double, easy on the ice. The trick is to seize that control and live it instead of looking for countless ways to deny our own responsibility. To do that we need to detoxify ourselves from our emotional addictions. Emotions like fear, guilt, resentment, anger, worry, depression and so on, are every bit as addictive as drugs and booze. People who are addicted to worry, for instance, are always searching for something to worry about because their system has become so dependent on feeling that energy that it needs its constant "fix". My mother used to say about some people: "It's being so miserable that keeps them going". In a way that is true. Being miserable and depressed is another emotional addiction that people find so hard to break. It becomes their vibrational state.

POOR ME

The "poor me" mentality is the most destructive state of mind it is possible to experience. It is the means through which we create unhappy, unfulfilled lives, and the state of mind that allows a tiny few to control the direction of the world. Poor Me = The Victim. And the victim mentality creates the victim reality. The spiral of despair. The Poor Me mentality is always searching for excuses for its suffering, failure, and lack of action to change its circumstances. The Poor Me prison is the most tightly guarded, has the biggest walls, and the prisoners show the greatest reluctance to escape. At times in our lives when we are faced with challenging circumstances, we all experience the Poor Me mentality. For many, however, it becomes their home, their permanent mental and emotional residence. This world is awash with victims because the world is awash with people conditioned to see themselves as victims. Poor home, no money, bad luck, bad parents, prejudice. The Poor Me, victim mentality has no shortage of excuses for its situation, nor people to blame for its plight. The worst thing we can do in these circumstances is to feed the Poor Me by sympathising with their "misfortune" and "bad luck". We can have empathy with their pain, but the last thing they need is someone confirming their Poor Me sense of self. Love takes many forms and telling people what will create further "misfortune" and pain is certainly not one of them. There are no victims. We just think we are and so we create that physical reality. We are persuaded that life is not for living, it is for surviving. We are so indoctrinated by this that any new vision in which people are happy, prosperous and fulfilled, is dismissed as "idealistic" and not living in the "real world". In the "real world", you see, people have to suffer and battle for survival. Anything else is "idealistic". The survival mentality abounds on planet Earth.

"How are you today?"

"Oh, you know, surviving, but there's a lot worse off than me, I guess."

We are not here to simply survive or exist, nor to judge our own lives on the basis that others suffer more and so we must be grateful for our lot. But if we think we are – and so many do – that will be the nature of our life. Throughout history we have been sold the idea that you have to suffer and sacrifice now to create the good things we desire in the "future". What we really want to have in our lives are always in the future, never the *now*. Religions have told us we need to suffer and sacrifice in this life to qualify for paradise...tomorrow. Politicians and economists tell us we need to make sacrifices now to create economic prosperity...tomorrow. The jam is always tomorrow. It is what I call the "one day" syndrome. One day I'll have what I want, but not now. If that is our reality, our imagination of self, we will never have what we desire because that energy is always projected into the future and not into the now. Hope is another example of living in the future. Hope is a future experience, not a *now* experience. As the Cretan writer, Nikos Kazantzakhs once wrote: "I am without hope. I am without fear. I am free."

No-one feeds the victim mentality more than people on the "left" of politics, the Robot Radical mentality as I call it. This state of mind occupies a mental world of "us and them", of victimiser and victim. The masses are victims because of the victimising few, this mentality believes. They see life in terms of the bosses and the bossed, the leaders and the led. The Robot Radicals' sense of reality, their imagination of themselves, is the fighter for freedom and justice for the victims. The way to do this, they believe, is to constantly tell people they are victims of circumstance, victims of someone else, and that only when that someone else is changed or removed will they cease to be victims of circumstance. The Robot Radical state of being actually needs victims to feed its sense of self. Without perceived victims, it would lose its sense of identity. If victims did not exist, this mentality would have to invent them. They also have so much anger within themselves that they are constantly searching for people and circumstances to get angry about. This is why you often see the same faces at every protest march and also why those of the Robot Radical mentality have protested against me without reading my books or hearing me speak. They want to believe that what is said about me is true. It allows them to get angry with someone to avoid looking at the source of that anger – themselves.

It is appropriate that the Robot Radical organisations often have "anti" in their names like the Anti-Nazi League, Green Anti-Fascists, etc. They are stuck in the negative and their view of life would change dramatically if they started to be "for" things. Most of the Robot Radicals do what they do out of the best of intention. I was on the fringes of that mentality at one time. I saw myself in the British Green Party as a "fighter" for justice for those less "privileged". But you don't "fight" for freedom, you "peace" for freedom. I am not challenging the Robot Radical mentality from a holier than thou position. Robot Radicals are not "bad" people and that includes those who have sought to give me a hard time personally. But, I would suggest, they are actually defeating their objective because they are feeding and fuelling the very mentality which is creating the ills they say they want to eliminate. Robot Radicals won't like what I am about to say, but I want to see people take back their own power. That's my motivation for what I do. I am not trying to win a popularity contest. Robot Radicals had better sit down, have a stiff drink, and, ideally, a whiff of oxygen...

Single parent families, those in poor housing and no housing, and the endless stream of other "victims" trotted out by the Robot Radicals are not the result of bad luck or misfortune. They are the creation of their own thoughts, their own imagination of themselves, or their own choices made before incarnation. They don't need people telling them how unlucky and victimised they are. They're already convinced of that. They need a new vision of themselves which will create a new and positive physical reality. They have thought their circumstances into existence and they can just as easily think them out again. "Get off your ass and stop feeling sorry for yourself" is often the most loving advice you can give to someone. They won't thank you for it at first and they might even become abusive. But true love is to say what people need to hear, not necessarily what they want to hear to confirm their sense of Poor Me. Whatever circumstances we are born into, we choose them before birth. The alternatives to this are that life is a random accident or that the consciousness is created with the body, neither of which stand up to serious discussion. That leaves an eternal consciousness deciding its own experience by choosing when, where, and with whom to incarnate. You didn't like your childhood? Then why did you choose it? What were you hoping to learn from those circumstances? Fine, so learn and move on. Look at things in that positive way and you can let go of the guilt and resentment from the past that does so much to destroy our present. You don't like your life now? Ok, what is it about your sense of self, your imagination of yourself, that is creating it? You don't deserve to live in poverty or pain. No-one does. We are all of equal worth, value, and potential. So why are you creating poverty and pain? I don't care who you are, you are an incredible, astonishing, aspect of God. Express that infinity and your life will reflect that. See yourself as small, insignificant, an "ordinary" man and woman in the street, and you will be. You can see life as a series of problems or a series of solutions. It's a choice and the lives those states of mind create will be very different.

Ironically, few states of mind need to understand this more than the Robot Radicals who set themselves up as freedom fighters for victims. In truth, they often create victims instead of freeing them. We can only free ourselves. No-one can do it for us. Robot Radicals see themselves as victims and they feed the victim mentality with almost every word and pronouncement. "You were born on a council estate in bad housing or in poverty in a New York slum? You are a victim. It's the bosses, you know. They're to blame for your situation. We victims must stand together in victimised solidarity. Raise the victims' flag brothers and sisters." I was brought up on a vast council housing estate in Leicester in a poor family and I remember the "us and them" indoctrination that went on. All it did was condition me to see myself as a victim of circumstance and someone who would always struggle financially because I was an "us" and not a "them". That is exactly what happened to me until I realised what a load of old tosh that is and I began to create another reality. How often have I heard this: "I was born working class and I'll always be working class."? Oh really? Not planning to evolve then? It's got so silly that where you stand in the Robot Radical league table of political purity depends on how badly off you are. It is the Robot Radical version of suffer little children to come unto me. Pain, which should only be a warning signal that something is out of balance, has been integrated into our minute by minute existence. Feeling pain is now "normal" in this crazy world our minds have created and to a Robot Radical, and many in the New Age too, pain has taken on the role of a medal, a symbol of your credibility as a fully fledged, official, mentioned-in-dispatches, victim. Ahh, poor soul. To win the championship in the Robot Radical league table you have to suffer more than anyone else! If you are a black, lesbian, single-parent, on social security, squatting in a derelict house, you go straight to the top of the Robot Radical league table of human victims. "It's not fair. That woman is so unlucky. She's just a victim of her own bad luck, poverty, colour, and sexuality."

No she's not. She is an incredible, amazing, aspect of all that exists and she can be whatever she wants to be. She chose to be black, just as people choose to be white, Arabs, Jews, and so on. She is *not* a victim. She has only been persuaded that she is a victim and so her life reflects that sense of reality. She needs a new vision of herself, not crocodile tears. Victims don't do anything about their circumstances because they believe they are powerless to do anything and so nothing gets done. It's someone else's fault so someone else will have to get me out of this mess. What are *they* going to do about it?, comes the victims' cry. Don't get me wrong here. I am not saying that we should ignore the circumstances of others, nor am I belittling the plight of some black people, lesbians, single-parent families, and the homeless. Quite the opposite. But I want to get to the real solution to the circumstances they are facing and that means wading waist high through generations of bullshit from self-styled "radicals" who have massaged their own sense of purity while avoiding the whole point: if we want our lives to change, *we* have to change them.

When people change their sense of self, when they stop seeing themselves as a victim, their energy pattern changes. It begins to magnetically attract to them the people, places, experiences, "coincidences" and "luck" which change their circumstances from the negative (a reflection of the old self) to positive (the new self). It is then, and only then, that people in trouble can be helped. While they retain the Poor Me mentality there is nothing anyone can do. Nothing will work no matter how hard you try, because their magnetic consciousness will continue to create the physical life that befits a victim. Throughout this century and before, we have seen a stream of people and politicians all over the world offering their physical solutions to what are, in truth, mental and emotional problems. This is why these "solutions" never work. All they do is create structures of dependency (control) and dependency diminishes our self worth, our imagination of ourselves, so creating the very circumstances the structures are supposed to be alleviating. The structure itself becomes a vehicle of control, not freedom. You can't change a mental state with a penny off income tax or another pound on social security.

Throughout this same period the number of "victims" world-wide has grown because those who say they wish to remove the problem go on feeding it. If you are born black or Jewish, for example, you are likely to be conditioned to expect prejudice. So that is what you get. If you are walking down the street, you will magnetically attract the racist mentality because you will be fulfilling your own sense of reality. The same with a homosexual. If you expect prejudice, if it is part of your imagination of yourself, you will not be disappointed. The mentality that imagines itself as a victim of prejudice helps to create prejudice because without it that sense of self, that imagination of self, could not be fulfilled. Attracting prejudice is no different to me attracting barking, aggressive dogs as a child while my friends had no such problems. Yet what do we see? "Community leaders" representing groups of collective "victims" like blacks, Jews and homosexuals, who tell their version of "the masses" that they are victims of circumstances created by others. Yeah, just what they need, that is, eh? It is all so self perpetuating and avoids the only solution – changing our sense of self.

If we love and respect ourselves and stop seeing ourselves as victims, that sense of self is broadcast in our magnetic vibration. That will attract to us people and circumstances that mirror back that love and respect. When those blacks, Jews and homosexuals, stop seeing themselves as victims of prejudice and let go of any prejudices they may have against other groups, the prejudice and victimisation against them will end. But not until.

Let us look at this from the global perspective. The sum total of individual human reality becomes the collective reality – the world. You can see that as human consciousness has become more globally uniform, this has been reflected physically in the way cities all over the planet, which once expressed their unique culture, are increasingly looking the same. As consciousness becomes more uniform, so does the physical environment it creates. Politics is another example of this principle. People condemn politicians for thinking only in terms of self interest and what's in it for me. But what is in the hearts and minds of most voters when they are deciding which party to support? Yes, precisely: self interest and what's in it for me. If that is our motivation when we vote, we will, and do, create that reality by electing politicians who reflect in their actions the very state of mind that we used to give them their power. If you want to change the kind of politicians that represent us, change yourself. If people still think it is worth voting in today's rigged system (I don't), then let us vote for what we believe is right and not only for what we believe is right for us, materially, in the short term. Then, if this is done by enough people, we will have politicians that manifest that state of mind.

The same principle applies to the pyramid of global control I described earlier. We created that too, without realising it. If we give our minds away and stop thinking for ourselves, we are allowing others, governments, Elite families, community leaders, priests, teachers, the media, and pseudo-gurus of all shades, to tell us what we are and how we should see ourselves. They are programmed to programme the rest of us. We are allowing them to condition our imagination of ourselves and the world and so allowing them to create our physical reality. When we concede our right to be unique and we accept another's version of what we should be, we allow others to control our physical experience. That is precisely what the human race as a whole has done and continues to do. The Hassle-Free Zone is populated by those who are projecting a programmed sense of self as a physical reality which we collectively call the "world" or "society". There are so few real differences in the basic mentality within the Hassle-Free Zone because people are getting their programmed sense of self from the same basic source, the pyramid of conformity, the Global Elite which controls the sources of "information" and indoctrination that hypnotise our consciousness. Today even more subtle forms of reality programming go on thanks to subliminal messages, often via the television, which speak directly to the subconscious in ways the conscious mind cannot see or hear. Make no mistake, those who work to programme human reality know exactly how to do it, because they are working with knowledge passed on secretly over thousands of years via the upper levels of the global secret society network, the origins of which go back to Atlantis and beyond. This is the same knowledge that has been kept out of the public arena by the twin responses of "mad" and "bad".

We can remove the means of this control by ceasing to conform and by using our own immense power to effect positive change. This can be done in very simple ways. You can sit quietly and visualise whatever you want to create for yourself. See it happening to you *now* in that moment. Thought creates exactly what you think, so if you visualise something happening in the future it will always be happening in the future and never in the *now*. You can use this same technique, perhaps with a group, to visualise and project the thought form of peace, love, harmony and the end of conflict. These visualisations do work because they are concentrated thought and thought creates everything. Only if what you desire is not appropriate to your life experience will a higher level of yourself block it. Also, it is important to remember the chain reaction of words and behaviour. What we say and do is like throwing a pebble into a pond. The waves continue to affect the water long after the pebble has gone. If you walk into a shop and you are nasty and unpleasant to the shop keeper, it will make him angry and wound up. After you leave he will be less than pleasant to his next customer or his wife and family. This will upset them and so it goes on. But this chain reaction can be used positively. If we knock on the door of the boss no-one likes and say we think he is doing a great job and what a pleasure it is to work with him, it is likely to make his day. Nobody will have said that to him before. He will be lifted by the compliment and this is likely to be reflected in the way he treats his staff. In turn, they will feel happier and enjoy their work, thus they are more likely to be pleasant to their families when they go home. It's only a choice and we constantly underestimate the effect on the world of the so called "little" things that we say and do. Every time we think or feel we affect the sea of electromagnetic energy and affect everything that exists. And, of course, if we are loving and pleasant to others because we feel happy and loving inside, that state of being will attract the same reaction to us. How we treat each other in the supermarket or the office may not appear to be revolutionary, but it is. If we are loving and pleasant to each other in our daily lives and if we use the power of our minds to think love, peace, and harmony, we break the very foundations that hold the pyramid of control together – fear, guilt, resentment, judgment[2], competition and aggression.

Today our generations are being offered an opportunity unprecedented for at least twelve thousand years and probably far, far longer. It is the opportunity for a mass evacuation of the human prison. If we choose to grasp it, we can be part of the Great Cleansing of Planet Earth and the human mind which so many are now experiencing. It is the moment we have prepared for over many lifetimes. This opportunity is not only for some "chosen people" or chosen few. No-one is chosen. We make the choices ourselves. This gathering transformation is for anyone and everyone. Once again, YOU are in control. You always were and you always are.

---

[2] I think it is worth defining what I mean by judgment, and therefore being non-judgmental. I do not mean looking the other way when we see things we don't like because to say anything would be "judgmental". That form of non-judgmentalism denies the right to have opinions and express them. By non-judgment, I mean to say what we think about attitudes and behaviour while realising that we are not challenging the people involved, but the thought patterns and states of mind which control those people. It is also to realise that we all need different experiences on our unique paths of evolution.

Chapter 6

Set The Genie Free

I magine a wine bottle standing on a light. Inside is a moth. The top of the bottle is open and the moth can escape any time. But the moth does not escape. It can't see the opening at the top because it stays at the bottom, mesmerised by the light. So eventually it dies, still unaware that the door was open to infinity all along.

For moth, read human race.

Our "light", the hypnosis that holds us at the bottom of an open bottle, is the invasion of the psyche by mantra messages of dos and don'ts, wills and won'ts, shalls and shan'ts, couldn'ts and can'ts. It also includes all those who accept and feed the victim mentality and the "scientists" who tell us that not only is the bottle tightly closed, there is nowhere outside to escape to even if we could. The bottle is all that exists. These messages constantly increase the energy which powers the light and disempowers the people. We are the genie in the bottle and it is time to escape. The cork was never there, we were just duped into believing it was.

The symbolism of the bottle is very appropriate because we exist, at this level of ourselves, anyway, in a vortex of energy which is shaped not unlike a bottle (*Figure 4 overleaf*). This spiral of multidimensional energy is like a cinema screen on which the game, the ride, we call physical life is played out. You could imagine this vortex of experience as a pyramid with a circle at its peak (*Figure 5 – see page 104*). You can see in a cinema how the projection of the picture is like a pyramid. When it leaves the projector the picture is very small, but by the time it reaches the screen, it has expanded massively. Look at a spotlight in a theatre and you will see the same principle. The beam of light widens the further it travels. The circle at the top of the pyramid in *Figure 5* represents the Oneness of where we come from. It is a "heaven" of

Figure 4: the Bottle Vortex

balance and harmony between what are, at this physical level, "opposing" forces of positive and negative, male and female. The Global Elite and the cult of the All Seeing Eye are the physical representation of the negative extreme in this positive-negative, male-female duality, but they are still part of the whole and therefore part of us. Oneness is the collective mind that created a vortex which separated the elements within the Oneness. It was designed as a spiritual university and a very tough school. It is within that vortex that our dense physical world exists. It is one of perhaps nine time-space planes or dimensions – "worlds" – within the vortex. These planes are the "many mansions in my father's house" which Y'shua (Jesus) is reputed to have talked about. All these levels are connected vibrationally and what happens to one affects them all. They each vibrate to a different "note" (wavelength), but all the notes are part of the same tune. Each higher dimension is responsible for guiding the one below which, again, is where the ancient idea of the guiding "gods" originates – from the dimension above ours. We are in a three dimensional world or the Third Dimension which is near the bottom of the pyramid. Each dimension has a "physical" level (gradually becoming less dense the closer they are to Oneness) and a non-physical level to where consciousness returns between physical incarnations. The diagram in *Figure 5* is very simple and there are many more wavelengths, worlds, and subtleties involved, of course, but it summarises the general theme.

When I say that we are God and that all is God, I don't mean that we are all at the same level of understanding. Within this infinite mind/energy that is everything, are infinite levels of love, knowledge, and wisdom. At the highest vibration, at the heart of God, is what I call the Source Consciousness. This is the mind from which all else has come. What is the Source? The Source is Love. And Love is Oneness, the balance of all. How do we return to the Source? We love ourselves and we love every other expression of God. We love and become love. Loving God means loving everything because everything is God. That includes the Global Elite and those exposed in chapter four. No-one needs love more than they do.

Understanding Oneness in the deepest sense comes from experiencing the division of Oneness. You only understand the balance between hot and cold by experiencing both hot and cold. You only know when you have achieved balance because you have experienced imbalance. This spiritual journey is like a pair of scales leaping from one side to the other until, with the passage of experience, the

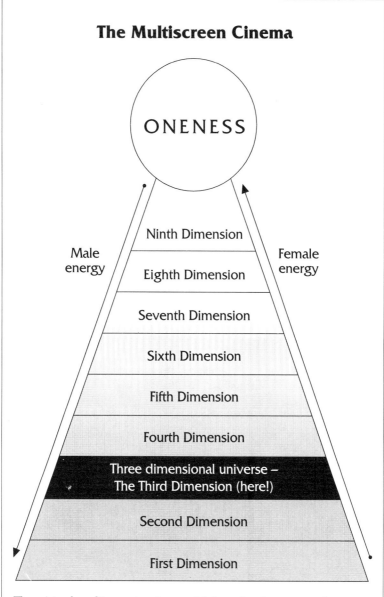

The virtual reality vortex/pyramid. Levels of our consciousness exist on all these planes of existence, including Oneness.

Figure 5

movement slows and slows and the balance point, Oneness, is found. This is why the ride can feel bumpy when the scales are flying around. The vortex, the movie picture projected from the level of Oneness, is symbolised by the concept of God breathing out, which you find in some Eastern religions and elsewhere. That symbolic "outbreath" was the projection of the vortex from the Oneness that caused the separation of male and female, positive and negative, which, when in harmony, make One. The "outbreath" of separation and creation is the male energy and the "inbreath", the nurturing back to Oneness is the female energy now re-emerging on Planet Earth. As with the cinema projector, the further away from Oneness the vortex travelled, the wider it expanded and the greater the separation of "opposites". The wider that separation the slower the energy vibrated and so at the bottom levels of the vortex (that symbolic bottle) the dense physical world formed. What we call "matter" is only energy condensed to a slow vibration.

You can see this expressed in the world around us. The rocks operate on a longer wavelength, a very slow vibration, and so their matter is very "solid". Our bodies vibrate to a shorter, quicker, frequency and so they are less "solid" than a rock. Our consciousness vibrates on an even quicker wavelength and is, therefore, out of range of the body's physical senses. We have to expand our minds, increase our vibratory rate, and use our psychic "third eye" sight if we wish to see such levels. The task of those who chose to take part in this learning experiment was, and still is, to experience division and through that to bring those "opposites" back into balance within us. As that balance is achieved, our vibratory rate quickens and we ascend up the frequency levels within the pyramid/vortex towards our real home – Oneness. Symbolically, the Prodigal Son returns home to "the Father".

Let us get this straight. People talk about living in the "real world" as if the divisions, pain, and control of this dense physical planet were the "real world". That is the last thing it is. The "real world", if you want to put it like that, is the level of highly evolved existence called Oneness. The world you see through your eyes is a holographic, three dimensional, virtual reality game created by Oneness as a vast learning experience. When you look through your eyes it is like donning one of those virtual reality helmets you get with computer games. We are looking at a cinema screen, that's all. This world is not real, it is a spiritual Hollywood. A movie set. A hologram is a three dimensional image created by the manipulation of light. You can buy holograms in gift shops and holographic images of people can be projected onto the stage in theatre productions. Creating a hologram is very straight forward. Also, every part of a hologram is an image of the whole. The only thing you lose, the smaller you go, is detail. That is exactly what we are, a part of the gigantic hologram we call the universe and we are a smaller image of the whole of that hologram – the universe. We just don't manifest all of the detail. In the same way, every cell in our body holds the information contained in the whole body. As above so below, as they say. Everything is a reflection of everything, no matter how small. There is actually no here or there, only everywhere. The here and there are merely the section of everywhere that our senses are perceiving at any moment. If you walk around a department store you are only seeing one department at a time. But go outside (symbolic of expanding our consciousness to higher levels) and you can see the whole building which contains all the departments.

Oneness created the foundations of this time space reality, the thought form and vibrational interaction which built the "movie set". But it is we who make the film. It is we who decide which parts we will play, who with, and in what setting. It is we who write the script and create a physical reality to match the imagination we have of ourselves and our part in the picture. It can be a nice family film full of love and respect or it can be a horror movie. We, you, all of us, decide that. No-one else. No "God", no "random accidents", we do it. You think your life is a horror movie? It will be. You think of yourself as the guy who gets shot early in the film? You will be. You think of yourself as one of those who end up laughing and happy in the last scene? You will be. What part do you want to play? Then think it and live it. Great, you got the job. Cue camera – action!

Now, let's stop fighting each other and condemning each other. Let us instead love ourselves, love each other, find balance, and get out of here! Let's go!

The opportunity to do just that is being presented to us like never before since the vortex was created. "God" is breathing in. We are being pulled back towards Oneness – if we choose to go. The effects of dividing Oneness so comprehensively were possibly underestimated. The division has become a prison within which the prisoners are so mesmerised by the cell that they can conceive of no other reality. Symbolically, I see people existing in an eggshell (*Figure 6*). Inside the shell is our conscious level, that part of us that looks through the eyes and experiences the conditioning of this dense physical world. Outside

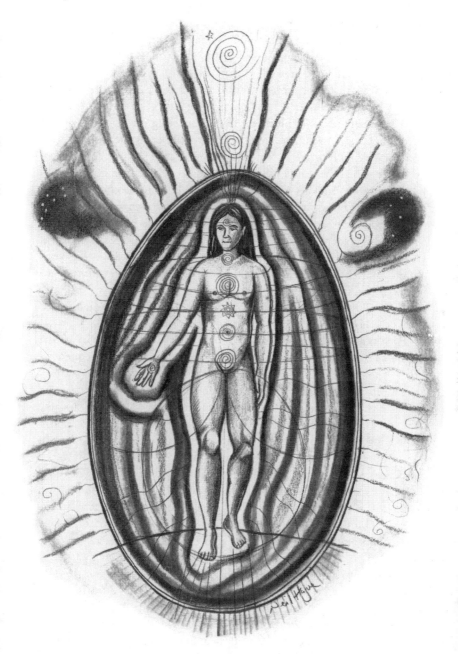

**Figure 6: The Eggshell of programmed thought and response –
the self-imposed barrier to our infinity.**

the shell is the rest of creation, the sea of electromagnetic energy and our multidimensional consciousness expanding into infinity. Keeping the two apart is the eggshell which is the veneer of programmed thought and response, created by lifetimes of fear, guilt and resentment, and of: you must, you should, you won't and you can't. The eggshell is our personal Hassle-Free Zone. We don't have to "seek" enlightenment, it is sitting there patiently waiting for us. It has always been there. Ignorance and enlightenment share the same space as each other. We simply need to remove the barrier, the shell of conditioned thought, which has caused the disconnection from our infinite self and the Source Of All That Is. Crack the eggshell, shatter it into a thousand pieces by changing the way you see yourself, open your heart and mind, and all levels of you will be reunited. A little help is required to speed this process and that help is here, not least in the form of "extraterrestrial" activity which will expand enormously in the years ahead until we eventually interact with people from other time-space dimensions in the same way that we mix with people of different countries on Earth. But, once again, within this free-will virtual reality, it is *we* who must decide if we wish to accept such support.

Each time-space dimension within the vortex/pyramid is sharing the same space as all the others, just as radio and television frequencies share the same space. They operate in different "worlds" unaware of the other's existence. However, frequencies very close on the radio band can interfere with each other. So it is within the vortex. On the dimension next to ours, what I will call the Fourth Dimension, are two opposing forces, male-female, positive-negative, which have fought over hundreds of thousands of our years for control of this dense physical world. Two of their manifestations on Earth were the civilisations known as Lemuria and Atlantis. This battle on the Fourth Dimension has been symbolised in ancient texts as the "battle in the heavens" and the "battle of the Gods". We see it symbolised by Hollywood in films like *Star Wars* and *The Empire Strikes Back*. It is a tussle between two elements of Oneness separated within the vortex. Light and Dark is the way that some people describe it, but it is really two shades of imbalance at war with each other. And it is this sometimes turbulent fourth dimension which has the role in the movie of guiding our third dimension back to Oneness! Someone there lost the script and if two sides involved in an enormous spiritual tussle have been guiding this dimension it does explain rather well how humanity lost its way. That does not mean that all of the fourth dimensional reality is in trauma, only some significant elements within it. Wonderful gifts of love, understanding, and discovery have been transmitted to us from that dimension which have enriched human life and there is a tremendous amount of support coming to us from that dimension today. On the Fourth Dimension is knowledge of technology beyond our dreams, but because of the divisions this has been abused at times. Knowledge without wisdom, technological invention without love, can be very unpleasant combinations. It is from this fourth dimension and higher that at least most of the "UFOs" come, both positive and negative. The scale of the UFO-extraterrestrial cover up is extraordinary and so is the manipulation of this phenomenon by the Global Elite. The fear of extraterrestrial "invasion" is being used to justify a world government and army. Hollywood films are being produced with this theme as part of the conditioning. The genuine space craft have the ability to change their vibratory state and "switch" dimensions. When they do, they disappear to our physical senses. They have not actually disappeared, they have merely left our time-space reality – the frequency range in which our physical sight and other senses operate. It's like moving the radio dial. Many of these craft and beings might even be thought forms transmitted from the Fourth Dimension which only manifest as "craft".

The Earth, the solar system, and the universe, exist on all the time-space dimensions within the pyramid. While the Moon and the planets of the solar system may seem to be lifeless to our physical senses, we are only seeing them from our dimension. On other dimensions those same planets are teeming havens of life. The same with the stars. We see the Earth from the perspective of our physical frequency range, but the Earth exists on all of these other dimensions, too, and it may look very different on some of them to the one we experience here. But it is still the same multidimensional Earth. Our consciousness is also multidimensional and levels of us exist on these other dimensions, too! We are like those Russian dolls, one inside the other, but we have become disconnected from most of them which is why our perspective has been so limited. I remember how a very sensitive psychic friend once had a vision of me addressing what she called millions of people. "It is you" she said "But it is you on another level, not this one". It seemed a strange idea at the time, but not anymore. What she saw was not the physical "me" which is tapping the keys of this word processor, it was that part of my multidimensional consciousness which is experiencing that other dimension. A level of us is experiencing every dimension within the vortex right up to Oneness. Each is another actor playing its chosen part on this multiscreen "cinema" within the vortex, learning and evolving with each new experience. Not only did the pyramidic movie projection separate into "worlds" of experience, it separated the Oneness of those who chose to take part in the experiment. As the pyramid rolls back into Oneness and we rise up the dimensions, we become One with each of our separated levels in turn until we are "whole" again. At that moment, we will be back to our state of Oneness and we will have access to the experience and learning that every level of us has absorbed. And, come to that, what every level of everyone else has absorbed within the vortex. The learning will be incredible and all of creation will evolve as a result. It is like one student separating into many students who then go off to different universities, studying different subjects, and experiencing different lifestyles, attitudes, and ways of hating and loving. Then they all return to each other and swap notes and stories. So while we may be experiencing a positive life here, another aspect of us may be a "villain" somewhere else. It's just an experience and it makes the judgment of others so ludicrous. While I challenge states of mind like the "far-Right", Christian Patriotism, and the Robot Radicals, the people tuned to those mental and emotional states are having an experience from which they, and all of us, will learn. It's a game, a ride. We are each other, no matter what any of those "others" may be doing. The extraterrestrials who are dubbed "aliens" are actually other aspects of ourselves. They are not "alien" at all. They are part of us. These vortexes of learning in specific, artificially created, conditions can be found throughout the infinite mind we call God. They are vortexes, eddies, within the river of consciousness that flows to infinity. These vortexes of experience allow God (us) to experience His/Her self and understand the extent of His/Her potential: we are all One consciousness experiencing itself subjectively.

If we are to evolve, to balance and raise ourselves back up the levels to Oneness, we need to remember who and what we are. Without that, we will remain like the moth in the bottle, unaware of the means of escape. And the pyramid of experience cannot roll back into Oneness again until the dense physical level moves. It will continue to be a lead weight holding down all the rest and the time has arrived for the experiment to move on It is time to become One again with our multidimensional selves and "God" in general. This could not happen without support and guidance from the level of Oneness because we have created such illusion within ourselves that we have forgotten who we are, where we came from, and what we are part of. We are the prodigal son who left "the Father" (Oneness) to experience and then lost his way. But, just as the prodigal son returned to a welcoming "father", so we have the opportunity now to do the same. It is my strong belief that a "team" of "volunteers" came out of the Oneness to help with the transition from separation and division to balance and harmony. These multidimensional volunteers (consciousness) are operating on all dimensions within the vortex offering information which will help people to remember that they are taking part in a game. It is not real. The toughest task is faced by those operating in this dense physical world because the density has added to the spiritual amnesia which has disconnected people from their eternal memory. They have forgotten who they are, where they came from, and what the hell they are doing here. I think that even some of this volunteer consciousness has become so hypnotised by the light at the bottom of the bottle that it, too, has forgotten what it is here to do! Many are called, but few serve. Enough have stayed awake, however, to do the job. Examples of this volunteer consciousness can be found throughout history and they include some, though most certainly not all, of the figures which later had religions founded in their names. Y'shua (Jesus) was possibly among them and the difficulties he encountered were caused by interference from the Fourth Dimension. When he left this world, his words were turned on their head and used as the foundations for a religion, inspired from the Fourth Dimension, which has been the epitome of everything he came to challenge.

Life on this dense physical dimension has been made more difficult by the interference from the Fourth Dimension. It is from there, as I have indicated, that the so called "gods" of ancient legend originate. Elements of this consciousness have manipulated this world throughout known history and before. It is the "Prison Warder" consciousness, as I call it in ...*and the truth shall set you free*, and I believe it has a physical extraterrestrial expression on, and under, the Earth today. What is the common theme that connects the thought control of religion going back thousands of years and the thought control of today's political-economic-military-media-industrial complex? The manipulation by elements in the Fourth Dimension via the minds of those here in the Third and maybe even more directly as a physical form. The negative consciousness operating on the Fourth Dimension created, either though direct incarnation or thought manipulation, the religions and various creeds which have controlled, divided, and ruled this world for thousands of years. It was also the source of the belief in this-world-is-all-there-is "science". It was behind the creation of the education system, the legal (in)justice system, the wars, the interest-on-money banking cartels, and it is the force that is pressing, via its physical puppets or direct, incarnate, representatives, for a world government, central bank, currency, and army, together with a microchipped population.

The Global Elite are either incarnations or physical projections of this extreme negative consciousness which people call Satanic, or, in other cases, they are possessed by it. So it has been for thousands of years going back to ancient Egypt, Babylon, etc. These Fourth Dimensional "Satanic" manipulators have their symbolism in all areas of society because they created all the vehicles of control. One of the main channels of interaction between the Fourth Dimension and its Third Dimensional representatives and puppets is the upper levels of the global secret society network in which the initiation ceremonies can create a vibrational connection between the initiate (puppet) and the Fourth Dimensional manipulators. Symbols like the Pyramid, All Seeing Eye and many others which go back into ancient times are still those of the secret society network today because they are the Satanic symbols of this highly imbalanced element of the Fourth Dimension. The Satanic rites and grotesque human sacrifices still going on today are designed to create huge amounts of extreme negative energy on which this consciousness feeds. This "Satanic" consciousness *is* extreme negative energy and so the more of this energy that can be produced in the three dimensional world, the more power the consciousness has to manipulate this planet. Humanity is then operating on a negative vibrational playing field within the vibrational range of the "Satanic" consciousness. This is why animal and human sacrifices which abound throughout human history still continue today. Some of this even goes on openly. What is a slaughterhouse if not a place for the sacrifice of animals, thus creating enormous terror and pain – extreme negative energy? The spilling of blood is very important to this consciousness and its Global Elite/extraterrestrial puppets on Earth. The United Nations building in New York is built on land given free by the Rockefellers. It is the site of a former slaughterhouse. The Satanic force is symbolised by the All Seeing Eye of Lucifer at the peak of the pyramid and it operates through the Global Elite. The same force has been controlling and manipulating the planet for at least hundreds of thousands of years, probably a lot longer. But it is vital that we don't react to this consciousness with hatred, fear and aggression. It needs our love because it is the absence of love that has led to its current imbalanced state. Hatred, fear and aggression are the emotions it *wants* to stimulate. They are its power.

At their highest levels those who control the secret society network knowingly serve their fourth dimensional and extraterrestrial "masters". Nor is it coincidence that the Pyramid and All Seeing Eye are on the reverse of the Great Seal of the United States and on the dollar bill. Representatives and puppets for the negative elements of the Fourth Dimension were behind the creation of the United States and control it to this day, as they do the global banking system, the intelligence agencies, political system, the media, and so on. Some people believe that another symbol of the fourth dimensional manipulators is the black gown. What is the attire worn by Christian clergy and representatives of many other religions? A black gown. What is the colour of the legal profession, barristers, many judges and such like? Black. What is the symbol of success in the education system or the top of the teaching profession? A black gown. The fourth dimensional thought manipulators inspired all of these institutions of control. In *Star Wars* and *The Empire Strikes Back* what was the colour worn by the "baddie", Darth Vader? Black – with a Nazi helmet, appropriately, because the fourth dimensional manipulators were the force behind the Nazis, too. If you read ...*and the truth shall set you free,* you will appreciate how and why the Nazis were created. Darth Vader was the symbol of what I have called the Luciferic or Satanic Consciousness, the fourth dimensional source which has manipulated our three dimensional world. Hollywood, especially the films by Steven Spielberg like *Raiders Of The Lost Ark*, are full of symbolism which betrays a wide knowledge of the true story behind the manipulation of this world.

The mentality known as the Illuminati or Global Elite, the few who control the direction of the world by conditioning the mass consciousness, have their origin, guidance and motivation in the Fourth Dimension and its extraterrestrial expression. This is how the same force that was responsible for the creation of religion is also the force behind the plan to microchip everyone and link them to a global computer. Ironically, those Christians who rightly oppose the microchipping of people and the other plans of the New World Order, are following a religious belief system manipulated into being by the same fourth dimensional consciousness which is behind the microchipping!

Look at the common objective between all of these apparently "separate", even "opposite" creations of the fourth dimensional manipulators: control of the human mind. It does not matter to them if we are mind-controlled by a religion, a political "ism", an economic theory, the "education" system, or a "scientific" belief in some after-life nothingness. You want your mind-controlled, sir? Good, come in, look around, I'm sure you'll find something that's just right for your state of being. We don't care which one you choose. All you do is pick your form of designer thought control, hand over your mind to us, and away you go. Couldn't be simpler. Oh, you fancy the Jesus-died-so-our-sins-could-be-forgiven model? Wise choice, if I may say so, and it also comes with an optional wave-the-flag-for-America, God-is-on-our-side, attachment and today's special giveaway, George Washington singing *Land Of The Free*. Thank you, sir, that will cost you only one mind and a thousand self-delusions. Next time you come, you can pay by microchip.

Those imbalanced elements within the Fourth Dimension can only control and direct events in this one if we give our minds away. That is why all the creations of these manipulators, be it religion, finance, politics or "science", involve the hijacking of the human psyche. In this way they also hijack humanity's sense of self, its sense of reality, and its physical experience. When we take our power back and stop accepting another's belief of what we should be, we remove the ability of the few to mind-control the "masses", the mass human consciousness. Beliefs are limitations of vision and prisons of the mind. We believe too much and feel too little. Only when we follow our feelings, instead of denying them, will we break the grip the manipulators have on so many psyches. Go with the flow without fear of what others will think. The most powerful way to set ourselves free of the believing, fearing, intellect, is to celebrate our own uniqueness, allow everyone else to do the same, and never seek to impose what we believe on another. I say anything goes unless there is imposition or pressure of any kind on anyone to do the same. That's freedom.

Part of the vibratory transformation now unfolding on this planet and this time-space reality in general, is to cleanse the negative energies in the Fourth Dimension and remove their abuse of human free will. The whole vortex/pyramid is being transformed and that includes the Fourth Dimension. The ability of this fourth dimensional "Illuminati" to impose its design on this world via the human "Illuminati" is being curtailed by the day. We are in the last years of this control and with its interdimensional power source rapidly on the wane, if not already withdrawn, the Global Elite will find it ever more difficult to achieve its end of global, political, economic and spiritual power over a microchipped, robotic population. The Global Elite have reached their peak of power because the human population have reached the depths of giving their power away. From now, the only way is up. This is already apparent to gathering millions who are awakening to a new vision of themselves and their destiny as their eggshells crack and they are reunited with higher dimensions of themselves.

Energies are being transmitted down from Oneness throughout the pyramid. These energies, thought forms, are designed to harmonise and balance the separation. As this happens the movie sets created by the interaction of separated polarities begin to change because the circumstances which created them are changing. If the dense physical world is created by the separation of negative and positive, female and male, which slow the vibrations and form dense matter, then as the scale of that separation is reduced, the vibrations will quicken and the dense physical world as we know it ceases to be. The movie sets manifest an ever closer connection with Oneness as the energies move closer to that state of being. Conflict becomes less, love and understanding becomes more prevalent, and so on until we are back at the balance point we came from: Oneness. Game over. What shall we play now?

This change is already well advanced. It has been creeping upon us unnoticed, just as the cracks in a dam can go unnoticed until just before the whole structure is about to give way. For those with eyes that can see beyond the physical illusions, the cracks are now very wide indeed and the dam is beginning to sway. A tidal wave of change is upon us and we can swim with that tide or against it. That is our choice, but the consequences of this choice will be very, very different. We can let go of the rigidity and limitations of our reality and potential, unload the emotional sewage in our subconscious, and fly, vibrationally, out through the top of the bottle and home. Or we can continue to be mesmerised by the light at the bottom and wage war against the vibrational change the entire bottle is experiencing. In my view, the consequences of that choice will be deeply unpleasant, but it's a choice we all have every right to make. These high vibrational energies have travelled down the pyramid from Oneness, affecting and transforming the other dimensions within the vortex. Hence, the imbalances and divisions on the Fourth

Dimension are being healed, and now that process is filtering down to
this dense physical world of ours. These energies are having a gathering
effect on the consciousness of humanity and life on Earth. Again we are
back to electromagnetic energy fields and the sea of energy with which
we constantly interact. As higher energies are introduced which raise the
vibrational state of the global energy fields, everything is being affected,
not least human thought and emotions.

It may not seem to be obvious when you watch the TV news that we
are in the process of transforming this planet from division and conflict
to peace and harmony. There seems to be more unrest than ever. There
is a reason for that. Whatever your state of being, it will usually settle
into a sort of equilibrium. Put something on only one side of the scales
and after a while the scales will settle down into what you might call a
balanced imbalance. The scales will be pushed down much further on
one side, but they will eventually stop moving up and down and come
to rest in that position. If you then put something of equal weight on
the other side to balance the scales, the balance does not come
immediately. Once again, the scales jump around for a while until they
settle down into the new situation, in this case, balance. So whenever
the scales change, it involves a rather chaotic period of readjustment.
But in truth it is not chaos at all, it is a natural, and essential,
prerequisite to change. If you take the symbolism of the scales to be the
energy fields of the Earth and ourselves, it expresses very well what we
are experiencing now. The old structures (balanced imbalance) have
reached the end of the line and they are crumbling in the face of the
energies ushering in the new world and new Earth (balance). I will talk
about the effects on humanity a little later, but the effects on the planet
and the systems of nature are already apparent. The increasingly
obvious changes in world weather patterns are not the result of the so
called Greenhouse Effect in my view. They are being caused by the
vibrational changes affecting the Earth's energy fields. The scales are
moving.[1] The effects on the weather will continue to grow in the
transitional period until, possibly, a pole shift completes the
transformation from old energy field (time-space dimension) to new.
These high powered energies, which manifest in part as a phenomena
known as the Photon Belt,[2] are now being measured even by

---

[1] It is also important to note, however, that the Elite now have technology to manipulate the
weather for their own ends.

[2] See *...and the truth shall set you free* and *The Robots' Rebellion*.

conventional "science". According to the London *Daily Telegraph* of July 5th 1995, energies have been measured that have shattered popular "scientific" belief. The article said:

> *"Something out there – no-one knows what – is hurling high energy particles around the universe, in this case the most energetic ever observed by scientists…Not even the power released by the most powerful exploding stars could account for them. Indeed conventional theory says such particles should not exist…"*

These energies, known by "science" as cosmic rays, are normally measured in the range of millions of electron volts power. Since 1992, the article said, they have been measured in a range of up to 320 billion billion electron volts. And these are only the energies that human "science" has so far developed the technology to measure. Most of the change is happening on vibrational levels unknown and unmeasured by "science". But the human mind, heart, and emotions can feel them far more sensitively than any technology. The Photon Belt, a field of highly, highly charged energy, is, I believe, responsible in part for this incredible difference in the gathering power of the energies being measured. Many people believe that the solar system is now moving into the Photon Belt and the effect of these energies will be felt more and more in terms of physical changes (weather, geological unrest) and, the root of all change, the awakening human mind. Another enormous source of change is the spiritual and physical heart of the solar system, the Sun. I was interested to read about the work of the researcher and writer, Maurice Cotterell, who studied the cycles of sun spot activity – the times when the Sun is emitting very powerful magnetic energies which travel to the Earth on what is known as the solar wind.[3] He later came across the amazing mathematical system of numbers and symbols left by the ancient Mayan people in Central America which claimed to measure the cycles of human and Earth evolution. He was fascinated to realise that his cycles of sun spot (magnetic) activity corresponded very closely with the Mayan cycles of human evolution, even those projected over thousands of years. This was no "coincidence". Life is the interaction of magnetic energy fields. Change the magnetism and you change the nature of the energy field. Change the energy field and

---

[3] See *The Mayan Prophecies* by Adrian G. Gilbert and Maurice M. Cotterell, (Element Books, Shaftsbury, England, 1995).

you change the nature of "life". That is happening now to Planet Earth. Look at so many of the ancient prophecies about great changes on Earth, be it native peoples like the Hopi tribe in the United States, the Maya, or psychics like Edgar Cayce or Nostradamus, and they point to enormous change in the time period we are living through today. According to the Maya, the last Great Cycle of the Earth's evolution began in 3114 BC and it is due to end in 2012 when another, very different, period of evolution will begin. Again same story, same basic timescale. The incoming energies have already awakened very large numbers of people to see the world and themselves through far more open and perceptive eyes by helping them reconnect with higher levels of themselves which, up to this point, they had shut out. Those numbers are growing rapidly by the day. Everyone can begin that same journey. It's only a choice.

No matter what the scale of change unfolding, this is not a time to panic. It is never a time to panic! Life is forever and we are going through a cycle within the vortex which will allow us to begin the journey home to Oneness. Just as the "death" of Autumn and Winter is followed by the "birth" and "life" of Spring and Summer, so in the greater cycles of evolution, whole dimensions go through this sequence of "death" and "rebirth". Spring, new birth and abundance, will follow this period of breakdown and change. No worries. How bumpy or spiritually orgasmic the transition will be depends upon you and me and our imagination of ourselves and the "future". If we think it will be catastrophic, so it will be. But it doesn't have to be. We can imagine something different and create that reality.

We are what we think and the world is what we *all* think.

Chapter 7

It's A Piece A Shit, Walk Away

If we are to complete our transition from ignorance to infinity, we need to float to the surface of the vibrational pyramid. That is easier than it may sound because our consciousness naturally gravitates towards Oneness, just as the deep sea diver would float to the surface without the weights to hold him down.

Our "weights" are the emotional gunge in our subconscious, our programmed sense of self and reality, and the endless mind-numbing claptrap that assaults our eyes and ears via the media, the education (indoctrination) system, politicians, economists, and all the other mind doctors selling us their view of what our reality should be. In short, the eggshell. Without those influences, that weight on our mind and emotions, the bird would have flown a long time ago. These are the influences that create the light at the bottom of the bottle, hypnotising us and keeping us in ignorance of our true and infinite self. I remember listening to a tape of the late Bill Hicks, the American comedian I mentioned before. He was talking about a film called *Basic Instinct*. His summary of the film: "Piece a shit". However, great debate ensued about the picture. Was it too this or too that? Much of this "debate" was hyped to promote the movie and Bill Hicks offered the following advice:

It's a piece a shit, walk away.

If humanity did that more often, it would not waste its energy day after day on irrelevant debate and argument over "issues" that are only there to divert us from what really matters – our own evolution out of ignorance and our own ability to love and be loved. But we get hooked in by these manufactured debates and diversions. We see irrelevant events and statements as vitally important, instead of walking away and seeing them for what they are: irrelevant diversions. It's

119

fascinating to observe, as your mind expands and the cell door creaks open, how the issues and concerns that occupy our minds, screw us up, and give us a bad sense of self, simply don't matter. We are just conditioned to think they matter and so we expend our energies and wind up our emotions worrying about things that others programme us to believe are important. Are we too fat? Are we too thin? Are we too tall? Are we too small? Are our breasts big enough? Are our willies big enough? Are we losing the hair on our heads? Do we have too much hair on our bodies? Are we wearing the latest uniform (sorry fashion) that someone we have never met has decided is "in"? We are deluged by advertisers and the television "programmes" funded by advertisers which tell us how we should be, look, and feel. You've got a wrinkle on your face? Oh, my dear, your life is over. It's the end of the road. Unless, that is, you buy this super-duper face oil named after somewhere that sounds exotic. It will save your life. Hey, look at this curvy, sun-tanned, blonde we paid vast sums to show her bum on a beach. Buy our oil and that could be you. (*Author leaves word processor in order to vomit.*)

In Hollywood, the home of self and mass delusion, there are more face lifts and hair transplants per square mile than probably anywhere else on the planet. It is no wonder. The Hollywood mentality is the ultimate illusion and it is obsessed with the physical senses. Its industry, its very reason for being, is based on illusion, with false backdrops, false sunlight, and plastic, artificial emotions, as two actors who can't stand each other come together for a warm caress. My darling, I love you (cut!)…you asshole. Hollywood is a wonder to observe and symbolises magnificently the illusions that keep the human mind enslaved. It sells to the mass psyche its version of history and of what is beautiful, successful, and important. This invariably relates to archetypal images of butch men with firm faces and plenty of hair (real or otherwise) and ideally shaped women straight out of wardrobe and make up. Some actors know all this isn't real, but many forget to leave the illusions on the set. They live them and take on that celluloid world as their reality. It is a world of fear, insincerity and insecurity: you were brilliant darling, what was I like? Oh Dorothy darling, I'm so glad you won the Oscar (lucky bitch). Their sense of self comes not from what they are, but from how they are perceived by those who control the illusion machine and by an audience conditioned by the illusion machine. So plastic surgeons (why don't they melt?) and hair transplanters have a licence to print money in this never-never-land. Yes folks, this is what you can aspire to. These are the stars, the image of what you ought to be, but aren't. Aintcha just so sad?

A few questions for those who buy this idea that there is somehow an ideal shape, height, weight, hairstyle, age or willy size. Who says? Who decided that? Did you decide that because it was your original thought or because that is what you have been conditioned to believe? The latter, almost certainly. What's more if your friends and family have been conditioned to believe the same (and most of them have) you feel an even greater pressure to aspire to that manufactured image of physical perfection. I saw a documentary about Hollywood men in which this guy's sex life had been destroyed by an operation that went wrong...an operation to fill his willy with fat from another part of his body to make it look bigger.

Uhhhhhh! I know, I know, my eyes are watering too. My God, what's happened to us? What happened to our infinity of understanding, Oneness and self love? I think it bought a movie ticket.

Is it just me? I mean what does it matter if someone has a larger or smaller body than the "ideal". Does it make them a bad person? No. Does it make them less intelligent? No. Does it make them less able to give and receive love? No. So what does it make them, then, what's the big deal? It makes them different to the conditioned version of "normality", that's all. And what is this "norm"? Is it normal to be a suntanned blonde with a polished smile showing her bum to a camera? I've just come back from town and I didn't see one of them anywhere. I would have noticed, I'm sure. All I saw were people of different shapes, colours and sizes adding to the variety of life and experience. Not a bare bum or sun tan in sight. And what's this terror that men have of losing their hair? Oh my life's over, women won't be attracted to me...save my hair, take it from my armpits, anywhere, Aaaaaaaaaaaaahhhhhhhhh!!! Let's just go through this again: when you lose your hair does it make you a bad person? No. Does it make you less intelligent? No. Does it make you less able to give and receive love? No. What's more, it doesn't even make you different. Look around you, most men lose their hair. And get this: what would be our reaction if we lived on a planet in which the physical body had no hair on its head and suddenly it started to grow? Oh my life's over, women won't be attracted to me...remove my hair, stick it under my armpits, anywhere, Aaaaaaaaaaaaahhhhhhhh!!! Exactly. It's just conditioning, that's all it is.

It's a piece a shit, walk away.

The irony of all this, and the knowledge that will end the manipulation of human emotions by the multibillion-dollar-hate-your-body industry, is that there is no need for all these potions and creams and willy surgeons. Our bodies are a reflection of our sense of self. They are a physical expression of our mind and emotions. You can see in the faces of people if they have been through extreme emotional pain. It is written in their features. People who eat a lot and create bigger bodies for themselves are invariably manifesting in their eating habits an emotional torment of some kind. For them it's food, for others its drink or drugs, just a means to escape temporarily from the emotion they wish to shut out. Our minds control our bodies and our bodies will reflect our state of mind. I have a close friend who has an astonishing connection between mind and body. Her whole face changes with her changing emotions. It's remarkable to see. The faces of the mind-controlled human robots often change as they switch "personalities". If we feel good about ourselves we will transmit the same energy to our bodies. If we feel unloved and unwanted, our bodies will manifest that, also. The same goes for aging. We don't have to age as we do. We expect to age because that is our reality and so we age. As we evolve towards Oneness, the aging process will slow down and we will live for what appears to us now to be incredible lengths of time. Impossible? Nothing, NOTHING, is impossible. Incidentally, returning to that Hollywood theme, those actors who fear losing their looks or their hair are far more likely to lose them. We attract to us what we most fear because overcoming fear is essential to our evolution. Relax. Whatever you are is OK. It's your role in the movie at this moment. You are what you are and you can change what you are by changing what you think you are. That, too, applies to our bodies. Anyway, you chose your body before incarnation in the knowledge of what that would mean in terms of size, shape and length of appendage. You did that for an experience that you believed would speed your understanding and evolution. It is just a temporary body – *you* are eternal mind and spirit. But if we get caught into the trap of accepting the manipulators version of what is normal and "sexy", we will have a lifetime of diminished self worth if we don't have a body that conforms to that.

Fundamentally related to the desire for some physical "perfection" or "norm" is the great myth that happiness can be pursued. The pursuit of happiness is even part of the United States Constitution and it is a system-serving device which encourages people to run around like terrified chickens chasing something that simply cannot be caught.

People are duped into pursuing happiness with a bigger fridge, or the latest car, or a bigger house. "If I just had this or that," they say "I'd be happy." But when they get it, they're still not happy. Most people go through their entire lives without being truely happy. Of course there may be moments when they feel blissful, but those moments are so fleeting. Their "happiness" is normally measured by levels of *un*happiness. The harder you try to find happiness, the more elusive it becomes. The reason is simple: if you are in a constant state of pursuing happiness you can never be happy. Your "now" experience is always the *pursuing* of happiness, never happiness itself. Your happiness is always in the future and not in your now. Its like sitting on one of those horses on the fairground rides. It doesn't matter how fast the carousel is turning, you never get any closer to the horse in front. John Lennon once wrote that life is what happens to you while you're busy making other plans. In the same way, happiness is constantly passing us by because we are spending all our time pursuing it instead of "being" it. The only way to be happy is to be happy. That is a state of mind within your control whatever you are doing. It doesn't require a new Ferrari or an extension to your dangly bits. Happiness is not a pursuing, it is a being. The harder you chase it, the further you push it away. It can be likened to chasing a butterfly. The more desperately you charge at it, the more it will elude you. But if you stop trying so hard, lay down on the grass and relax, there is a chance it will just come and land on your shoulder. A similar example is the swimmer trying to reach a ball in the water. The harder and more desperately he swims, the more he disturbs the water and the ball gets further and further away. If, however, he is patient and relaxes, he will reach the ball using a lot less effort and emotion. We are called human beings and yet we have become human "doings". We are conditioned to chase everything, including, most significantly, happiness. This constant state of pursuit obscures the truth that life is a lot easier than we are conditioned to believe and does not require the enormous expenditure of physical and emotional energy that we observe every day. Instead of chasing our dreams, we can use our multidimensional powers to attract our dreams to us. Flowing with our intuition is a great deal more effective than living our lives as if someone had just shouted "fire".

Another thing that hooks us in emotionally and seeps our energy for no good reason is the way we are offended by what others say or do. People are offended by different things because they are programmed by different Hassle-Free Zones (a religion, a political "ism", what we were told was "right and "wrong" by our parents). What offends one person won't offend another because they will have been conditioned to be offended by different things. Tell a Christian that Jesus was an asshole and they will be mortally offended. A Muslim will not. Tell the Muslim that Mohammed was an asshole and he'll be offended, but not the Christian. It's all in the mind. There are, however, some universal taboos which seem to offend vast numbers of people of all beliefs because society as a whole, the main Hassle-Free Zone, has decided that we should be offended by them. So we are. We do as we are told like fully paid up robots. There may be some people reading this book who have been offended by my use of the word shit. If you have, it might be worth asking yourself why you are offended. Shit is merely the one syllable sound which has been accepted to mean a substance we all produce and if we didn't produce it we would eventually explode. Very messy. I use the word shit because the nature of the substance it describes is brilliantly symbolic of the propaganda we are pressured to accept as our reality on this planet. If anyone is offended by the word shit, it is not because I am being offensive because that is not my intention. It is because you have chosen to be offended. It is all taking place in your mind, not mine. Even if I was trying to be offensive, you still don't have to take it on and be affected by it. You have a choice. Well now I've offended you, I might as well go all the way. In for a penny, in for a pound – you know me. How about the word fuck?

My GOD! Did you hear what he just said?
You know…ffff…the "*F*" word.
Disgusting! Outrageous! What an awful man!

I said the "F" word? Oh, you mean fuck? Yes, that's right, I did. So? It's funny that the same people who do not get offended by American warplanes bombing the crap out of people in the Middle East, Vietnam, and elsewhere, killing children by the score, will be breathless in their indignation when someone says the word "fuck". The end of the world is not ushered in by warplanes and atomic bombs, but by people saying "fuck". "The moral fibre of society is crumbling. Bring back hanging and conscription, that'll sort it. Put 'em in the army, make bomber pilots of them." What a hoot it is, all this plastic moral hypocrisy. You have "news"papers selling themselves by using naked women and sexual titillation and that's OK, it seems. But when the word fuck comes into a story, it is always written as "f★★★" because this is a "family" newspaper as you can see by the lady showing her tits on the inside page. What's with this f★★★ business? When you see f★★★, what word goes through your mind? Fuck, exactly. So what's the difference? Ah, I get it now. It's fine to *think* the word fuck, but not to say it or write it in full. Gotcha. F★★★ that. See, its easy.

Give me strength.

I was thinking: what if the slang word for sexual intercourse had turned out to be something else? It could quite easily have been so. We call two pieces of bread placed together a sandwich because a guy called Sandwich was supposed to have "invented" them. What if his name had been Willie? Or Sidebottom? We'd now be eating willies or sidebottoms. It's just a word, a sound. What if the slang word for sexual intercourse had been, by a quirk of fate, sandwich? And what if the word for two pieces of bread placed together had turned out to be fuck? Today if you go into a sandwich bar and ask for a cheese and tomato sandwich no-one turns a hair. But if you ask for a *fucking* sandwich, everyone is mortally offended. Imagine if the words were the other way round, as could quite possibly have happened. You would then go into a fucking bar and ask for a cheese and tomato fuck. No-one would turn a hair. But if you asked for a *sandwiching* fuck, everyone would be mortally offended.

My GOD! Did you hear what he just said?
You know...ssss...the "*S*" word.
Disgusting! Outrageous! What an awful man!

I've got a great idea. Let's grow up shall we?

I'm not advocating that everyone goes around using the word fuck or any other just for the sake of it. I actually think the word is a travesty of the true experience of sexual union, which at its peak, with the right person at the right time, is for me, the ultimate experience in this time-space reality. But it is also a very expressive word which conveys brilliantly your state of mind when you drop a hammer on your foot, or the car won't start, or the events of the day have wound you up. A few more "fucks" and tears and a few less stiff upper lips and a lot of people would occupy their bodies for a great deal longer. The overall point I am making here, however, is that if you are offended at anything and have your emotions stressed as a result, it is you who have chosen to be offended. It's a thought form, a state of mind, which you are in control of. People constantly get offended and wound up about things that don't matter. Just whisper slowly…f…u…c…k… There, are you any better or worse a person? No. You have just shaped your mouth and lips to say a word, just as you do when you say sandwich. It is just a sound. It is the intent behind a word, not the word itself, that is positive or negative.

The way so many are offended by the sight of the naked human body never ceases to make me chuckle. Religion has conditioned the collective psyche to such a degree that to display what we were born with, live with, and die with – our physical body – is considered highly offensive and an arrestable offence! It is illegal to show your willy or fuzzy bits on a beach, but legal to blow the shit out of defenceless people in faraway countries under the banner of freedom and peace. To say our "values" have become desperately confused is the understatement of eternity. This is one reason why I decided to appear naked on the front cover and even then I had to hide my doo dah with a sticker to allow the book to be displayed in the shops. Bookshops, it seems, have been designated doo dah-free zones. It's just a body for Christ's sake and we all have one. If you are offended by a naked body, again you might ask why you are offended because that's your choice, your problem, and no-one else's. The same applies when people attack us or hurl abuse at us. We can take on their problem or leave them to deal with it. If they have a problem with us, that's exactly the situation. *They* have a problem. It only becomes *our* problem if we choose to get hooked in and be offended by what they say or do. When we react negatively to someone who offends or hurts us, we are making a two-way magnetic connection with them. We become hooked into their vibe. Their problem is now ours. We are playing on their negative playing field, on their terms, and by their rules. When we choose not to be offended or hurt, there is no magnetic connection and so we don't take on another's problem or create a problem that isn't really there. You don't have to be offended, it's up to you. But for those who are easily offended I can only say:

It's a human waste product, walk away.

Another irrelevance we take terribly seriously is the so called "education" system. It is nothing of the kind. It is an indoctrination system, a key form of mind-control. Its job is to mould our consciousness into the shape of a four-legged animal from which we obtain wool. Teachers pass through the indoctrination system and they go off to schools and universities to indoctrinate the next generation. At the peak of the "education" pyramid, this is done knowingly, but the overwhelming majority of teachers and lecturers are just programmed people programming their students. It is a self-perpetuating cycle. Those teachers who know they are caught in a web of indoctrination and conditioning only go so far in pointing this out because if they say what they really think they are out of a job. In the United Kingdom, we have a "National Curriculum" which insists that all children and students are the same, or must be made to be so. Everyone is taught the same subjects in basically the same way and the measurement of success of both system and student is based on how adept they are at transferring mental garbage from mind to paper. Sorry, how adept they are at passing "exams". The education system is the mind-mould production line for the Hassle-Free Zone. The curriculum is, in its themes and at its core, merely the view of life and ourselves which the Elite and their manipulators on the Fourth Dimension wish us to have. Students are taught about politics as if democracy was freedom and choice actually existed; they are taught that the financial system is sane and sensible and not an enormous sleight of hand; they are told that this world is "real" and not just an illusion created by thought – their thoughts; they are conditioned for the world of "work" and a mind numbing life of serving the system. One slave reporting for duty, sir! One mind for the use and abuse of, sir! Atteeen-tion.

A most powerful form of reality conditioning is what is called "history". What is really meant by that term is the *official* version of history. How we see the past has a massive impact on how we see the present and the future. Official history tells a story of black and white events in which the good guys fight the bad and win victories for "freedom". Hiding what really happened in the past is essential for the manipulators if they are to hide what is happening now. Nowhere are students taught, or even asked to consider the possibility, that the same people might have been manipulating and funding all "sides" to create divide and rule, start wars, and change the nature of the post-war society. Even though this is provable, children and students all over the world continue to be told a very different, manufactured, story. Teachers are told this version is true when they go through the system and they tell their students it is true when they become an indoctrinator (teacher) for the system. No-one has to intervene to directly manipulate schools and teachers once this structure is up and running. It runs itself. In the same way all the knowledge about an alternative view of life, consciousness, healing and creation, are kept out of the classroom unless a rare, enlightened and determined teacher finds a way of introducing these subjects outside of the official curriculum. This curriculum is, in the UK and doubtless elsewhere, so packed with "information" which the system insists must be taught that there is no time in the day for an alternative to its imposed reality. The education system is about teaching and tuning minds to see only the world of physicalness or some religious "afterlife" that involves doing as you are told to avoid being handed the coal shovel.

But, and here's the point I am making in this chapter, billions of people have bought the idea that passing exams set by the system for the perpetuation of the system is a measurement of a child's or student's success. Young people worry and sweat and have their lives blighted by the fear of not passing this or that exam and getting the grades the system has decided confirms your level of intelligence. Some youngsters even commit suicide if they fail to achieve this and they feel incredible guilt at "letting down" their parents. My friends, if your parents are going to feel let down or think you are a failure because you have failed to recall the trash the system was asking you to recite, they deserve to be disappointed. It'll do them good. It's time they grew up. For goodness sake what is an "exam"? It is the system saying "tell me what I want to hear, otherwise you fail. Do as I say or you'll be a loser, kid". Exams are actually a measurement of how indoctrinated you are! Exams are a colossal irrelevance, except where they relate to a specific job or task. They don't matter. Your personal learning, your understanding of yourself and your potential, is what matters and the education/indoctrination system suppresses, not caresses, that understanding. You're not a clone, you are an amazing being of light and love with an astonishing uniqueness to express. What are you doing worrying about examinations set by a system which wants to condition you, clone you and crush your sense of uniqueness?

It's a piece a shit, walk away.

Still today, despite all the evidence from past and present, people continue to argue about party politics, even though the same Elite has funded and manipulated virtually every major party in the world into existence. People turn out at the mass rallies waving their party flags, clapping and cheering as dictated by the spin doctors playing to the cameras, and then off trot their heroes to Downing Street, the White House or wherever, to pursue policies that are a virtual mirror-image of the "opponents" they replaced. What we call "democracies" are merely One Party States with the same force, a Global Elite, either controlling directly, or dictating by events, the decisions of presidents and prime ministers who only appear to be in charge. They are not. They are puppets. Look at the background, for instance, to Bill Clinton and George Bush and you see that they are members of the same organisations and controlled by the same clique.[1] Yet they appear to be opponents with one proclaiming to be a "Democrat" and the other a "Republican". Again, it's an illusion, some more special effects to dupe the audience watching the movie. We have to think we have choice otherwise we might realise we live in a dictatorship that is only decked out to look like freedom.

In many ways I feel for politicians. They are pawns being moved around the board by manipulation and events until they no longer know their arse from their elbow. They become so focussed on the dream of power that they have no idea what they really think or stand for – if anything. The pursuit of power becomes the sole decider of policy and "opinion". It is policy by yesterday's headlines or the latest, manipulated opinion poll – both of which are dictated by the Elite. In truth, politicians, even presidents and prime ministers, have no real power. They are at the mercy of events controlled by those much higher up the pyramid, those who manipulate public opinion – the very opinion the politicians seek to pander to at election time. This means that all their "policies" and attitudes are basically the same (the One Party State), and this has turned politics into a sickening farce in which insults are preferred to insight and discord to debate. Twice a week in the House of Commons in London, the Prime Minister hosts something known as Question Time when he or she is questioned by the leader of the opposition. I will give you a flavour:

> **Opposition Leader:** *"Will the Prime Minister please explain why his government is the most useless, unfair administration, in the history of this parliament, and why he is such a jerk, incapable of running a whelk stall on Camden market?"*

---

[1] See *...and the truth shall set you free*.

(Sits down amid loud cheers from fellow party members who are waving bits of paper and shouting silly yah boo remarks.)

Prime Minister: *"What hypocrisy for that to come from the most useless, talentless opposition party in the history of this parliament, led by a man who is such a jerk that he couldn't run a fish and chip shop on Brighton sea front."*

(Sits down amid loud cheers from his fellow party members who are waving bits of paper and shouting silly yah boo, remarks)

I don't claim that to be verbatim, but you get my drift. Two people trade insults and it is seen as a virility contest for which one is best equipped to run the country. I thought the Prime Minister looked more authoritative and in control today, you know. The way he said "You're just a lily-livered berk" right at the end was a master stroke of timing. He'll win some points in the ratings for that! Often these mutual insults are the lead story on the television news that night: (Fade loud, ominous music, and cue stern, concerned looking newsreader with stern, concerned sounding voice): "The Prime Minister and the Leader of the Opposition clashed in the Commons today over which one was the biggest jerk. A report coming up."

ZZZzzzzzzzz!

No, wake up. We're supposed to take this seriously. We are supposed to ponder long and hard over which one we will vote for as the next puppet of the global dictators and the manipulators on the Fourth Dimension. Come on, this is serious. We can't just ignore elections because we know that whoever runs for president on both "sides" is funded, controlled and selected by the same clique who use the media, which they also control, to make sure the guy they really want wins. How can we call ourselves free if we don't use our vote to decide which of these guys will be the next puppet of the Elite? My pappy died fighting for the right to vote, y'hear? You can't ignore "free" elections. No? I beg to differ.

We will only loosen the weights on our consciousness and rise towards Oneness when we let go of the irrelevant diversions that take our eyes off the ball. It doesn't matter which party is in the White House or which one has a majority in Congress or the House of

Commons, or any other parliament. It's all a con, anyway. They are all of the same basic mentality, oppo-sames playing the game, a game which ignores who and what we really are and the solutions that come, and only come, from that knowledge. The party political system, like the financial system, is going to collapse because its structure is a physical expression of the old global energy field, the old imagination that humanity has had of itself. To support this system any longer by voting at rigged elections (also known as democracy) is to give it an energy which will prolong its death and the human prison it underpins. It is wasting energy which could be used to create another reality to replace the old. Let it die, its day is gone. We are growing up now. As the spiritual transformation gathers pace and the sense of human reality changes, the old structures of party politics and interest-bearing debt are being thought out of existence. This will manifest on the physical level as people losing confidence in the system, refusing to play by its rules, and the edifice of control will be denied the power (our power) which it needs to survive. It is already sprinting to stand still, or rather chasing its own tail. The time is approaching when it will disappear up its own backside, like some giant black hole, never to be seen again. Halleluyaaaah. How quickly that happens depends on how quickly we withdraw our energy from it and stop taking seriously the sight of boys and girls playing silly little games while trying to look important. Politics is an illusion of freedom, it is imposition parading as choice, and it only survives because we give it our energy by playing the dummy at the one party ballot box. Those who get to the top in politics are the least qualified people for the job because of what they need to do, and the attitudes they need to have, to reach the summit of the greasy pole.

In 1996 Bill Clinton said he supported a curfew for children and young people up to the age of 17. This was, he said, to reduce juvenile crime (problem-reaction-solution). In fact it was a stepping stone to the much wider use of the curfew (control) in the adult population. Juvenile crime is obviously not desirable, but it pales in the face of the violence and crime created and perpetrated by politicians and those who control them. A 16-year-old breaking into a house is deeply unpleasant for those involved, of course. It hardly compares, however, with the murder and maiming of thousands of people by US and NATO aircraft, or the death and misery of billions in the Third World caused by abuse and manipulation by governments in the "west". Therefore if curfews are such an effective response to violence and crime, it is only right that we should have them for the President of the United States and his equivalents across the planet. If they spent their days tidying their rooms and doing their homework, the world would be a much safer place. Amazingly, that is actually true! Party politics should carry a health warning: Danger, not to be taken seriously.

It's a piece a shit, walk away.

Two other areas I would raise in this context are economics and the media. We can get seriously hooked into sterile, diversionary, debates about economics and money. Economists are wheeled on nightly to tell us how important some irrelevant financial development is to our lives and why this or that must happen to compensate. It usually involves bigger taxation, holding down wages, or higher prices. We then worry about money and attract what we fear. It is a vicious circle. We have a "can't do" economic system which reflects the system as a whole. It's designed as a prison. By "can't do" I mean that anything that really needs doing to fundamentally improve life on Earth cannot be done, according to the mind doctors, because of its effect on "economic stability" – in other words it doesn't suit the Global Elite and their controllers on the Fourth Dimension. "I know what you suggest would help people," they say, "but look at the effect on inflation or the public sector borrowing requirement". You name it and the system will offer you a long word to justify why it can't be done. There is nothing we can't do. It is only that we choose not to do it and because the economic system is designed to prevent positive change. It is a prison because it is meant to be a prison. We have people in need and people who have the skills to help them, but the rigidity of the economic (Elite-created) structure seeks to stop the two getting together. When they tell you that something can't be done because it would harm the economy, they are lying to you or betraying their own misunderstanding of what is going on. Economic-speak seeks to confuse us and diminish us because we don't understand the language and what seems to be such a complex web of figures and data. In fact, it's dead simple. You lend people money that doesn't exist and charge them interest on it. Everything over and above that is a smoke-screen which is built on the foundations of lending people money that doesn't exist and charging interest on it. Without that global conjuring trick, it all comes tumbling down. And yet when we hear predictions that this system will collapse there is enormous fear among those who are enslaved by it. I can understand that, given the way we are conditioned. But why are we desperately trying to shore up the walls of our own prison? Let it go, the quicker the better, and then we can create a system of interest-free money and exchange that is based on abundance for all, and not, as today, on manufactured scarcity which leads to dependency – control. If we think abundance, there will be abundance.

Everything is made from energy and energy is infinite. There is no shortage of anything. Scarcity only comes when we accept the conditioning that life is about struggle, scarcity, and mere survival. Again, if that is our imagination of ourselves and the world, there will be scarcity, but we can just as easily create abundance. There is nothing to fear about the imminent collapse of the global financial prison. There's no need to waste your energy and emotions worrying about the consequences. You will always have whatever you need if that is your imagination of yourself. And there's no need to divert your attention from your multidimensional self by getting caught up in economic "debate" and argument about the best way to resuscitate a dinosaur. Trying to stop the collapse of this economic insanity would be like rearranging the deckchairs on a sinking Titanic. A waste of time and energy. Much more sensible to climb in a lifeboat. This is your sinking prison we are talking about and it's falling apart. Why aren't we rejoicing instead of searching for the glue? The economic structure is going to fall anyway because the energy field or "matrix" which created the structure is imploding with changing human consciousness and the energies now encircling this dimension. The economic system which we see as our security is really a ball and chain. Let it go. Think it out of existence.

It's a piece a shit, walk away.

I guess nothing powers the light at the bottom of the bottle more than the global media. I worked in newspapers, radio and television for many years and I can honestly say that in all that time I never had a single conversation with a fellow journalist that was not related to the version of life promoted by the Hassle-Free Zone. I cannot recall those daily conversations producing one original thought. There are few more programmed, conditioned professions than the media. And yet it is this myopic mentality which writes and edits the "news" that you read and hear every day! You don't have to control every journalist personally to force them to publish the Elite version of "truth". It's much easier than that. You create the mentality and perspective from which the media sees the world and from that point the manipulation virtually runs itself. For instance, the media judges everything from the perspective of the status quo, the "norm" accepted as reality within the Hassle-Free Zone. Whoever decides what that "norm" shall be at any point, effectively decides how the media will report the world. The status quo – the accepted norm – a few centuries ago was that the Earth was flat. Today's media, in line with the "scientific" and religious status quo at that time, would have ridiculed or condemned anyone who dared to suggest it was round. But once the evidence became so overwhelming that the status quo reality had to change, suddenly it was those who said the Earth was flat who were laughed at. So it is with the modern media and this is why anyone who challenges the fundamentals of the accepted "norm" is immediately jumped upon by the media monster. In effect, the media is the police force of the Hassle-Free Zone. It frightens people into conforming to imposed norms. Meeting so many mainstream journalists and seeing their attitudes to life has served to confirm this to me more times than I care to recall. That is not to condemn them as people. They, like all of us, are incredible beings of light in their multidimensional form. But, in my view, they have switched off their multidimensional self and chosen to work on a fraction of their potential to understand and "see". This makes them a manipulator's dream and the ideal mentality for a journalist within a system designed to control and misinform.

The media is part of the game and reports the players in the game without ever questioning the game itself. The "big name" correspondents and news presenters are nothing more than sports reporters. They report a different game, that's all. They report on the ups and downs of teams in the game, the political parties, the banks and the financial exchanges, and they interview the managers, the players and the pundits. They call this "reporting" or "investigative journalism", but it only "investigates" those areas which will not expose the game itself as the reason for our global plight. They never question the game because the media is part of the game and owned by the game. It is fundamental to the game. Any journalist who sought to really expose the game as rotten to the core or, God forbid, that it is controlled by a relative handful of people, none of which are ever elected, would be looking for another job. If anyone tried to explain that we create our own reality and that we live in a virtual reality vortex, they would be clearing their desk with a recommendation that they see a shrink. The mental and emotional divide between the view of life expressed in this book and the media mentality is not only a chasm, it's a universe. The media is another example of oppo-sames promoted as choice and diversity. The only real difference between the so called "radical", "intellectual" London *Guardian* and the tits and bums London tabloid called *The Sun* is the size of the paper, the length of the stories, and the approach they use to defend the status quo. Oh yes, the *Guardian* and its like around the world will pontificate about poverty and freedom and criticise players and teams in the game. But on the foundations that shore up the game it is at one with *The Sun*. They are status quo protection sheets.

The same goes for the BBC, an organisation I used to work for. It sticks its nose in the air and talks of pursuing truth, but it is really just another arm of the Global Elite's propaganda network. In December 1995, the BBC produced a "Review of the Year" in which the "reporter" proceeded to tell the story of the year according to the official version of events. One section talked of the "enemy within" and opportioned blame for the Oklahoma bombing and the Japan underground gas attack to groups and individuals who had yet to even stand trial! They simply took the government line of what had happened and who was to blame. No other view was reported. When I wrote to the Director General of the BBC asking how this could be justified, there was no denial of the points I made, only that the whole story could not be told due to pressure of time. That was a nonsense because in the time they gave to these items a balanced picture could have been reported. But here we had the BBC, this so called legendary broadcasting network, unable to deny that they gave only one version of events – the official one. The same is happening in newspapers and on radio and television stations the world over every day with all the television networks like NBC, CBS and ABC in the United States owned by the Global Elite, as is the global cable news network, CNN. It is called news, but it is propaganda, designed at source to manipulate the mass consciousness. Only a comparatively few journalists knowingly manipulate. Most of those who report this propaganda are duped into thinking it is news and truth. The media is the myopic leading the partially sighted.

But again, how often we allow ourselves to be sucked in by manufactured and meaningless debates stimulated by news items designed to manipulate our view of ourselves and others. And we judge people and events on the basis of information presented to us by this controlled, closed minded naïveté, we call the media. It's lying to you minute by minute, day after day, and yet those lies are used by people to condemn and ridicule others and pressure them to conform to the limitations of the Hassle-Free Zone. "It must be true, I read it in the paper and saw it on the news." (In that case it is probably not true.) "No, no, *all* the papers and television stations are saying it." (In that case, it's *definitely* not true). I observe the media because it is a major player in the game, but I don't believe a single word it says unless it is confirmed by other independent sources. If the media in general wants us to believe something it is because those who manipulate the world want us to believe it. Those who manipulate the world control the media and the global news agencies that provide much of its information. The news programmes tell us *what* to think and the mental cancer of game shows and soaps urge us *not* to think. It is a telling combination and it has created a resident hypnotist in the homes of billions of people. It may be called a television and what it spews out may be called news and entertainment. But it is really a hypnotist whispering its thought control. It is after your mind and its mantra messages tell us what we should think, be, and do. Of all the elements that make up that light at the foot of the bottle, the media, and especially television, are among the brightest and most seductive...

Listen to meeeee. Look into my screeeeen. This is realiteeeee. Shut down your psycheeeee. You are freeeee.

It's a piece a shit, walk away.

You can find diversions everywhere to lead us away from the simplicity of understanding. The so called New Age movement has done some excellent work in offering people alternatives to the system's view of life, but it, too, is becoming a prison of the mind. Across the New Age you find endless pseudo-gurus setting themselves up as "teachers". It is good that people are beginning to speak out and offer a new vision as long as they don't become another crutch for those who follow them. Giving your mind away to some New Age "teacher" is no different to handing it over to a priest, politician or economist. Surely we are looking to take back our responsibility, not find a new home for it. Yet so many people I meet who talk of the need to think and feel for ourselves, still look to someone else for answers. They move from guru to guru, teacher to teacher, seeking the very enlightenment that has been there within themselves all along. You don't need to find an "enlightened one" to tell you what to think – *you* are an enlightened one. We all are. We've simply forgotten and switched off our connection to that enlightenment. Listening to all views, including those of the New Age "teachers", is a good thing if we filter their information and take from it what we believe is right while leaving the rest. The danger comes when people take everything that someone says and, in effect, take on another's belief system in full. I have found quite an arrogance among some in the New Age who insist that what they say must be accepted by all of us. There is even a New Age fashion which is nothing more than the uniform you find within other areas of the system. For me, the New Age has become bogged down with irrelevant ceremony, jargon, and bullshit masquerading as enlightenment. People give their power away to Ashtar Commands and Maitreyas and a stream of other "masters", so ignoring the real master within. This is an example of how the pendulum or the scales swing from one extreme to the other before settling down to balance. I feel also that the same fourth dimensional manipulators who created the religions, party politics and the global financial system, are manipulating parts of the New Age and it is a warning of how the same old hierarchical structures can be dressed up as new. I have great sympathy with the view that the New Age movement is planned to evolve into the World Religion, another global centralisation and imposition on the Elite's agenda. There is a consciousness that has moved beyond the New Age which has accepted the themes of reincarnation and the eternal, multidimensional nature of consciousness, but has rejected the complicated explanations and the New Age-speak. It has seen the simplicity of everything and realises that much of the New Age is another diversion from that simplicity. I feel we need to be constantly selective and allow our own intuition to make that selection. There is a great deal in the New Age which is highly commendable and makes an important contribution to the awakening of the human heart and mind. But there is even more in New Age dogma to which the following would be highly applicable:

It's a piece a shit, walk away.

When I use the term "walk away", I don't mean that we should never pamper our bodies, observe the political scene, go to a school, listen to the view of New Age "teachers", or use the financial system as it stands today. I would not dream of telling you what to do, that's up to you and no-one else. The thoughts in this book are mine, an expression of my reality. They don't have to be yours. By "walk away", I mean to walk away mentally and emotionally. If you know the media is lying to you and seeking to manipulate your thoughts, you watch the television or read a newspaper from that detached perspective. You don't get fooled into taking it seriously or seeing it as important or true. You know what the game is and you're not playing. The same with "education". You can go to school, enjoy the parts that stimulate you and accept the information that feels right to you, but still walk away mentally and emotionally from all the rest. You know it's an indoctrination machine, so you can observe it in the knowledge of what it is seeking to do. You can filter everything you are told and not be indoctrinated. *You* take control of what you absorb and accept, not the system. You can also see exams for what they are and refuse to be emotionally affected by how the system judges you in that way. It doesn't matter. My boy Gareth is coming towards the end of his school life, but he is not indoctrinated. He has taken the information that feels right and rejected the rest because he knows that schools and universities are primarily there to condition, not to inform.

I use the money system at the moment to live, travel, and do my work. But I know it is all a big illusion, a joke. You take away its power by not taking it seriously or seeing it as "real". The money system is hilarious. The moment you let go of the fear of being without the means to provide warmth, food, shelter and clothing, the system loses its grip on your psyche and you cease to feed it with your energy, your power. What's more when you lose the fear of being without, you will always have what you need. Once the twin emotions of fearing the financial system and seeing it as important and real are removed, the structure will naturally collapse because its energy source is gone. In the meantime, we can use it as necessary, without taking on its fear and "values". We take control of it, not it of us. Again, if you want to have a hair transplant, wear a wig, or have your face lifted, fine. So what? Good luck to you. But who is making that decision? Is it society instilling fear and pressuring you to conform to "norms" or do you genuinely want to control the way you look because you, and only you, have decided that's the way you want to be? You want to lose weight? Fine, good luck to you. But who is deciding that? Is society telling you to conform to the "norm" or have you, and only you, decided that's how you want to look?

This is what I mean by walking away. Detaching emotionally and making our own decisions from our own values and delinking from manufactured diversions that keep us in the spiritual dark and imprisoned in the illusions of physicalness. I repeat: most of the things that cause us emotional pain, occupy our attention and demolish our self esteem, simply don't matter. We are only told they matter because that will keep us captivated by physical illusion and delinked from our infinite self. Here's a little exercise. First remember that you are an infinite aspect of eternal consciousness on an endless journey of evolution and that other levels of you are playing different roles in the movie on other screens (dimensions) in the cinema. You are not just a body, you are consciousness experiencing various situations and emotions to speed your return to Oneness. Right, keep that in mind and take a deep breath. Now take another look at whatever it is that is screwing you up at the moment, be it a relationship, your body, fear of the future, whatever.

See what I mean?

It's a piece a shit, walk away.

Chapter 8

I Love Me

What's that you say? I love me? What are you, some kind of egomaniac? Who do you think you are, for goodness sake? You need taking down a peg or two my lad or lady.

You're not supposed to say you love yourself. You are supposed to be humble and keep putting yourself down. Then people won't feel threatened by you or be forced to face their own self-imposed limitations. You tell me your inadequacies, I'll tell you mine, we'll both agree on how self-righteously humble we are and then go back to sleep. ZZZzzzzzzzz. It's not yourself you should be loving, it is others – the world. That's the street cred approach. You tell people how humble you are and that your desire is to love the world. Oh, what a lovely man. He's ever so humble, always putting himself down, and he loves everyone.

No he doesn't. He doesn't love everyone because he doesn't love himself. And if he doesn't love himself he doesn't love *anyone*.

How can we give out from within what we do not have within? Love, true love in it's widest sense, does not discriminate. It doesn't say I love this person, but not that one. It just loves. Sure, people can feel what they think is love in the narrow view of that word on Planet Earth. They can say they love their partner or children and they can feel a powerful bond with them. But they can't feel true love – cosmic love, you might say – until they feel cosmic love for themselves. What you don't have within, you can't give without. And continuing the theme of creating your own reality, if you don't love yourself in that total, unconditional way, you will attract to you people who will see you in the same light. They won't love you unconditionally until you love yourself unconditionally. They will go on saying I love you as long as you conform to what I think you should be. That's not love, it's possession and manipulation, dressed up as love. How many of us truly love another to the extent that we would support them and love them

140

in whatever they need to do for their own learning and evolution? If what they feel they need to experience or what events lead them to experience happens to conflict with our view of what they should be and do, our "love" for them can start to run very thin. You can't be you if you want my "love". You have to be what I want you to be. That's the deal, isn't it? Welcome to my jail, lover, give us a kiss. We have the same conditional attitude to loving ourselves. If we follow our hearts, that intuitive energy that expresses our uniqueness, we feel guilty and diminished when others react against us or appear hurt by our actions. But if we don't love ourselves and respect our right to be who we are, how can we expect others to love us for what we are? Self love is that balance point when we allow ourselves the freedom from fear and guilt to be who and what we are. In turn, true love for others is to allow them, without resentment and judgement, to be who they are, even if it differs from what we would like them to be. I love you because you are. I love me because I am. Now that's love.

When I look back at my life I can see so clearly how my journey towards self love has been mirrored in my physical experience. For the first 42 years I didn't think much of myself at all. I was the classic angry man, my temper always simmering just below the surface as my frustrations at the world I saw around me bubbled like some steaming cauldron in my psyche. I didn't like me and I didn't like the world. Planet Earth was a shitty place, populated by too many shitty people. This was a replica of how I saw myself. I lived life on an emotional knife edge, wishing to love, but so often feeling only anger and "pity" which I believed, quite wrongly, to be an expression of love. That attracted into my life many people who mirrored back at me what was going on inside. My life was a stream of angry confrontations with people, born of my own inner anger. I wasn't angry with them, in truth, I was angry with myself and they were the means through which I could express that anger outwardly instead of dealing with the source within me. After my spiritual alarm clock went off at the start of the 1990s, I began, slowly at first and then at great speed, to see myself in a very different light. For the first time in this incarnation, I started to like myself. Crikey, call the police. That's a crime, isn't it? It's not a case of looking in the mirror, brushing the eyebrows, and saying "Oooh, I'm a bit of alright", although there's nothing wrong with that, either. It was more that I began to respect who I was and what I was seeking to achieve. I liked being me. I didn't want to be anyone else. As this evolved into a much wider appreciation of love – a never ending journey – my whole sense of self was transformed. I saw the areas I needed to face and work on because, as always, they were manifesting before my eyes in the people and experiences I attracted. But I knew who I was – an ever evolving consciousness which, at its core, in its natural state of being, is love, pure love, an aspect of the Source of All That Is. So are you. We all are. I began to see that whatever I was doing at any time, whatever I was experiencing or helping others to experience, was what I needed to do at that moment to face myself, help others face themselves, and so gain greater insight and understanding. When my sense of self changed, the people I attracted into my life changed also. The angry confrontations with others (myself) began to subside and along came people who loved me for what I am, not for what they wish me to be. I stopped trying to be what I thought others wanted me to be – the mask – and I have found peace with what I am, a unique aspect of God making a unique contribution to the human tapestry of experience. I have changed my sense of inner reality and therefore I have changed my physical reality. I have started to love myself and that is mirrored by others back to me in return. What's more, as I have loved myself unconditionally, I have found it easier to love others without condition. One person in particular has challenged me in this area of unconditional love and, as a result, helped me to travel further along that road. Feeling these powerful emotions in my life like anger, fear, guilt, resentment, and a lack of self worth, has been vital to what I am doing now. My lifeplan is very simple: experience, learn, communicate. I couldn't write these books unless I had lived and felt so deeply the emotions I am writing about. Nothing happens to us by accident. All happens for a reason, although it may be only years later that we realise why.

There is so much conflict in the outer world that we see on the television news because there is so much inner conflict within people. The physical world reflects exactly what is going on within the human psyche. The inner turmoil and conflict creates its outer reflection – everything from a family row to muggings, rape, terrorism and war. Conflict will only end in the outer world when we find peace within our inner world – our consciousness. There will be peace and love on Earth when there is peace and love in our hearts. And that begins and ends with self. When we love and respect ourselves, we will create a personal – and together, a collective – reality that will mirror that inner love and harmony as an outer love and harmony. We will have thought and felt into being a new heaven and a new Earth. Not one gun will have been fired, not one new political "ism" established, and there will not be an economist or banker in sight. It doesn't need new economic systems or parliamentary legislation to change the world. They only reflect the world as it is. All we need to do is change ourselves and everything will flow from that. Heal yourself and you heal the world.

But is it any surprise that we have such a lack of love and respect for ourselves and why we find it so difficult to find the inner peace that will bring heaven to the Earth? From the time we are small children we are being conditioned to judge ourselves harshly and to think of ourselves in negative terms. We are being told what we should be, how we should be, what is right and wrong, sane and insane, good and bad. Our self esteem and our sense of uniqueness are conditioned out of us under the onslaught of messages invading our psyche from programmed parents, priests, teachers, journalists, politicians and bankers. This is how we think you should think and if you don't conform we will brand you ...naughty, lazy, stupid, mad, bad, a disruptive influence, a danger to society, a sinner, or a threat to the economic stability of the world. You get back in that sheep pen, y'hear? Woof, woof, woof. Be a clone, your country needs clones. What do you think you are, unique? My God, if we let you get away with having your own mind, where will it end? They'll all want to do it.

The foundations of our subservience and lack of self esteem were built a long time ago. Most consciousness in the world today has been caught in a cycle of incarnation and reincarnation...physical life, followed by a return to the non-physical realms – "death" – and then reincarnation into a physical body. In this way, we have all had experience in different cultures, colours, creeds and life situations on the journey of learning through experience. This makes racism ridiculous. And as we attract to us what we need to find balance and return to Oneness, the racists of today will be the racially persecuted of tomorrow. We get what we give out until we learn and evolve. We have all been men *and* women in our various incarnations because consciousness, in its harmonious state, is a balance of male and female. Each of the planes of existence within the virtual reality pyramid/ vortex has a physical and non physical level. You could see this as a sort of hour-glass shape (*Figure 7 overleaf*) with the realms of the spirit at the top and the dense physical world below. The narrow tube, the "gate" between the two levels, is a neutral point where the vibrational frequency of the spiritual merges with the physical. It's like a black hole. This is represented as the tunnel with a light at the end which

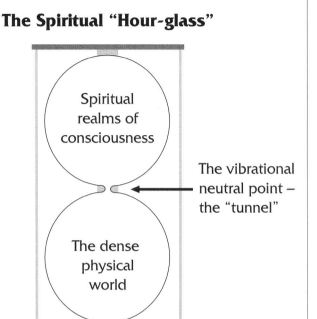

The Spiritual "Hour-glass"

Spiritual realms of consciousness

The vibrational neutral point – the "tunnel"

The dense physical world

Each time/space dimension has physical and spiritual levels. These can be likened symbolically to an hourglass or egg-timer. When a physical life is over, our consciousness returns through the "tunnel" to the realms of spirit.

Figure 7

millions of people have described after a near death experience. When people "die" and leave the physical body they do not necessarily move on to enlightenment. Death is no cure for ignorance. Consciousness continues to create its own reality. Many psychics have made contact with departed "souls" who are still floating in a limbo land of their own creation waiting for God to judge them, so programmed is their psyche to believe that will happen. If such confused souls are listening, I've got some good news for you. The priest was spinning you a yarn. God isn't coming to judge you, gang. God doesn't judge anyone. Pure love (the Source) doesn't understand judgment. He/She only understands love. So find that tunnel and get out of here! What we often call a ghost is consciousness that is so confused or mesmerised by the physical world and its conditioned sense of reality that it does not return through the "tunnel" to the realms of spirit. Some of the more imbalanced of them have manifested as the "demons" of legend. But these lost souls are not to be feared, they are just confused minds.

The point I am emphasising here is that our consciousness has experienced a long stream of physical lives in many different circumstances on the journey of evolution and at the point of "death" our psyche departs with all its knowledge, misunderstandings, and emotional debris. When you look back through known human history it is a story of people (inspired from the Fourth Dimension I would say) using fear and violence to impose their version of life on the masses. Religion played the major role in this to the point where non-believers were burned. The impact on the evolving psyche of this constant pressure to conform and do as it was told – or else – has conditioned humanity over scores of Earth-lives to submit to a perceived "authority". Today, the human race is so easy to herd into the pen because it has been in the pen before; life after life. It is not just one lifetime of conditioning that we are addressing here – it is thousands of years of them. When I talk of letting go conditioned responses, I am talking about attitudes and fears ingrained over vast periods of what we call time. The intense fear of expressing our uniqueness is not the result of only this life experience. It results from the sum total of our human experience, including those times when to say what you really believed was tantamount to a death sentence, as indeed it still is for many people. When we have intense fears and phobias that have no "rational" explanation, it is events in this life, often quite innocuous events on the face of it, triggering memories of deep emotional trauma caused by a past life experience. We need to be kind to ourselves. It's been a tough journey through this dense physical world, but now we have a golden chance to complete it.

Also, the misunderstandings and manipulation of the three dimensional world have turned experience, without which we could not evolve, into a nightmare of resentment, guilt and recrimination. Not only that, with each Earth "life", the unresolved, unbalanced, emotions are carried over in the psyche to the next one. So by now, the human subconscious is a sewer of unresolved emotional turmoil which must be released if we are to achieve the vibrational leap that the Earth is currently embarked upon, the quantum jump to a whole new state of consciousness. These emotions are the weights on the feet of the diver which stops him naturally floating upwards to the surface. For many they are more like a collar around the neck connected to ropes hooked into concrete, so all consuming are the angers, resentments, fears, and guilts which have resulted from previous experience over many lives on Earth (*Figure 8*). We will never release our psyche from its dense physical prison until we release ourselves from our emotional prison. The two are actually the same thing. It is vital to understand this because as we get closer to the big switch, the quantum jump, our inner self will be attracting to us more and more experiences to give us the opportunity to face our emotional turmoil and release it. This is already happening to vast numbers of people. Their status quo, their false sense of personal security, is being challenged by business collapse, loss of employment, the break up of long term relationships, and so on. If we have a false sense of programmed security, that will come under challenge from events that we, repeat *we*, are attracting to us. On the face of it, from the physical perspective, these seem to be very negative events and I can understand that. But we are not physical bodies at our core, we are timeless, eternal, evolving consciousness and these experiences and challenges are designed to help us reach the vibrational state that can make the jump from physical prison to spiritual freedom.

If we don't see our experiences in this light, the release of such longtime, big time, emotional trauma could turn the world into a swirling sea of turmoil and conflict in the transition period that has been winding itself up for many years and is now entering its critical stage. It doesn't have to be like that if we take a step back and view our emotions and our interaction with others from a much wider perspective. Using the movie example again, we need to get off the screen more often and into the audience. I'll explain what I mean. The build up of emotional baggage through each Earth-life experience into what is by now an explosive mass of negativity, is the result of believing that this world is real. It is not. It is a three-dimensional, virtual reality, holographic, movie screen designed to provide us with the opportunity to experience the separation of Oneness as an aid to our further exploration of ourselves. We have also been under the illusion that we are separate. We are not. We are all aspects of One consciousness, God, experiencing itself subjectively through its constituent parts – all of us. In truth, one actor is playing all the parts and sometimes this actor kicks the crap out of itself. Imagine standing in front of the mirror shouting abuse at yourself or hitting yourself around the head with a baseball bat. Only a madman would do that? The last time you screamed abuse or were violent to someone, you were actually doing it to yourself! The

Figure 8: Without the weights of negative emotion, we have the freedom to fly.

separation of Oneness in the dense physical world has been so challenging, that we have forgotten that it's a movie. This separation has manifested in the separation of humanity into different relationships, groups, beliefs and lifestyles, each seeking to impose their version of right and wrong on everyone. Once you stop respecting your own right to be you, whatever you may be, and you stop respecting everyone's right to be them, the circumstances are there for emotional warfare to unfold on the personal and collective level. You have inner emotional turmoil because you are suppressing who you really are and submitting, through fear, to another's design; and/or you are seething with anger and resentment with people who won't live their lives as you believe they should.

There are two main types of people, it seems to me. Those in the movie and those in the audience. The most effective approach, I would suggest, is to keep switching between the two. Then you enjoy both perspectives. Those stuck entirely in the movie (the overwhelming majority) believe that the movie is real. Learning experiences become enormous emotional catastrophes and the guilt and resentment this produces is held throughout that lifetime and into the next one. Far from removing baggage and moving on, each Earth-life simply collects more. Those stuck entirely in the audience (the few) realise that this is a virtual reality game, but they withdraw themselves so far from the intensity of physical experience that they don't "feel" the emotions that lead to such a greater understanding of self and Creation. They cop out, you might say. There is a balance point here. It is to feel the emotion of physical, separated interaction in the moment it occurs and to react in whatever way seems right, but then to detach from that close-in view (the movie) and observe why it happened from the wider perspective (the audience). From this more detached view, you can refocus on the understanding that you created the experience, whatever it was, because of something going on within you, or something from which you were hoping to learn. It is so important to detach emotionally from the movie, but not so far that we lose the true power of the experiences it offers. I always find it more effective to scream "Aaaaaahhhh, bollocks to it" when I hit my thumb with a hammer than to quietly whisper "Oh what a wonderful learning experience". But once I have hurled abuse at the hammer, I realise that while the hammer was the apparent cause of my pain, it was in my hand at the time. Experience the movie, then observe from the stalls. This approach can release emotional garbage and stop us taking on more.

We can also see those emotional cancers, fear, guilt and resentment in a very different light.

Let us take guilt to start with. It's incredible what makes us feel guilty. I have met people in their fifties and sixties who are still screwed up with the guilt of "failing" to achieve in their lives what their fathers or mothers wanted them to achieve. I remember when my own soccer career ended with arthritis, how I felt worse about the effect this would have on my father than I did for the loss of my own dreams. I felt guilty about getting an illness that ended the career I had dreamed about since childhood because of the pain it caused my father. My own pain was far less important to me. Mind, I spent most of my life feeling guilty about everything and anything. I could have represented England at feeling guilty. This creates a vicious cycle of interreaction. I remember that my own cycle, or rather downward spiral, was getting angry, feeling guilty about getting angry, and getting frustrated at the way I felt about myself as the guilt destroyed my self respect. This stimulated further anger, which made me feel even more guilty...on and on it went year after year. How could I be me? I didn't know who "me" was. "Me" was submerged and drowning in a sea of anger, guilt and plummeting self worth. As I look back it is clear that I hated myself, to be honest. There was this David Icke chap, the television linkman appearing on the screen smiling, confident and chummy. And yet behind those eyes and within that heart sat a little boy, lost and imprisoned by the turmoil of anger, guilt and self-disdain that swamped the love at the core of my being, the love that is me. How can we love ourselves and therefore love others unconditionally, cosmically, in the face of that deluge of inner negative emotion? It is this emotion which is reacting and interreacting with itself in what we call "life", the world we see around us at home and on the television news. Life on Planet Earth has become the interaction between programmed, emotional eggshells. The real us, love, hardly gets a look in. It is often just a horrified spectator. True love rarely has the chance to communicate its wisdom, balance, and harmony and the world reflects precisely that situation.

The people we meet are mirrors of ourselves or actors playing a role which can teach us something about ourselves and the world. We attract them to us because they mirror the vibes we are broadcasting from within or because their states of being create an experience which can lead to greater understanding. When we see conflict anywhere, be it an argument in a supermarket queue, a family upset, or a world war, we are looking at inner turmoil being projected outwards and expressed as a physical event. When we get angry with others, we are getting angry with ourselves. It's interesting how often you hear the comment: "It's alright for so and so to do that, but when anyone else does the same he/she goes crazy". This response comes when we see a characteristic of ourselves which we don't like, expressed by someone else. We often react to that person in a really over-the-top way because they are mirroring at us something we don't wish to face about ourselves or their behaviour has pushed emotional buttons deep within us that trigger memories of past life experiences or those from this life, especially from the emotional minefield we call childhood. I have seen people become vicious and violent when this happens to them. The focus of their anger is not the person involved, they are just the mirror. It is themselves they are attacking. But most people don't realise that – they are stuck in the movie and the separation and they think it is real.

But now look at guilt from the more detached view – the front row of the stalls. When we act negatively towards another person, that is a reflection of our own sense of self, our own imagination of ourselves, at that moment. OK, if we are sensible, we learn from the consequences of what we did, evolve, and move on. That's a positive experience for which we should be thankful. It has given us understanding. But, from the wider perspective, the person on the receiving end of that behaviour should be grateful too, once they have felt the initial emotional hurt. We create our own reality by attracting to us magnetically the energy fields, people, experiences, which match the imagination of ourselves that we are broadcasting. Our behaviour is a reflection of our state of being and that also applies to the experience of our "victim". They attracted our state of being to them at that moment, and not another person who would have reacted very differently, because they needed to face what our state of being could give them. Instead of feeling guilty about what we have or have not done to others, we need to learn from the experience, know that it was a gift, a learning experience for ourselves and for the other person or people. They created it just as much as we did. Experience is how we evolve and we need the full range of possible experiences for a balanced evolution. If we are going to hold on to guilt with every negative experience we have attracted, we are going to be swamped with the stuff. And we have been. Look at us. Let us see guilt for what it really is – the unjustified emotional hand luggage that slows down our journey to Oneness because it destroys our sense of self. Guilt is merely the negative side of experience. It is valid in that it is an emotion we can feel and learn from. But it is not meant to be in permanent residence, squatting in our psyche. Let it go. Let the weights fall off. It's time to fly. There is nothing to feel guilty about. No, not ever. A big movie star doesn't feel guilty when he plays out the part of the "baddie" does he? Of course not. Then why do you? You're a bigger star in a bigger movie. If you don't like the part, change the script.

The same applies to resentment. Just as we hold on to guilt for what we have done to others, so we seethe with resentment, consciously and subconsciously, for what others have done to us. We seek revenge, sometimes conspiring to bring that about, most often just wishing ills and "come-uppance" for those who dare to give us an experience that aids our evolution. How dare they help me to evolve? I am so angry. If the focus of our resentment does face a karmic reaction for their behaviour, the temptation is to laugh and feel that sense of satisfaction inside that says "they got what was coming to them". We can hold on to resentment from childhood for an entire lifetime. And who suffers for that? Certainly not the people we are resentful about. They might be having a great time while we suffer and seethe to an early grave through cancer, heart attacks, and other physical expressions of suppressed anger and resentment. Not very clever is it, really? Resentment has multilevel consequences. It can mean that children and parents don't talk to each other for years, that neighbours ignore each other in the street, or that resentment passed on and indoctrinated from parent to child perpetuates violence between communities for hundreds or even thousands of years. There is nothing more destructive that a parent can do than to bring up a child to resent other people or beliefs, because in that way the imbalances of the parents are visited on the children which are, in turn, collectively visited upon the community. Look at Northern Ireland, the Balkans, the Middle East, and other long term intergenerational trouble spots around the world. When the parents grow up to the extent that they cease to see divisions of race, colour, creed, religion or income bracket, the cycle of violence will end because the children will inherit that balanced view of life. If you no longer wish to live amid violence and fear generation after generation, or you no longer want the anger and resentment to continue with your parents, neighbours, children, or friends, the answer is within you. Let go of your own resentment. Go to the focus of your bitterness, look him, her, them, in the eye and say how much you love them and you want the conflict to subside. How they wish to react to that offer is up to them, but you have ended the conflict because conflict cannot exist without two sides full of bitterness for each other. If you no longer project bitterness the conflict must end because love and bitterness are never in conflict. They cannot be because love is without judgment, bitterness, guilt or resentment – the very fires that make conflict possible.

It is the same with fear. It is our creation. Ask a group of people what most frightens them and you will get a stream of different answers. It may be boats, planes, small spaces, big spaces, spiders, snakes, speaking in public. The list is as long as human experience. What terrifies one person will have no effect on the other. Why? Because fear, what we fear, whether we fear, is our individual choice, our creation. It often has a past life origin and it is always an expression of something within us that needs dealing with. This is why we attract to us what we most fear because we need to face those terrors and work through them, otherwise our evolution in the area of our lives related to the fear will come to a dead stop. Fear is like a cruise missile to our self esteem. It explodes it apart. We are embarrassed at being frightened of something and as that leads to low self esteem and frustration, it creates an emotional cocktail that often affects our whole lives. Fear can also become so panicked that it thrashes out first in violent confrontation, like some cornered rat. I seem to have been frightened of everything as a child. I made room for the fear between all the guilt, you know. I should have organised a rota: 9.00am to 9.30am – feel guilty for not being what my father wants me to be; 9.30am to 10.30am – be terrified by the thought of the lesson with that horrible science teacher; 10.30am to 12.30pm – feel guilty for how I treated my mate three years earlier; 12.30pm to 1.30pm – lunch; you think I'm kidding? I was like an emotional road traffic accident. I could have feared for England, too.

I guess the four biggest fears in my life were going to the dentist, flying, being ridiculed and speaking in public. My worst nightmare would have been having a tooth out on a plane while making a speech to the laughing passengers. But I am the living proof that fear is our own individual creation. I don't fear any of those things now. In fact I don't fear anything on a scale that limits my actions and certainly nothing that is long term. Those fears, like all fears, were an expression of my sense of self. The dentist represented the fear of pain and being out of control; flying was the fear of death and again, having my destiny in the hands of another; ridicule related to my sense of inadequacy; and the fear of speaking in public was the focus of my lack of self esteem, self love and self respect. What we fear and how we fear is not some random accident, it reflects what is going on inside. I let go of the fear of pain after years of agony from the arthritis, a condition that dramatically improved as I began to ditch all this emotional baggage. My fear of death disappeared (and so of flying) when I realised that there is no death. My fear of having my destiny in the hands of another dispersed when I knew that our destiny is never in the hands of anyone, but ourselves. It is our imagination of ourselves, our personal vibe, that decides if we are attracted to a plane that is going to crash or whether we are attracted to another flight that will get there safely. There are no accidents, only human creations within the universal law of what we think is what we create. My fear of ridicule was dealt with when I was a national figure of fun in the United Kingdom after going public with the story of what was an extraordinary and explosive spiritual awakening for me in the early 1990s. And my fear of speaking in public disappeared when I looked to myself for confirmation that I am an OK person and not to an audience of people outside of myself. That is why so many people are frightened of speaking in public. They are looking for their self esteem outside of themselves in the reactions of other people to what they say and do, instead of saying: I am what I am and I have a right to be what I am and express what I am. I am me, I am free. When you do that, you respect the audiences' right to be them, and to take whatever you say as they see fit. But you are not nervous, frightened or intimidated, no matter how big the attendance may be or even how hostile they may be to what you are saying. You know who you are, you have a right to be what you are, and to express that. When you get your power and self esteem from within, you don't need the audience to massage your sense of self. With that, the fear of expressing yourself publicly is gone. Experiencing these fears and eliminating them has given me so many gifts of understanding.

These are not navel contemplating issues we are talking about here. This is not some peripheral add-on or marginal subject we are addressing which can be put aside until the more important problems of the "real world" are sorted out. That isn't the real world, it is a movie screen and the script is being written by the emotional bilge within us. If we don't let that go in a controlled way we are looking at a seriously unpleasant period of transition as the collective emotional build-up of thousands of years of Earth experience explodes in a frenzy of conflict and turmoil. But that doesn't have to be. Everyone's deeper, unconscious self, is going to be attracting the experiences and triggers necessary to remove the emotional anchors that are holding us back, vibrationally, from the level necessary to make the quantum jump to a new state of consciousness. If we remain hypnotised by the movie and think it is real, the way we perceive these experiences will be very destructive. If we react to the people (mirrors) who provide these experiences for us from a perspective that leads to resentment and the desire for revenge, all bloody hell will break loose. Individuals, groups, countries, the world, will be tearing themselves apart as the uncleansed emotions of centuries war and collide. The vibrational stability of the planet will be severely imbalanced by such a scenario and the weather and geological consequences could indeed be catastrophic for those on the three dimensional level of the Earth. What we do, in other words what we think and feel, fundamentally affects the planet.

You only have to look at how the Earth is abused by human activity to see how deeply that understanding has been lost. This Earth exists on all levels within the virtual reality pyramid/vortex projected out of Oneness, just as we do. The Earth consciousness, Gaia, the Earth Spirit, Mother Nature, whatever name you prefer, is the equivalent of our conscious level expressing itself through a physical body. She feels what we individually and collectively feel. What state would you be in if your physical body was being abused as hers continues to be? Or if your body was sucked clean of this liquid or raped for that mineral? What would be your mental and emotional state if you lived among people who constantly bombarded your energy field with negativity, conflict, guilt, resentment, fear and ignorance? You would be in serious emotional turmoil. Well, so is the Earth consciousness and she also has a subconscious sewer of pent up emotions that need to be cleared and cleansed. Again, if they are released in an uncontrolled way, they will combine and conflict with the collective emotions of humanity and goodness knows what mayhem that will mean. Certainly geological activity and weather extremes unprecedented in modern times. Our emotions have a physical expression as tears, shaking, sweating, sickness, skin rashes, shouting and violence. The Earth also has those expressions through rain, tidal waves, rising sea levels, earthquakes, diseased land, winds and volcanic activity. These we are going to see in vast extremes unless we emotionally step back from the movie and widen our understanding of who we are, what we are doing here, and how we relate to the Earth and the rest of Creation. On top of all this emotional release, the vibrational state of the planet is also being transformed by the quantum jump to another dimension of consciousness.

There are two approaches here which can smooth this process along. First of all, we need to appreciate what is happening to us. The vibrations of the planet are rising. If we are to rise with them, up the neck of that bottle and out of jail, we need to let go of the emotional baggage and the negative sense of self and others that we have been conditioned to accept as reality. We can release these emotions in the catastrophic way described above, or we can withdraw to the stalls and view this process very differently. We can see the people who press our buttons and release our emotional sewage for what they really are – teachers bearing the gifts of self understanding which will release us from the emotional prisons which have blighted human existence for so long. Putting it another way, we can love our "enemies" and "forgive those who trespass against us". This way we release the emotions triggered by such experiences without adding yet further resentment to the sewer by resenting those who provide the experiences. We can also see ourselves as teachers as we, too, act as triggers for the emotional release of others. Again, we help them to cleanse their emotional burdens without adding to our own by feeling guilty at what we do to them. We can deal with fear in a positive way by welcoming the opportunity to face our fears in the knowledge that we are fantastic beings of light to which nothing is impossible. There is nothing to fear. We live forever, whatever. Love is the energy that will smooth the transition more than any other. Love *is* the transition. There is no greater gift that we can give ourselves, our fellow men and women and the Earth, than love. The planet is feeling unloved because the planet has been unloved. It is the same with humanity. You know how you benefit from love during your emotional crises and the Earth is no different. Send her love whenever you can, just think it and she will feel it. And respect her body and her gifts. Make her feel loved, wanted and appreciated. You know how love reduces anger, resentment, pain and frustration. Love her, love yourself, love everyone, and the journey into a dreamland of balance and harmony need not be as bumpy as it will be if we stay asleep.

Our emotions have been the means through which the fourth dimensional manipulation has been possible. The stimulation of fear has led to people giving their power away to those they believe will protect them from whatever they have been encouraged to fear; the stimulation of guilt has diminished self-love and self-respect, so diminishing our sense of potential; the stimulation of envy and greed has encouraged the few to monopolise wealth and power by violent acquisition; the stimulation of resentment has turned one violent or negative act into a cycle of violence and turmoil begetting more violence and turmoil in return; the stimulation of self-righteousness has created manufactured divisions and conflict between religions, kingdoms, political and economic systems, sexual preferences, parents and children, bosses and bossed, men and women, as each self-righteous dogma seeks to kick and cuss its way to the point of domination at the top of the greasy pole. How silly it all is. We are each other. We are the same actor playing all the parts. It's been an interesting movie and we now have the chance in the final scene to learn the lesson we set out to teach ourselves:

All you need is love.

And love is boundless and infinite. There is no shortage of supply, no matter what the demand. You just think it and feel it and there it is. As much as you want, whenever you want. Love is our golden key and it is under our control. Don't tell me we can't get out of here when we have in our possession all that we need for the great escape. The key, the ladder, and the getaway car, are just a state of being away. A state of being called love. You can love yourself or hate yourself. You can love others or hate others. You can love the Earth or abuse the Earth. You can race to the stars or stay in the stocks. These are just choices – choices that carry with them spiritual and physical consequences. And those choices are yours and mine.

Chapter 9

By 'Sin' To The Stars

When I began to realise that this world has been manipulated from the Fourth Dimension for thousands of years, it became clear that anything that would free us from our three dimensional prison has either been suppressed or its true meaning perverted and twisted.

Nothing has been manipulated and twisted more than sex and so, I decided, this must be at the very heart of our understanding of self and the reconnection with our multidimensional infinity. And so it is. Sex is not a quick bonk...wham, bam, thank you ma'am. Nor is it sordid, dirty, and something to feel guilty about. In its highest expression, it is an ultimate spiritual experience between two people in the dense physical world. It is a means through which we can connect with the highest levels of ourselves and access our fantastic creative power. We have been diverted from doing this by another group of oppo-sames – religion, the tabloid media, and the pornography industry. Religion, the tabloid papers, and pornography on the same side? Yes, in their effect, certainly.

To understand why, we need to look at the nature of physical experience and the genetic spacesuit we call the body. What you see is only the physical level of ourselves, that face and body that stares back from the mirror. On levels unseen by the physical senses is our eternal consciousness, the aura, as some people call it (*Figure 9 overleaf*). The aura is the amalgamation of the energy fields which together make up the thinking, feeling, emotional us. Or at least that part of the eternal "I" which is working directly through the body. One of these levels, the etheric, is the intelligence which organises the replacement of cells, controls the electrical system of the body, and generally governs the body's activities. When the etheric energy field is imbalanced, as it is through emotional disharmony, the emotional dis-ease becomes physical dis-ease. Some etheric imbalances, for example, disrupt the smooth replacement of cells and this is known to us as cancer. What we

Figure 9: the Aura

call cancer is cell replacement gone haywire. So called "modern
medicine" continues to treat cancer by cutting away the rogue cells and
dosing people with radiation. This reflects the "scientific" obsession
with the physical level of being and medicine's obsession with treating
symptoms rather than causes. The cause of cancer is etheric disruption,
usually stimulated by emotional disruption, although contact with
electromagnetic energy fields, like power lines and electrical
equipment, can also trigger cancerous cell replacement because the
electromagnetism destabilises the magnetic balance of the etheric
energy field. The immune system is also controlled from the etheric

and so emotional or electromagnetic influences can seriously damage our body's natural defences and make us more prone to illness. Dying of a broken heart is to be so emotionally traumatised that the etheric is thrown out of balance and the body reflects that in a terminal illness or heart failure. We literally die from emotional hurt and during the writing of this book I felt emotional pain that gave me an insight into how this is possible.

The means through which our balances and imbalances are transferred through the levels of being is the chakra system. "Chakra" is an ancient Sanskrit word meaning wheel of light. The chakras are vortexes of energy which intersect our levels of self, and therefore an imbalance in the emotional energy field will be passed through the chakras to the mental level (we stop thinking straight), and via the etheric to the physical (we become dis-eased). We have many of these chakra vortexes, large and small, but there are seven main ones in the body, and others outside the body which connect us with the higher realms of our consciousness. Each vibrates to the frequency of a particular colour and sound. The seven main body chakras are positioned at the bottom of the spine through to the pubic bone (base or root chakra); just below the navel (sacral or splenic chakra); between the navel and the chest (solar plexus chakra); the centre of the chest (heart chakra); the throat (throat chakra); the centre of the forehead (third eye chakra); and the top of the head (crown chakra) (*Figure 10 overleaf*). I also believe there are major chakras in the feet which connect and "ground" us with the Earth. Each of these chakras represents one level of being. The lower three chakras are of the Earth, the top three are of the spirit, and the heart is the centre of balance between them. The root chakra (red) roots us into the physical and through the genitals creates physical life. The second chakra (orange) is closely related to the root chakra. It is our sexuality centre and has a powerful connection to the etheric body. The solar plexus chakra (yellow) is the seat of our emotions, hence we feel our emotions in that area of the abdomen. The heart chakra (green) is from where we express the energy called love and this is how the ancient connection between the heart and love originates. Today, in our obsession with the physical, this link is made to the physical heart, but its origin comes from knowledge of the spiritual heart, the heart chakra. The throat chakra (blue) governs our ability to communicate and express ourselves. The Third Eye chakra (indigo) on the forehead is the centre for our psychic senses, the ability to see, perceive, and

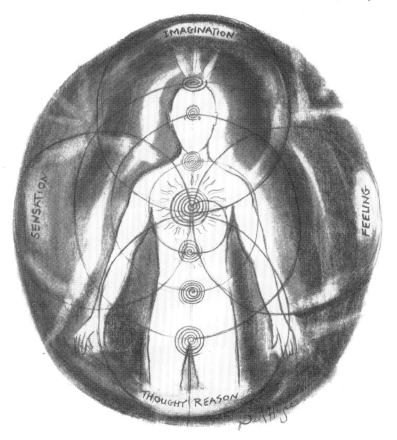

Figure 10: the Chakra system

access information from beyond the physical. The Crown chakra (violet) is our connection with the chakras outside of our body – the rest of the cosmos.

The "halos" depicted around the head of "Jesus" and other figures portrayed in religious art are in fact the light energy emitting from the crown chakra. As you become more psychically sensitive, you can see this light around the heads of people. It is the same, too, with the idea of angels with wings. The "wings" are energy pouring out of the crown chakra like a fountain. I have seen this in some people during a heightened sense of awareness and it can look like two white wings. They are not physical wings, they are energy wings which can lift us to the stars. The chakras transmit their state of being directly to the physical through the glands of the endocrine system. The control centre for this system is the pineal gland in the centre of the brain, which connects with the "third eye" chakra, our psychic sight. The pineal is also closely connected with the physical eyes and it is true that indeed "the eyes are the window on the soul". When we look into someone's eyes we are looking deep into their multidimensional consciousness via the eyes-pineal gland-third eye-cosmos connection. You can tell so much about a person by looking into their eyes. The pineal and the other glands of the endocrine system release hormones into the body in response to the changing state of the chakras and these hormones affect the body in positive and negative ways. It is at this point that mainstream medical science enters the scene, with the release of the hormones and their effect on the body. They have closed their minds to what happens before that, the instructions transmitted from the chakras to the glands, because to recognise the existence of the chakras would lead to the acknowledgement of the multidimensional levels of being and their effect on the physical body. In other words, the whole basis on which medical science operates (drugs and scalpels) would tumble and so would the profits of the multinational drug companies which control the "medical" system. It is self interest which has created the disinterest in seeing the human being as far more than a physical body.

Appreciating the existence of the chakra system is vital to understanding the real significance of sex. The root chakra at the base of the spine draws in energy from the Earth known as the kundalini, another Sanskrit word meaning serpent or sleeping snake. Throughout Eastern, and indeed many other religions, you will see the serpent used to symbolise the kundalini energy. Look at the story of Adam and Eve as just one possible example and how funny that the symbol of the modern medical profession is an ancient serpent representation of the kundalini – an energy that profession does not even acknowledge to exist! The kundalini is part of the lifeforce and it provides the sexual energy that triggers our creative potential. The energy people use to create an inspired painting, book, speech or piece of pottery is the same energy that stimulates sexual activity and explodes into orgasm. It is the creative force, the same creative force that creates new life. As a friend of mine says: we are walking, talking, sex bombs! This is one reason why the Satanic sexual rituals involving the terrorising of adults and children are constantly performed by the All Seeing Eye and its Global Elite – to access and trigger the creative force in its most negative form.

If the creative energy is suppressed, by the suppression of sexual feelings and natural talent, its power becomes imbalanced. This will manifest in other ways – through violence, rape, crime, wars and depression. More spiritual sex = less global violence! Also, when people are allowed and encouraged to express their own unique creativity, the kundalini flows in harmony, and the conflict, within and without, subsides. Dumping people in mind-numbing factories and office blocks creates the seeds for inner frustration, and so outward disharmony and conflict because the creative energy is being denied and suppressed. Appropriately, the word "evil" is the word "live" in reverse! But when the suppression of the creative energy leads to crime, violence and disharmony, what is society's response? To impose stricter laws and more restriction, so further suppressing the creative force and leading to more crime, violence and disharmony. When the creative force is suppressed it becomes destructive. That certainly applies to sex.

Through our childhood, the kundalini trickles up the central channel (the spiritual spinal column) triggering and activating the other chakas at a relatively low level. This is why most children are not stirred sexually until adolescence. It is also how their true potential to think and create is suppressed until their bodies are capable of manifesting what their minds know are possible, a point I made earlier about why the consciousness of a child does not express its real self until many years into a physical life. An adult mind in a baby's body would produce unbearable frustration. Around the time we call puberty, however, the kundalini begins to unfurl from the root chakra in much greater quantities. It activates the genital areas and we begin to acknowledge our sexuality. We start to see boys and girls in a rather different light. It is the evolution from "come and play with my train set" to "Cor, I don't half fancy her". As we know, puberty triggers massive hormonal changes and this is the kundalini stimulating the chakras, which then cause the glands of the endocrine system to release the hormones.

The unwinding of the kundalini affects us far more than just sexually. It resonates to the colour red and is symbolised as fire. This is very appropriate because as it flows through all the chakras it sets them ablaze vibrationally. When the kundalini is flowing smoothly and powerfully, we become more sensitive, and our minds become more alert, inquiring and open. The kundalini stimulates our memory and our ability to retain information. Our creative potential soars. A powerful kundalini gives us a strong magnetic connection with the Earth and as it shoots out through the crown chakra at the top of the head it connects us with our other chakras at the higher levels of our being. We become both of the Earth and of the spirit, the perfect balance. That's the process as it is meant to happen, anyway. That's what human beings are supposed to be, the balance of the physical and spiritual. Instead, we are dominated by one or the other, usually the physical, or we are out of sync with both of them.

What happens for most people is that the kundalini does not transform them in a smooth and balanced way. In fact it can be a nightmare. We are back to the manipulation of this world from the negative elements of the Fourth Dimension where the effects of the awakening kundalini are well understood. If you want to turn the human race into prisoners of this three dimensional reality it is essential to stem, or massively imbalance, the flow of kundalini. You disconnect them from both a powerful link with the Earth and the higher realms of spirit and themselves. To rise through the chakras and connect us with our higher levels of spirit, the kundalini must pass through the sacral chakra, the centre of our sexuality, and the solar plexus chakra, the centre of our emotions. These can be such a mass of denial, fear and negative emotion, that they act as a vibratory dam, turning the kundalini back on itself and creating a lifetime of turmoil in that lower abdomen area which often results in physical dis-ease. These "dams" also prevent a powerful flow of kundalini from activating the potential of the higher chakras, the heart, throat, third eye and crown, so making impossible a true connection with the higher spiritual dimensions of ourselves. We operate on the level of the spaceman in the spacesuit delinked from Mission Control and we become a manipulator's puppet. People in this state (the vast, vast majority) are neither of the Earth or of the spirit. They are of the limbo land somewhere between them. One means by which this is achieved brings us back to sex.

The same fourth dimensional force which created and used religion, particularly Christianity, Judaism, and Islam, to destroy the truth about sex, also inspired the culture of pornography and the quick "bonk". The common theme between these oppo-sames is closing down the root chakra, imbalancing the sacral and emotional chakras, and stemming the flow of kundalini, which if left alone would activate and connect all levels of being into wholeness. Religion has turned sex into a focus for an explosion of guilt of atomic proportions. The institution of marriage is at the heart of this, but it is not the only reason by any means. Marriage institutionalises separation. He's mine, she's mine. I marry you, therefore I own you. This is the spoken or unspoken reality of marriage and relationships in general. It is the means through which people buy into a manufactured sense of security and a desperately limited version of "love". They buy the fairy stories about wedding days and happy every afters. Most marriage is not about love, but possession and control. Only a tiny few marriages are fulfilling the partners. They may not realise why they feel empty and unfulfilled, but it's because their real potential to expand and create is being suppressed by this institutionalised prison. The consequences of walking away are too much for most people to contemplate and that is the only reason why the divorce rate, already rising rapidly, is not a tidal wave. Soon it will be.

I am not suggesting that it is not right to live with someone for whom you have great affection, even love, or that there shouldn't be some publicly spoken commitment to each other, if that's what the couple desire. I am saying that to institutionalise that commitment, to bring the church and state into it, and to create penalties for withdrawing at a later stage, is utterly ridiculous. How can you turn a human relationship into something regulated by the state? How can someone be expected to commit themselves at the age of 20 or 25 to another person for the rest of their lives? Who knows what lies ahead or how the two will change in their attitude to life and each other? The whole idea is crazy. Yet for thousands of years that is the mockery of love and relationships which religion has visited upon the human race. It is considered better to suffer your pain and stay in a marriage than to say you have grown apart and it's time to move on. In countries under the fiercest religious domination, like Ireland, it has been against the law to end a marriage! And yet Ireland has still called itself a free country. I don't remember even Josef Stalin suggesting that marriage could never be ended. A referendum in 1995 voted by a very small majority to repeal that law in Ireland, but still people battle to retain the right of church and state to dictate to the population who they will and will not have an official relationship with. According to this mental state, it is better to continue a marriage which both partners hate, than to bring it to a natural conclusion and free the partners to find love elsewhere. It also creates the unbelievable situation in which children at the moment of birth are dubbed "illegitimate" because their parents are not officially connected by a piece of headed notepaper. There is no such thing as illegitimate life. It doesn't exist except in the padlocked human mind. I would suggest that anyone who sees life in terms of legitimate and illegitimate, is in need of some serious help. Just as religion has survived through hypocrisy of an olympian scale, so I guess it is appropriate, that its institution of marriage should demand so often the same hypocrisy to hold it together. Surely love should be the bond which holds two people in a relationship, not a piece of paper and a sense of duty. Most marriage is not based on love. Its reason for being is companionship, financial security, habit, social conformity and fear of the alternative. What a basis on which to live your life with someone. Perhaps the most destructive element of the marriage game is that it institutionalises and makes a part of the law of the land the belief that you can only love one person at a time, preferably for life. It makes official the law of separation and denies the law of Oneness.

This has fundamental effects on the flow of the kundalini. Sometimes you need to interact sexually with more than one person in your life, even after marriage, because different people affect you in different ways. One person's consciousness – energy fields – will activate yours in a slightly, sometimes dramatically, different way to another. The kundalini is not just one blob of energy, it has many different elements which need to be stimulated and awakened if we are going to enjoy our true and infinite creative potential. It is not only sexual activity which opens the kundalini, but it is one very powerful and rapid way to trigger the serpent transformation. I had a very close relationship with my wife, Linda, after we met and married within a few weeks in 1971. I was 19 and she was 21. She is an amazing woman and I don't regret one second of the years I have spent with her. The fact that I married her is irrelevant. Getting married was something people were supposed to do when they loved each other, so we did. The bond which held between us through some experiences that would have shattered most relationships into a thousand pieces is not marriage, it is love. You only know the true strength of a relationship when the bond is challenged by events. So many "ideal" relationships fall at that point because they are built on conditional love and self delusion. The biggest challenge to my bond with Linda came in 1991 when I had a sexual relationship with another woman amid front page headlines. I had no idea at the time why I did that or why it happened. My life in the weeks before and after was lived in some dream-state. I didn't know where I was or what was happening to me. I reacted in the way we are programmed to react in such situations. I was consumed by guilt and remorse so massive I thought it would destroy me. It took me years to work it through and cope with the assault on my self-esteem and the self-love which I found so hard to feel. But I see things differently now.

From the perspective of the kundalini, that situation can be viewed from a much higher level of understanding, the stalls, not the movie.

Within two weeks of that sexual relationship starting my whole consciousness had erupted into a new sense of self and reality. Every fibre of my being was going through a transformation which opened my mind and my eyes to so much. As I was staggering, physically, emotionally and mentally, to cope with a mass of new knowledge and understanding pouring into my consciousness, I went public with what I was experiencing and began my period of immense public ridicule – the "turquoise period" as I call it – when I was obsessed with that colour for more than a month. I didn't know what was going on and I didn't for many years that followed. But now I do. The sexual relationship with another consciousness had, in part, created the vibrational trigger which helped to open the root and sacral chakras and allowed the kundalini to flood my aura, activating my emotional, mental and spiritual chakra centres as it rose through my body. Suddenly each of those chakras was also opened, including my "third eye", so flooding my aura with their knowledge and connecting me with higher levels of myself from which my mind had been delinked, at least consciously, until that moment. Is it any wonder I was in such a spin at the time? It was like sitting in a room with 50 televisions blaring out at once and all tuned to a different station offering different information. The kundalini doesn't have to affect you like that, it can happen much less traumatically, but it was an immense learning experience for me and those around me. It also happened at exactly the right time. Had that transformation happened any earlier, I would not have experienced life in the programmed world with all the delusions and emotions that come from that. It was so important to live those experiences, given what I am doing now.

Because of the abuse of sex by the church, state, and tabloid media, it has become a "sin" and a reason for enormous guilt and condemnation to have a sexual relationship with more than one person at the same time. If you are married as well, aaaaaahhhh! String him up, put him in the stocks. He's unfit to be alive. While the church parrots the clichés about the world needing more love, the moment you express that love physically for more than one person, it suddenly becomes a terrible thing. Of course love does not have to take a sexual expression, and in all but a few cases during our lives, it will not. But it can be reflected physically if that is right for the evolution of the people involved and if we and society cannot accept this, we are revealing just how immature we are as a human race – and how insecure. You *can* love more than one person at the same time. Many people, even those on the spiritual path, tell me it can't be done – but it can. It can. You love them in different ways, that's all. The focus and nature of that love may change at different times, but it is still love. This is not easy in the world today, I know. However, I believe it is possible. We are One Consciousness. Are we really saying that we can only love, physically, mentally, emotionally and spiritually, one aspect of ourselves at one time? Are we really? My God. Many people who say they love someone unconditionally, later reveal otherwise as the "league tables" start to appear: "You spend more time with this person than me" or "You do this for that person, but not for me". Relationships which begin (or think they do) on the basis of no-agenda love so often degenerate into league table love and their purity is lost. Unconditional love does not have league tables, it just loves. Totally and always.

Each person gives us something others cannot, because everyone is different. If we celebrate the fact that we are unique, we can see how we can gain knowledge, understanding and a greater insight into love and ourselves, by experiencing and interacting with different people in different ways. Our love for one does not have to diminish our love for another; indeed that love can grow as we truly understand what love is, and our power to express love expands. I know from my own journey these past few years that as the kundalini flows and opens us to our multidimensional wonder, parts of our personality emerge that we didn't know we had. It's like pulling the cord on one of those automatic life rafts. Suddenly our consciousness, locked and folded away for so long, unfurls and expands to produce a structure so large that you would not believe it was achievable when you look at the small space (the closed mind) from whence it came. These newly-freed parts of us need a focus of expression through people who are compatible with them. Different parts of our eternal self sometimes need stimulation by different people. This way all elements of self are activated, stimulated and challenged to grow and not only those which relate to the state of being of one person or partner. This goes both ways. One person can't give me all that I need to grow multidimensionally and neither can I do that for them. No one person can provide everything another will need for their evolution to Oneness, but – and this is the point – the manipulation from the Fourth Dimension over thousands of years has made society think this is possible and this myth has even been institutionalised and made part of state law. This is crazy. What are we doing to ourselves?

The effects on human life and intelligence of this ignorance of sex has been fundamental to our plight. It has created another vicious cycle of fear, guilt and resentment. Here is just one scenario to make the point. If a man or woman feels the intuitive urge to become close with a person other than their marriage or regular partner, they can either suppress that urge because they fear the consequences in a society that doesn't understand, or they can go ahead and feel terribly guilty because they, too, have been conditioned to believe that this is seriously wrong. Either way their root, sacral and emotional chakras are thrown into vibratory turmoil and the flow of kundalini becomes diminished and imbalanced. When the marriage partner finds out about the relationship, he or she will be overwhelmed with resentment and as that resentment relates to sexuality, their root, sacral and emotional chakras close down or imbalance the kundalini. This will not only affect the sexuality of the three people, it will diminish them emotionally, intellectually and spiritually as the other chakra centres lose their powerful connection with the energy that fires them on the physical – the kundalini. Yet it is not that these relationship situations are wrong, merely that society is conditioned to believe they are wrong. These situations are not right or wrong, they just *are*. They are part of the unique journey of learning and experience for all involved. Others won't need that experience and so it won't happen to them. They'll be challenged in other ways. If we were all born into a world in which the wider understanding and openness about sex were accepted, the pain caused by relationships and sex would plummet. As it is we are programmed to feel pain when certain circumstances arise and so we do. This is why it is such a challenge for those seeking to expose this imprisonment. We are doing it within a collective consciousness that has been programmed to condemn, judge, and see the world and themselves through a microscopic tunnel vision. But this will change and it is changing. You watch.

Religion has been the major force for the fourth dimensional manipulation to delink humanity from its true destiny and the abuse of sex has been at the forefront of this. They have gone so far in some religions as to make celibacy a virtue. How do you find the key to heaven? You cross your legs, bite your lip, and have buckets of cold water at the ready. Hello, is that the fire brigade? Bishop's palace speaking. One of our erections is ablaze. How soon can you get here? The legacy of fear and guilt which religion has passed across the generations in its arrogant, childish and manipulative view of sex beggars belief. Once again poor old God gets the blame for insisting we deny our feelings. But am I really supposed to believe that the God who made this incredible multidimensional universe, with its perfection down to the last ant and blade of grass, is sitting somewhere in torment worrying about what I do with my dangly bits? If people choose to be celibate, that's fine. We should all do what we feel is right for us and we don't have to have sex to awaken the kundalini. It can be done through meditation and visualisation too, and it is also triggered by astrological influences. But if people practice celibacy without understanding about the kundalini some very unpleasant events can ensue. If the kundalini is suppressed because of the sexual urges it is stimulating, this creates an energy "war" between the kundalini which wishes to unfurl and the person's mind and emotions which are seeking to push it back. This vibrational conflict can manifest as severely imbalanced sexuality and other mental and emotional disharmony. It is no mystery why, as is now evident, the sexual abuse of children in the Roman Catholic Church has been so rife. It is an expression of an imbalanced kundalini caused by suppressing a natural process of human development and, on many occasions, the Satanic manipulation of a child's sexual energy in line with the black magic practices of the Cult of the All Seeing Eye. Nor is it a mystery why that church, from the Pope down, has such a limited vision of life, humanity and creation. Without the kundalini flowing powerfully to activate and open the gateways to intellectual and spiritual infinity, the vision must always be barely one dimensional. Also, that which feels fear will project fear. Most religions fear sex and therefore use the fear of sex to manipulate and control.

But what is true of the church is equally true of the tabloid media and pornography. If people want to pose naked for photographs doing things with their bits and bobs, that's OK by me. And if others want to buy those papers and look at those pictures, that's equally OK. I'm not seeking to judge, merely to point out what I believe are the consequences of certain actions. The hypocrisy of the tabloid media mirrors that of the church. They sell their papers through sexual titillation, but then moralise about the sexual behaviour of the very people whose "exposure" sells their newspapers. When I was a journalist working for a news agency in the 1970s, I had a call from the London *News Of The World* to ask me if there had been any court cases in my area that week involving rape. The *News Of The World* did not, I was told, have enough rape cases for that week's paper. This is the mentality that publicly judges the lives of others! The tabloid media seeks to arouse its customers sexually while, at the same time, telling them that sex is outrageous and naughty. They want the erection, but condemn the connection. They have turned sex, the most beautiful and ecstatic state a physical form can produce, into the equivalent of artificial insemination. The cosmic orgasm has descended into "Cor, I'd give 'er one". This view of sex is equally destructive to that of the church if it doesn't evolve into something much greater. Sex is not a series of quick gropes which momentarily satisfy merely physical desires. That is not of the spirit because it denies the spirit and diminishes the spirit. The sexual experience stays in the root and lower chakras because it is operating overwhelmingly as a physical exchange. This, too, suppresses and perverts the kundalini with all the effects that has on the emotional, mental and spiritual development of that human being. The misuse and manipulation of sex by these apparent "opposites", religion and the media, has led both to massive guilt, fear and resentment in our attitude to sex, and via a suppressed and imbalanced kundalini, to a disconnection from our higher mental and spiritual potential. Put another way, root chakra sex, as promoted by religion and the tabloids, can keep you in a mental and emotional prison while cosmic sex can lift you to the stars. It is appropriate that tabloid newspapers which are obsessed with quick-bonk sex also treat their readers like intellectual buffoons. One is a consequence of the other.

So what is sex at the cosmic level?

Sex has become for so many a physical event when it really has the potential to be a multidimensional ecstasy. There is root chakra sex, an overwhelmingly physical experience, the goal of which is ejaculation – the outward projection of energy, an energy loss. This leaves the partners tired and often with a sense of anticlimax and emptiness. Was that it? This is the view of sex found in the tabloid newspapers and pornography. Then there is multichakra sex which takes us soaring into the spiritual realms of being. This is when the energy stimulated in the root chakra rises through all the chakras and explodes outwards into the aura as a spiritual orgasm rather than just physical ejaculation, although it can be a combination of both. This is spiritual love rather than sex because it is predominantly spiritual, not physical. It is when both partners merge into a male-female wholeness which raises their collective consciousness to vibratory levels which connect them with higher states of consciousness – Oneness. Sex at that level of awareness takes us into timelessness when we are without thought, fear, guilt or resentment. We just "are". We are out of our bodies and into our deeper self, out of our heads and into our feelings, our spirit (*Figure 11 overleaf*). We withdraw from this programmed world and access levels of consciousness far beyond this physical planet. When I have experienced spiritual love in this way, I have felt a fantastic flow of information, love and insight, pouring into my mind in the minutes and hours that followed, because the multichakra orgasm has lifted my consciousness to the vibratory levels which hold that information and love. It is like making love during an earthquake! Such an amazing level of spiritual love and vibrational connection between two people is so rare. Mostly we travel through many lifetimes without feeling that indescribable, multidimensional harmony with another human being which explodes as an immensely powerful creative force – love in its purest expression. When you have felt that with someone you may no longer need or desire to express love physically with another. You know instinctively that nothing could compare with the connection you have with that person. So you see I am not calling for a sexual free for all here. Not least because when we have sex we merge to a larger or lesser extent with the energies of the other person. We absorb, vibrationally, part of them, their very essence. Who we make love with, and on what level it is expressed, has consequences for both partners long after the actual event. All I am saying is that, it is not right or wrong to make love with more than one person. It is merely an experience along the road to finding that spiritual-sexual ecstacy. Once you have experienced that – and you'll know when you have! – you can often spend the rest of your life with that person and never need a sexual union with anyone else. There are no norms, only experiences on the road to Oneness. Everyone is different and needs to experience different things.

Cosmic sex leaves you ablaze with energy, rather than tired, and this is transmitted to every cell in the body, stimulating them to vibrate quicker and so make us feel "alive". There is an energy gain rather than a loss. This provides us with more creative energy to express in other areas of our lives. There is nothing wrong with ejaculation, there's nothing wrong with anything as long as it is not imposed against another's will, but there is a much greater meaning to sex than the very narrow idea of sexual release and relief that we are conditioned to accept. A mixture of all possibilities offers the range of all experience and potential. Children conceived in such high orgasmic states can incarnate on a very high vibration, too.

Figure 11: "Cosmic" sex is an explosion of creative energy.

To reach these cosmic levels of sex we need to stop trying so hard. Sex, like everything, has become a competition, a contest, a symbol of our manhood and womanhood. Is he any good in bed? Is she good between the sheets? Do I satisfy my man/woman? Am I good at it? This has brought yet more fear to the sexual experience because each partner is trying to "perform" for the other. Sod that. It is not a performance. It is not a doing, it is a being. If you relax and just "be" without trying to do or achieve anything, you begin to let go of the programmed responses of what sex is or isn't. If you don't focus your mind on the end goal (ejaculation and orgasm), you enter timeless, relaxed states of higher consciousness for far longer. You can only enjoy each moment to its greatest potential if you get your head out of the past and the future. Ejaculation and orgasm are in the future and if that is in your head from the start, you lose the power of each moment. To do that, means simply to "be" without thoughts of what may or may not be to come, if you'll pardon the expression. Sex is not a stage show, it is a unique experience every time if you allow it to be unique instead of playing out the script provided by religion, the tabloid media, and the guys down the bar.

The attempts to diminish us sexually even include the myth and manipulation called AIDS. The scare stories about AIDS have created tremendous fears over sex. We are told that the HIV virus causes the destruction of the immune system known as AIDS and that HIV is transmitted sexually. Both claims are simply a lie. HIV is a weak virus and the last thing it does is destroy the immune system. Thousands of people die of "AIDS" who are not HIV positive and millions who have been HIV positive for ten years and more are still perfectly healthy. The figures have been cooked! If you die of, say, tuberculosis and you are HIV positive, you are said to have died of AIDS. If you die of tuberculosis and you are not HIV positive, you are said to have died of tuberculosis. The myths and lies are even built into the diagnosis.

Dr Robert Gallo, the man who said HIV causes AIDS, has since been accused of scientific misconduct and two of his assistants have been charged with criminal offences. Gallo patented the test for HIV antibodies and he gets a royalty for every one. And that's another point. They don't test for the HIV virus, only for the antibodies which the immune system produces to fight the virus! AIDS has many causes – but not HIV. Anything which breaks down the immune system causes AIDS and that includes recreational drugs and the drugs, like AZT, used to "fight" HIV, a virus which does not cause AIDS! It's all a con and what a time bomb it has been for our attitude to sexuality.[1]

The reason that humanity's spiritual evolution has been much slower than it could have been is that we have denied ourselves and each other the right to experience. The course of evolution is very simple: experience, learn, evolve. The rules and regulations, the dos, don'ts, musts, and mustn'ts, imposed over the centuries by religions and other thought controllers, have narrowed dramatically the depth and breadth of experience that we are allowed to have before meeting the resistance of ridicule or condemnation. We have become afraid to experience and this has become ingrained as a fear of change because change = experience. We cling to ways of life and attitudes which will not bring new experience because we have been conditioned to fear experience. Life becomes a series of tedious repetitions and it is this very repetition of thought and behaviour that makes us so easy to control. Western society's view of sex is a most potent example of this. Once you have a marriage certificate, you are no longer supposed to have any sexual experience with anyone except your official partner. This seeks to deny a massive area of experience, therefore learning, therefore evolution. Many people are so insecure within themselves that they hold their partner in emotional handcuffs and go crazy if they even talk to another man or woman. Others are more open and don't so much mind an intellectual interaction between their partner and a member of another sex. But all, except a tiny, tiny few highly enlightened beings have a major emotional block with the thought of their partner making love physically with another. It is the physical experience that stimulates all the pain, guilt and resentment. I understand this and I'm not saying that sex with other partners is good or bad, nor right or wrong, only that it is a choice that people have a right to make without condemnation. The body is the outward expression of the mind-emotions-spirit, the mind made physical. It is a way for two human beings to express love for each other and share their energy if that is what they choose to do. Again I ask: what the hell is the big deal? Let's remember here that all is one and one is all. When we make love to another human being we are, in effect, making

---

[1] I strongly recommend a book about this and other health issues called *The Medical Mafia* by Guylaine Lanctot MD. It's available from Here's The Key Publishing, P.O. Box 113, Coaticook, Quebec, Canada.

love to part of ourselves. When we reach the stage of cosmic, multichakra orgasm, we are making love to the universe, to Creation, to all that exists, and we are making available more creative energy for all to use and benefit from.

And that is a crime? That is immoral? That is a reason for guilt, resentment and condemnation?

What on Earth have we come to? Rock bloody bottom, that's where we've come to – and the only way is up.

Morality always means limitation and hypocrisy. Morality = you can't. It denies a basic human right – the right to experience and to be who and what we uniquely are. Morality sets out someone else's view of the perfect human being and demands that everyone conforms to that. Such morality requires an arrogance of genuine world class. Because no-one matches the blueprint of this "perfect" human (including, often especially, the moralist who makes the blueprint), everyone goes around denying their real feelings or feeling guilty for not conforming to the blueprint. Because society gives a hard time to anyone falling below the standards set by the moralists, people put up the masks and try to kid everyone that they are living "moral" lives even when they are not. It is a world of denial, fear, lies, hypocrisy and secrecy. It need not be. It only happens because we fear what other people think of us and what other people think of us is conditioned by the few who decide the so called "standards".

We are back to the Hassle-Free Zones again. Yet who are these moralists who tell us what we can and can't experience? From my observations, they are seriously screwed up emotionally and, ironically, screwed up about the very issue they are moralising about. When you suppress something, it takes on a much greater importance. When you want to lose weight, food is on your mind far more than when you are eating what you choose. Denial always stimulates an obsession with whatever you are denying. Instead of the energy flowing through you in a harmonious, natural way, as it does when you allow yourself to go with that flow, it recycles itself around your energy fields, so staying at the centre of your thoughts. If you seek to deny your sexual feelings, you will be thinking of sex far more than if you flow with your feelings. The moralists who seek to suppress their own sexual feelings because of fear and guilt, then become obsessed with the sexual activity of others. You recognise the type: "This sex movie is a moral outrage and I should know – I've seen it five times". Their denial of their own sexuality makes them obsessed with sex. These are the moral guardians who tell us what to think and seek to dictate what we can and can't do, watch and say!

Never be afraid to experience if your intuitive self, the flow of energy within you, is leading you in that direction. We live forever. What is one experience? If you don't like it and it doesn't work out, you learn from the experience and evolve. If you do like it and it does work out, you also learn from the experience and evolve. Again, experience is not good or bad, it just is. One thing is for sure, the more you deny yourself the experiences your inner self is leading you into, the more turmoil you feel as the conflict ensues in your psyche and the longer it will take for you to reach higher levels of understanding. I feel we need to let go of the absolutes which deny us so much. These absolutes show themselves in phrases like "right, that's it, it's over forever" or "I'll never talk to that person again" or "I would never do that, not ever". Apart from life itself, nothing is forever and nothing is for never. All is there to experience on the road to Oneness. Everything in Creation is constantly moving, every expression of energy is dancing to the changing rhythm of life. If we seek to stand still and to turn our lives and attitudes into concrete thought patterns and rigid predictability, we are in fact trying to stand still in a fast flowing river and soon it will be a tidal wave as the vibes continue to quicken. We seek to be static eggshells while surrounded by a vibrational sea of movement and flow. No wonder that life is such a mental, emotional and physical battle in those circumstances. You are literally using all your energy just to stand still! But whether you welcome and celebrate experience or whether you deny it, doesn't really matter. Either way you will get there in the end. Denial just means it takes longer and causes you a great deal of emotional turmoil which you could avoid if you allow rather than deny your feelings. The point I am making is that we should have the right, without pressure, ridicule or condemnation, to make our own choice about what we experience without some moralising know-it-all dictating what we can and can't do. For instance, what is homosexuality? It is an experience, that's all it is, a way of expressing love for another human being, another aspect of ourselves. Two men or women loving each other deeply and sexually is considered a moral outrage, while a man and a woman hating each other and living together in a marriage they are both too frightened to end, is considered acceptable. My philosophy is to allow all experience as long

as the people involved have made that decision from their own free-will
without pressure or imposition of any kind.

(I guess becoming a member of the Christian Moral Crusade is now
out of the question? It is? Phew, thank goodness for that.)

Creation consists of a sea of relationships. Creation *is* relationships –
the relationships between atoms, electrons, vibrational states, people,
communities, countries, stars, planets, galaxies, and so on. There are
also the relationships, often forgotten, between people and the rest of
the Earth family like the trees, flowers, air, water, animals, insects and
the spirit of Mother Earth. So many of these relationships have become
based on domination rather than love. Whether it is a man dominating
his wife or partner (or vice versa) to impose his views and beliefs on the
relationship, or humankind seeking to dominate the animals and the
natural world, the picture we see is of one "side" of a relationship
seeking to change and mould the other to fit in with their view of how
things should be. Of course this is not always the case, there are no
absolutes, but it is overwhelmingly what I see happening. You cannot
divorce the way we view our relationships with other lifeforms on the
planet from the way we view our relationships with each other. All are
manifestations of the same state of mind – a wish to impose rather than
to respect and love. When we stop abusing ourselves, we'll stop abusing
the planet. Marriage and partnerships in general have become a prison
of imposition and denial. The insecurity of one partner, sometimes
both, wishes to preserve its misguided sense of security by dictating the
terms of the relationship with another. This leads to a "love" which
says: I love you if you conform to what I believe you should be. This is
light years away from: I love you whatever you say, do or think. Love in
its purest, most magical form, has no ifs or buts or maybes. Love is to
desire what is best for another, even if it is not what we wish to happen
from our own standpoint. Love in its purest form can also step back
emotionally and allow someone to go through a negative experience
rather than protect them from a learning opportunity that will speed
their understanding of life and themselves. The greatest love anyone
can have for another is to let them go, if that is what is best for them,
on their journey of evolution through experience. It is certainly to
allow them, without judgement or withdrawal of love, to experience
whatever they need to experience to speed their journey to Oneness.
Love is not only to say: I love being with you or I love to go to bed
with you. Love is to love someone so completely that nothing they can
ever do could destroy the way you feel about them. How many people

on this planet love each other by that definition of love? Exactly. We want to impose our blueprint on others and only if people conform to that do we love them, or rather *think* we love them. Needing someone and loving someone are not the same thing.

As the consciousness of humanity continues to awaken to its full and glorious potential, these relationships will fade and die. They reflect our old, narrow sense of self and reality, not the one we are moving into. Relationships have been replicas of the fear and insecurity that has swamped the human psyche for thousands of years. This insecurity has led to the prison cell marriage and the submission to another's will for fear of losing them. Marriage and relationships have also become Hassle-Free Zones. We fear being alone if we express our uniqueness because we lack self esteem and inner security. We have lost our "wholeness" because we have switched off our multidimensional selves. Relationships, like marriage, have consisted of two "halves" seeking to make a whole. The male seeks to balance himself in a relationship with a female rather than balancing his male-female harmony by accessing the female within his own psyche. Macho man denies his female polarity and searches for that polarity in a woman. This has created relationships which suffocate and imprison rather than set free (*Figure 12a*) because the partnership becomes one entity in which two halves struggle for dominance or submit to dominance. The same applies to the woman searching for her male polarity in a man instead of in herself. This is about to change dramatically and, indeed, is already doing so. People who are evacuating the Hassle-Free Zones and opening themselves to their multidimensional wholeness do not need to secure their "other half" in a relationship with a man or a woman. They are already whole or moving that way, thank you very much.

In the face of this, relationships are going to experience a colossal transformation. Suddenly two "wholes" will be relating to each other and once we evolve towards wholeness, balance, and completeness, there is no way we will accept the imposition upon us of another's blueprint. Wholeness celebrates its uniqueness and refuses to be a clone of someone else. These new relationships look, symbolically, very different to those we see today (*Figure 12b*). Instead of one partner dominating, both respect the other's right to be unique. This respect and acknowledgement of another's right to be themselves and to follow the experiences that come their way creates a fantastic bond between two people. The love between them is so great, so total in its widest sense, that each wishes the other to experience whatever they require

The Old Relationships

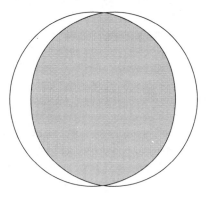

One partner dominating and suffocating the uniqueness and potential of the other. Often both partners suppress each other.

Figure 12a

The New Relationships

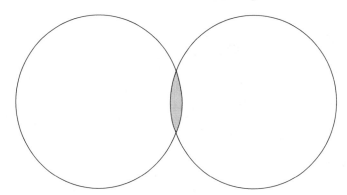

Two whole people enjoy a tremendous bond, but both respect and encourage the other's right to express their uniqueness and experience whatever they need to experience.

Figure 12b

to speed the journey to enlightenment, understanding and evolution. The point at which they meet, symbolised by the two circles in the illustration, holds a magnetic connection which is unbreakable, but they both have vast areas of their lives in which they can express and explore their unique path and individuality. Many people will not live together and even those who do will insist on their own "space". This might also mean relationships, even sexual ones, with other people. I'm not saying that it *has* to mean that, only that it can. But because such people have accessed the real meaning of love and the bond between them grows rather than diminishes, with the passage of time and experience, whatever it is. As I said earlier, I hear people talk about the need for unconditional love and they even lecture others on how important it is. But they don't live it themselves. Their own love is still conditional on another person conforming to their blueprint. My partner for 25 years, Linda, is one of the small number of people I have met in my life who understands the meaning of unconditional love. She is living it, not bullshitting about it, and that makes her an astonishing woman. Our relationship is in the process of great change and maybe we won't be together as we have been in the past. But the bond of love between us remains and will always do so because the love is without condition. Whatever happens to either of us on our journey to Oneness, that love and connection will be there, no matter what the distance between us in either miles or attitudes. People may change, even partners may change, but unconditional love lives on, no matter what. Unconditional love is not some trite phrase, it is a state of being that will transform the world. But only if we stop just talking about it and start meaning what we say and living what we say. Equally vital, it will only happen if we allow everyone to live unconditional love without moralising or seeking to frighten and hassle them into conforming to the blueprint of another.

GREAT EXPECTATIONS

This brings me to the greatest destroyer of relationships and a prime creator of emotional distress: expectations. We go through our lives thinking we are living in the present when in truth we are living in the past and the future. There are those who believe that the past, present and future are happening at the same time and I agree with that, but they are happening on different vibrations. We need to decide which of those vibrations we wish to occupy. We live in the past because of the guilt and resentment we hold onto and we live in the future because we fear what is to come. Expectations also keep us, mentally and emotionally, in the future. All the time we have expectations of what will happen, how a person will behave, what they will do and say. Then, when that person does not react in the way we expected, we are disappointed. We may lose our temper with them or sulk or tell our friends how disappointed we were with someone's behaviour. He or she was nothing like I expected, we say. But hold on just a second. It's not that person's fault that they did not "come up to expectations". They had no input in deciding what those expectations were going to be. They were just being themselves, which is all anyone can be. It was the person who created the expectations who created the subsequent disappointment. This disappointment is caused by someone not conforming to the expectations created by someone else. If there were no expectations, there would be no disappointment. And without expectations we live in the present, not the future, and we enjoy each moment as it happens without destroying that enjoyment with the disappointment of unfulfilled expectations. You go to a soccer match expecting your team to win and they don't. You are disappointed. You go to the same soccer match just to enjoy the game with no expectations of who will win, nor any great emotional attachment to either team, and you are not disappointed, whichever team loses. You just enjoy the game as it happens. So it is with life. Expectations = disappointment. No expectations = living each moment in that moment. Expectations also focus our minds on a very narrow area of potential experience – what we expect the experience to be. Once we let go of expectations, our mind walks free from that limited vision of possible experience and opens itself to all possible experience. We see this phenomena in action when people go to a film expecting not to like it and, because of that state of mind, they usually don't. If, however, they had gone to the cinema with no expectations they would have allowed that openness of mind to enjoy the picture because there were no expectations of unenjoyment which they were trying so hard to fulfill.

If you enter a relationship with expectations, sexual or otherwise, you are almost certainly going to be disappointed because people are not clones of our expectations of them. Why should they be? What arrogance that we should demand of people that they be what we expect them to be rather than to express what they really are. If we love someone unconditionally, without demanding that they meet our expectations, the relationship takes on a whole new dimension and becomes much more stable and permanent. My symbolic representation of the new relationships, the two circles connected at the centre, is the figure of eight – the symbol of infinity. This is appropriate because relationships founded on unconditional love with no expectations of each other are the only ones capable of infinity. The others either collapse because of unfulfilled expectations or the suffocation of individuality, or both partners accept the suppression of individuality and constant disappointment because they are too frightened to walk away from their perceived "security". Fear of the alternative is what keeps most, yes I would say most, relationships together. However, fear diminishes on the road to wholeness and Oneness and we are going to see an explosion of partnership break downs as we evolve from relationships based on conditions and expectations to those based on unconditional love and respect for another's right to individuality and uniqueness of experience. When we do this, we will live each moment as it happens without determining beforehand what we expect that moment to be and then being disappointed. We will live in the NOW, not the past or the future, and we will accept people for what they are and not for what we expect them to be. In the words of a Chris de Burgh song: Live every moment before the moment's gone.

I have realised from experience that one of the greatest obstacles to expressing our true selves is the desire not to hurt someone. We suppress our feelings because we want to avoid the emotional hurt that we know our actions may bring. This is particularly applicable to relationships of all kinds. People stay in marriages because they wish to protect their partner and children from the pain of divorce, or they worry that their parents will be upset if they follow their heart. But all this does, in the end, is to cause even *more* pain and distress because a person suppressing their real feelings and desires is at war with themselves. Part of the psyche wants to go with the flow while another part is desperately trying to dam the flow. The frustration and damage this creates often manifests as simmering anger and resentment, which destroys the relationship in a much more long term and painful way than simply being honest from the start and saying: "It's time to go". At its most extreme, the suppression of our uniqueness and the urgings within us can cause so much pent up frustration that it explodes as violence, crime, depression, illness and even suicide. Suppressing uniqueness with a stream of rules, regulations and "moral" absolutes is supposed to protect society from violence and crime when, in fact, it is *causing* them. In a world in which people are conditioned to accept such a narrow version of "life", there are bound to be people who are hurt and upset when we express our real, unconditioned selves. The alternative to that is to stay in jail forever and a day. The point is this: is it your *intention* to hurt someone? No, of course not. You are just being you and going where your heart leads you. If you suppress that you are allowing your life to be controlled by the attitudes of another and not your own. You become a puppet on the strings of another person's emotions and beliefs. It is hard to say and do things that you know will cause hurt to someone you care for, but often you are also creating an experience which sets them free, too. In the process of expressing your real self, you are helping to shatter their status quo prison of the mind and give them the opportunity to regain and express their true and infinite power. How often do we hear people say that an experience which was traumatic in the moment has turned out to be the best thing that ever happened to them? In this era of change and self re-appraisal, it is time to be honest with ourselves and honest with others about the way we feel.

For all this to happen in a harmonious way, it is necessary to let go of our emotional dependency on each other. By that I don't mean that we cease to love people and feel wonderful when they are around. That is an incredible and blissful feeling. I mean to still be OK within ourselves when they are not around. That is not easy in a world conditioned by the guilt-resentment-fear-expectation view of relationships, but it is possible if you are prepared to work through the initial and understandable pain in the transition period. And as we attract to us what we most fear, if we don't let go of the fear of losing another, we will lose them. Only in that way can we experience that loss, find our own inner strength and self esteem to stand alone if necessary, and let go of that fear. When we release the fear of being alone, we will no longer be alone because the lesson will have been learned and the evolution achieved. That's the idea behind creating our own reality – growth, not punishment. The only person who punishes us is ourselves. Untying our emotional dependency on another person or lifestyle, is to stop taking on other people's problems. We tend to lock into the emotional ups and downs of each other. When one partner is depressed or wound up, the other starts to feel the same. But all that creates is two people feeling depressed rather than one. What good is that? What is making one person feel down is their own problem and it is for them to sort out. Also, people emerge from their emotional traumas far more quickly when those close to them stay "up" instead of taking on the emotions of their partners and loved ones. Other people's emotional problems are not yours, they are the creation of the person involved no matter what the circumstances. That means only they can sort them out. If we take on their emotional states, we actually hinder rather than help them to emerge through that emotional mire. If you stay independent from people emotionally you will be in a better position to give them what they most need in those circumstances...love in its truest and widest sense. I am having some t-shirts produced which say:

"Piss off, I'm having a bad day...don't take it personally."

That's a key to harmony in relationships of all kinds, whether it be a marriage or parents or people at work. When people act towards us in ways we don't like, they are expressing their sense of self at that moment and they are mirroring back at us something that we can address and learn from. It's a movie playing to an ever changing and evolving script. You can love all the other actors in the movie without taking over their parts or reading their lines. Don't take it personally. It is never personal. It is always someone dealing with their own emotional garbage which far from relating directly to you may go back thousands of years. You are just the trigger for that suppressed emotion and others are triggers for you. Let's get out of the Earthly personality and into the eternity of it all. However people behave towards us or anyone else, just love them. The more negatively they act, the more love they are crying out for. We don't have to approve of their actions to love them. Yet what do we do? We give our love to those who conform to our blueprint, our expectations, and deny love to those who don't. As almost no-one conforms to that blueprint we truly love almost no-one, usually no-one. Because others are insisting that we conform to their blueprints, almost no-one, usually no-one, truly loves us. This is why the world is so short of love. Everyone is laying down the conditions for it. We'll have lawyers producing contracts which say "I promise to love you in return for the following...". Love is about loving without conditions of any kind. Love is never, never, never about the possession and ownership of another mind, body, emotion or spirit. Love is independent from emotional ties which diminish love in its greatest and most unconditional form. Only without that emotional dependence can love give us what we need to experience and not necessarily what we want to experience. In my first book on these subjects, *The Truth Vibrations*, I quoted a channelled[2] message which sums up all that I have said here about love and relationships:

> *"True love does not always give the receiver what it would like to receive, but it will always give that which is best for it. So welcome everything you receive whether you like it or not. Ponder on anything you do not like and see if you can see why it was necessary. Acceptance will then be very much easier."*

Love is to become independent of someone emotionally to the point where you can help them experience what they need to experience to speed their evolution to Oneness. What we have called "love" in this world has often been the very opposite of that definition. It has sought to deny experience, not to encourage it; to possess, not to set free; to ex-pect, not to re-spect. A re-evaluation of love is emerging to sweep away the limitations and launch us into limitlessness. After all, those limits are of our own making. If we didn't create them, they could not exist.

What I have said in this chapter is fundamentally different to the views of sex and relationships which you will hear in what we call "society" – the Hassle-Free Zone. Many will think that what I say is a moral outrage because the thought of people loving each other unconditionally, including sexually sometimes, is outrageous to moralists and those who take their off-the-peg opinions from them. But that sense of outrage speaks volumes about the state of being of the moralist, not my own. I believe in allowing people to be what they are, to learn, and to evolve to something greater. I believe that people can love more than one person, even physically, at the same time and that the energy called love is without limits. The flow of love can never run dry. Whether we express it or suppress it is merely a choice that we all make in every moment. The right to love and be loved is in our own minds and our own hearts. Love is on tap whenever we choose. It is

---

[2] Channelling is when someone tunes their consciousness to another wavelength of reality and becomes the vibrational bridge between that wavelength and this one. Thought fields are sent from a higher wavelength through the "medium" or "channeller" who turns those thought fields into spoken or written words. It is a means for one dimension to communicate with another. Some channelling produces inspired information, some a load of old nonsense. It depends on the levels with which the channeller is communicating and how skillfully they can suppress their own personality and thoughts to allow the information to come through in the form that it was sent.

only a choice. If saying all that is an outrage, then I guess I must be outrageous. Good.

The abuse and denial of love and its physical expression have done serious damage to human evolution. It has suppressed and imbalanced the kundalini and in doing so it has delinked us from our true sexual, intellectual, emotional and spiritual potential. The imbalanced, uncontrolled power of the kundalini, caused by fear, guilt and denial, has also led to sexual abuse, aggression, hatred, suicide, inner conflict and global war. It has been like trying to stop a flow of water by pressing your thumb against the tap. The water spurts everywhere, out of control. So it is, symbolically, with the kundalini when you try to hold back its natural, God-given flow. This has scrambled the human psyche when, if it is allowed to flow naturally and without emotional hindrance, the kundalini has the potential to take us home to multidimensional Oneness. Relax. What you are and what you do needs no excuses. Only when we grow up as a human race, and stop dictating to each other what we should be, do, say and experience, will people begin to relax with themselves and have the inner peace to allow the kundalini to do its work without fear of the experiences that will bring.

And we can grow up now, today, this second. Like everything else, it's only a choice.

Chapter 10

The Past Is Over – Goodbye

We stand on the threshold of the most incredible change. Nothing and no-one will be the same again. We can flow with it and go with it, or we can cling to our sense of programmed security. Either way, it's going to happen. It *is* happening. The past is over. It's time to move on.

Most people have forgotten how long we have all worked for this. We have played our parts as goodies and baddies, victors, victims and villains, and we have learned so much about the consequences of separation. We crave once again for a return to the Oneness we remember deep in our consciousness, a memory that makes so much more painful and frustrating the world we observe today. We turn to drugs and booze to shut out that pain and to escape all too briefly from the emotional turmoil that separation has created. Deep inside we know what is possible and it hurts to see how far we have fallen into the pit of ignorance. Most don't feel this consciously, of course, but that is the foundation of the emotional distress that plagues the human heart.

Come on, gang. We can do better than this. What are we doing hanging around here? We've got a home to go to and it's called paradise.

We have reached the point in the cycle of evolution within the multiscreen cinema when a fantastic shift is taking place. The Third and Fourth Dimensions of consciousness are merging into the Fifth Dimension. It is like a ladder being pulled up until, eventually, the whole vortex/pyramid returns to Oneness. The structure which creates each of the dimensions is an energy "net" or "web" called a matrix (*Figure 13 overleaf*). You might think of it as the steel structure of a building. The multiscreen cinema is a series of matrixes or energy grids interconnecting with each other. The whole "building" (vortex) is one matrix and so is each dimension, galaxy, solar system, universe, and planet within that

Figure 13: the Matrix

overall structure. The human body is also a matrix and the energy lines of the body matrix provide the basis of the ancient healing art of acupuncture. Again you could relate this matrix structure to those Russian dolls, one inside the other, with the biggest one encompassing all of them. The matrix energy web sets the format and nature of each dimension, universe, galaxy, solar system and planet, and everything that exists within them. It is a gigantic thought form created by Oneness. It's the movie screen, if you like. The matrix is the blueprint, the "computer" program, which creates and holds together this three-dimensional world and interconnects with all the other matrix levels. When a matrix changes, everything within it changes, and our matrix is changing...now! In fact they all are, on every level of the vortex and we are heading for a fantastic multidimensional galactic orgasm.

A matrix is the collective mind of all that exists on each dimension and so it is with every level. The Earth matrix, for example, is the collective mind of all that exists on this planet. It is the collective mind of humanity. Our thoughts are absorbed by the matrix "computer" and at that level all that has happened on the Earth is recorded and stored. This is one source of the so called Akashic Records which many psychics access when they are recalling past events and past lives. They are tuning their consciousness to the vibratory "library", the matrix, which holds that information. I guess this could be an origin of the ancient idea of "God" recording our every move. Sure beats a notebook. The matrix is also a source of information for the "prophets" and psychics, ancient and modern, who "see" the future. It is not the future that will definitely be. It is the future that will be if we don't change. Each matrix mind takes all information available, including current human attitudes and behaviour, and projects forward how the future will turn out on current trends. This is the "future" which people like Nostradamus and others have connected with. It exists as a thought field created by a matrix mind. The future is not set in concrete. If we change, it changes, because we create the future reality as we create our present reality. Our thoughts and attitudes are affecting the Earth matrix and, through that, affecting the thoughts and attitudes of everyone connected to the matrix – all of us. You could see it symbolically as everyone connected to a computer program and each of us slightly rewriting that program with each thought, word, and action. Researchers have documented the "hundredth monkey syndrome" which very much relates to the matrix structure. They have shown that once a certain number of a species has been taught something new, suddenly all or most of that species can do the same purely by "inspiration" and without being shown. How does this happen? Simple. A few members of a species learn something new until the critical mass point is reached where the sum total of their knowledge is powerful enough within the Earth matrix for the rest of the species to access the information. As a result they "know" how to do something without being shown. This appears to be a mystery, but it isn't. They are tuning into the matrix, the collective mind.

This process can also affect us negatively of course and the Earth matrix has become a prison of programmed, imbalanced thought. The Earth matrix has long been dominated by the herd mentality and other classic human reactions and responses explored in this book, because so many "individual" minds have chosen to think like that. This can be self-perpetuating because the matrix absorbs this mentality and then feeds those attitudes back to the human race. It has set in motion a cycle of individual minds thinking limitation, which together create a sense of limitation in the collective mind, the Earth matrix, which then feeds limitation of thought back to human minds, which then think in even more limited terms, which then...you get the idea. The Earth matrix has become a global eggshell which has closed down the channels to other levels and dimensions of creation. It has been like living in a vibrational box with the lid locked down. This is the process through which humanity has become stuck in a rut of intergenerational non-thinking and desperately limited vision. Billions of people who choose not to think for themselves become dominated by the deeply ingrained patterns held within the Earth matrix. In effect, the matrix mind thinks for them. They are its robots and they have been able to live out an entire physical lifetime without having a single thought that originated with them. Patterns of fear, guilt, resentment, judgment and low self esteem are repeated generation after generation in this way. It is the symbolic record needle stuck in the groove. This has been the consequence of the cycle of limitation looping between human minds and the Earth matrix mind. That is the cycle we are now in the process of breaking. With every mind that opens and sees life in a new way, the matrix mind is affected. Eventually there comes the point of critical mass, the hundredth monkey, when enough people have changed their attitudes and sense of reality to "switch" the Earth matrix reality from limitation to limitlessness, from can't to can, from wanna-be to gonna-be. At that point the global reality is transformed and the vibrational rate begins to climb rapidly up the octave scale. We evolve very, very quickly because the global eggshell has gone. Oneness here we come. How do we change the world? We change ourselves.

What has happened to the human race has happened to the Earth matrix. It has closed its mind and lost its most powerful connection with the solar system matrix centred on the Sun, and certainly with the galaxy matrix and the ones governing the entire Third Dimension and higher dimensions. This has been caused by all the mental and emotional gunge that has swamped the Earth matrix mind. As a result of this, it has acted a little like a dam, holding back from most human consciousness all that exists beyond the dense physical reality. Some people on the planet have expanded their consciousness to access levels beyond the Earth matrix and at that point they see life with a totally different perspective. The prison door opens. But for the overwhelming majority of people, they are accessing only the Earth matrix with all its limitation of thought and emotional sewage. Just as the human subconscious needs to be cleansed of its emotional crap, so does the Earth matrix. Indeed the two are the same. The Earth will therefore be releasing her pent up emotions in the same way that humanity is now doing so. Strap in and hold tight! The shift is hitting the fan! It is the emotional imbalances in the Earth matrix which has made it so much more difficult to connect with our multidimensional selves. When all the matrix levels are in powerful connection, it means that to tune to one is to tune to all. Connecting with the Earth matrix offers the potential for your consciousness to be as big as the Earth. But when, as will happen again, the Earth matrix is powerfully connected to the solar system matrix, and it with the galaxy matrix, and so on, we have the potential for our minds to be as big as Creation. In *...and the truth shall set you free* I spoke of the probability that the Earth was trapped in some sort of vibratory prison which was detaching us from our infinity of knowledge, understanding and love. That vibratory concentration camp is the Earth matrix and I feel that manipulation from elements in the Fourth Dimension have conspired to bring this about. When the present Earth matrix is replaced by a new grid during our lifetimes, WOW! Our minds will expand so rapidly we will need a seat belt because we will then find it so much easier to connect with the higher matrix levels, too. Symbolically the human mind and sense of perspective is expanding from the size of a pea to that of a hot air balloon – and then some.

Across the planet today are millions of people working to change the thought patterns in the present Earth matrix/grid and to introduce the new one for the next era of human evolution. Sometimes this involves going to certain points on the Earth's surface, many, though certainly not all, of which are the places held sacred since ancient times. These include stone circles, mounds, hills, mountains and pre-Christian earthworks which are sited at chakra and "acupuncture" points on the Earth matrix/grid. Peoples of thousands of years ago knew far more about the cycles and structure of life than do the letters-after-your-name scientists of today. The sacred sites, as they are often called, are points on the grid network of energy lines around and through the planet which have become known as ley lines or meridians. Acupuncture involves putting tiny needles at certain points on the meridian lines of energy that circle the human body. This balances the flow of energy and so keeps us free from disharmony, dis-ease. The same basic principle applies to the Earth. She has a grid of energy lines, acupuncture, and chakra points, at which people can become walking, talking, "acupuncture needles" and affect enormous changes in the balance and imbalance of the energy flow within the Earth matrix. The fourth dimensional manipulators have inspired the destruction of so many major points on the grid with the siting of cities, power stations, roads and battlefields. The Cult of the All Seeing Eye systematically arranges black magic rituals on these sites to fill them with negative energy. They know that if they can hold down the vibration of the grid and imbalance it negatively this will ensure that humanity as a whole is operating within the "Satanic" frequency range. This delinks people from their multidimensional selves and makes them so easy to close down, control and manipulate. The Earth matrix has been reduced to tatters and as we constantly interact with this grid without realising it, the negative, imbalanced energy flows this has created have fundamentally affected human thought. This is one reason for the mysterious crop formations or "circles" which increased dramatically after the end of the 1980s. Some have been hoaxed to divert our attention from the genuine patterns and the realisation that they are harbingers of enormous change. The crop formations are created by a higher intelligence using magnetic energy and the symbols they represent can often be charted back to the ancient world. A symbol, a pattern, is also energy, as is everything. These formations often appear on ley lines and on, or close to, Earth energy points. They are stimulating and winding up the power in the grid, the Earth matrix, and raising its vibration. Also they disperse blockages in that flow.

The positive elements of the Fourth Dimension and those even higher, particularly the fifth, are working to coordinate and guide the transformation of humanity and the Earth. The new grid has been created on a higher dimension and it needs to be "grounded" in this one to replace the old grid controlled by the Cult of the All Seeing Eye. The transformation, in fact, is the introduction of this new matrix. The new grid has been created with heart energy – pure love – and it can only be grounded by human beings vibrating within this frequency range known as love. When people open their hearts and allow their unconditional love to flow, they lock in vibrationally to this energy field and "earth" it in this Third Dimension in much the same way as lightning is earthed by people and trees. More and more people are awakening to their higher guidance, opening their hearts and following their intuition to energy sites, the acupuncture points on the Earth's surface. They then allow themselves to be used as channels to ground the new love grid at those points. As this progresses – and it's already well advanced – the Global Elite's control of the world will cease to be because their power to do it will be gone.

Everything is electrical and magnetic energy. It is only that some things are more powerfully electrical and magnetic than others. Quartz crystals, for instance, are especially sensitive and powerful and this is why you find quartz-based stones used for stone circles around the world. The ancients, probably with extraterrestrial inspiration, knew what they were doing. They didn't choose those stones at random, they understood at least the basis of what they could do. Quartz can store and transmit energy and act as a receiver for energy frequencies. Research has also shown that at least the vast majority of standing stones and circles are built on or very close to faults on the Earth's surface which produce particular electrical and magnetic effects. Of the 286 stone circles in Britain, 235 are built on rocks more than 250 million years old, the statistical chances of which are in excess of a million to one.[1] Most UFO sightings are made on or very close to stone circles and other sacred sites and ley lines. Many people believe that this is because of the electrical and magnetic "fuel" they provide for these interdimensional craft, but it could also be that the electromagnetic effects of ley lines and power points increase psychic awareness and make it easier to "see" what we call UFOs on other dimensions and wavelengths. So you can see that the plundering of the

---

[1] Serena Roney-Dougal, *Where Science And Magic Meet*, (Element Books, Shaftsbury, England, 1991) p156-157. This is an excellent book which shows how "paranormal" phenomena can be explained scientifically once scientists let go of their fundamentally flawed "laws" of physics and their obsession with this-world-is-all-there-is.

Earth for rocks, crystals and minerals, is not only damaging physically, it is disastrously rewiring the planet by moving and destroying the natural energy stores, transmitters and receivers. These rocks, crystals and minerals are not where they are for their health – they are there to play their roles in the electromagnetic balance of the Earth's energy field, *our* energy field.

The power of the energy waxes and wanes as the seasons and planetary influences affect the Earth's magnetic field, thus the ancients had their ceremonies to celebrate different points in nature's cycle of birth and death, the ups and downs of the energy field. Sun rise and Sun set are powerful times because of their effect on the energies. The Moon, especially full Moon, affects people because of its magnetic effect on the Earth's energy field and human consciousness. This is how it draws the tides in and out. A friend used to have a migraine headache on every full Moon until she made the connection. She concluded that her consciousness was being "pulled" out of her body by the effect of the full Moon magnetism. She went outside in bare feet to make a strong magnetic connection with the Earth (no rubber soles) and the headache immediately disappeared. When you touch a standing stone or any rock, indeed anything, you are making an electrical and magnetic contact which allows the two way exchange of energy to occur. This is what is happening with hands on healing and, of course, sex. Sick people have been shown to have diminished power in their energy fields while the best healers have extremely powerful fields. Alternative healing methods, psychic phenomena, dreams, strange sounds or lights in the sky, stone circles, crops circles, pyramids, and an endless list of other "mysteries" are all caused or inspired by electrical and magnetic energy fields and their relationship and interaction with each other across the dimensions of consciousness. People accept that lightning exists because they can see it. But that is merely an electric-magnetic phenomena happening within the frequency range of our physical senses. "Paranormal" phenomena are only the same principle at work on wavelengths that our physical senses often can't see or feel, but our higher psychic senses can. The knowledge of how to access this infinite electromagnetic power for free energy is already available, but the technology is being suppressed by the Global Elite who control the global fossil fuel industry.

The current transformation of human consciousness is being inspired by energies introduced to the Earth's electrical and magnetic fields – the Earth matrix. These are increasing the vibrational state of the global energy field. This must affect human consciousness because we are part of that field and it must affect weather patterns, etc, which are also an expression of that field. It is all very simple. The positive elements in the Fourth Dimension, and higher, are working with those millions of humans who have opened their minds to this knowledge to make the transformation of the global energy field as smooth as possible. These people have been guided by higher dimensions of themselves to repair the old energy grid and, at the same time, help to "ground" the new one in this dimension. The plan is to raise the vibrational rate of the Earth to the limits of the old grid and then switch in the new. It is the same principle as switching from one computer program to another. Ideally this is a smooth process, like lock gates on a canal. The vibrational rate of the energy flowing through the ley line network is raised to the highest level of the old grid; the symbolic lock gates then open; and the switch is made to the lowest level of the new grid. From that point, the vibratory levels of the new grid will be gradually wound up as human consciousness expands and is able to take that power of energy without being mentally and physically blown away. However, because of what has happened, this is no ideal situation. The old grid has been in such a state that there is a gap between the highest vibrations it is capable of taking and the lowest levels of the new one. At switchover time there will be a sudden vibrational "jump" across this gap which could send shock waves through the Earth, very much like a sudden surge of electricity through your electrical system at home. Fuses may blow! How big that vibrational leap has to be depends once again upon us. Are we going to heal the grid with love or further diminish it with conflict? Are we going to speak our truth so that others may hear or are we going to stay in the shadows and hide how we feel through fear and insecurity? We are back to our old friend – choice.

Speaking and thinking your truth is vital to this transformation. Every time you think in ways that challenge the limitations, you are transferring that knowledge to the Earth matrix and making another step towards critical mass. When you speak in public, your words and thoughts are also absorbed by the Earth matrix and, more than that, they offer the audience the chance to hear the information. This opens their minds to reject their sense of limitation and their thoughts also add to critical mass. It's the same with books. The process gets quicker and quicker and this is happening today. For many years I have been travelling Britain, and increasingly the world, talking of these things and after a while I noticed how often my apparently "random" speaking venues were positioned on, or very close to, acupuncture and chakra points on the ley line network of the Earth matrix. This is because, like an acupuncture needle, when words and thoughts are created at these points, they enter the matrix very powerfully and they pass around the planet on the global energy network. In this way, words spoken at a point in Scotland can affect someone living in China. That knowledge becomes available, via the matrix, to the guy living in Peking. Of course he won't stand there accessing every word of the speech, like listening to the radio. It will be more in the form of an "inspired" thought or a sudden questioning of the status quo. If you simply stand and project thoughts of love, as a group or by yourself, the same effect applies. This is the principle which allows telepathy to happen – the reading of another person's thought fields. You think love in New York, you think love to the world. We are all One.

The global energy network has a central point, a heart, which pumps the energy around the spiritual veins and arteries of the Earth. This is, obviously, the point where you can most effectively change planetary consciousness. That heart at the present time is, I believe, in the British Isles and the Republic of Ireland. I feel this heart centre will move to the United States when the new matrix structure switches in. By then the US will be a very different place to the one we see today. The system as we know it, the one typified by a culture of mass consumption developed in the United States, will be rapidly collapsing.

Within our generation we will reach critical mass, the moment when the Earth matrix – the collective mind of humanity – switches from limitation to infinity, from fear to love. We are hurtling towards it now. Not only are vastly more minds and hearts opening, energies of unimaginable power are filtering down from Oneness into this time-space dimension to transform the nature of thought and reality here. These energies and changing human consciousness are affecting global weather patterns and will, quite possibly, lead to unprecedented (in modern times) geological activity. Vibrational codes are also being emitted from the Sun to challenge the limitations of the Earth consciousness. These codes are picked up by the chakras of the Earth and the human body and they are making subtle changes to our thinking and our DNA, the body's genetic library and control centre. The Third and Fourth Dimensions of consciousness are merging and as the transformation proceeds, these will in turn merge with the Fifth Dimension. Three separated levels of us will become One and our perceptions of life and self are heading for an unbelievable change. People with the most fixed and programmed attitudes will change in ways that would seem impossible now. I have seen this trend so often in the people I meet on speaking tours and at workshops, and in the thousands of letters from around the world. This transformation of consciousness knows no boundaries of race, colour, creed, or income bracket. It recognises no "chosen ones" or "chosen peoples". It is there for everyone and everything. All it requires is for us to open our minds and open our hearts. In other words, to open the door on our mental and emotional prison, to shatter the eggshell around us, and allow in the energies that will set us free. That means evacuating the Hassle-Free Zones, letting go of fear, guilt, resentment and judgment, and celebrating our right, and everyone's right, to be unique. This is a time to be joyous. We're going home. We are returning to multidimensional Oneness and we are being drawn to our vibrational "home" on Planet Earth. This will involve changes of location, even countries, for many people as the eggshell cracks.

There is no need to allow the magnitude of it all to stimulate fear or panic. You are an incredible aspect of multidimensional consciousness. You are capable of anything. People talk about the time of the apocalypse as if it is all death and destruction. But when you take the word apocalypse back to the Greek language from whence it was translated, it means something very different: the disclosure, the uncovering, the revealing. That is exactly what is happening now. What we are experiencing and will experience is part of the natural cycle of learning and evolution. We live forever and we learn forever. There's nothing to fear. A friend of mine, Jack Watters, put it very well when he wrote:

> "Nobody panics when the Sun goes down at night. We know it comes up again in the morning. Nobody panics in the season of falling leaves, we know there'll be another Spring. If we didn't know about Spring we'd probably try and superglue the leaves back on the trees. If they should be green then better to paint out the russet, copper, and gold of Autumn.
>
> "If we understand a game, we know where it starts and where it finishes. By forgetting the point of the game – in the playing of it – we lose the how, when and why of finishing it. By forgetting the point of the game we forget about the natural transitions which end it, resolve it, and transform it. How and when were we going to finish this unusual,

planetary improvisation of ours? Whenever would we let one cycle go to
replace it with another? Or would we, in the depths of our
misunderstanding, keep inventing bigger, better glue?" [2]

And that's what we have done. Humanity has had such a fear of new
experience, if the experience is at odds with the view of the Hassle-
Free Zone, that we have clung to status quos of all kinds as our sense of
personal security. We would rather expend massive amounts of emotion
and energy supergluing together these matchstick structures, than
allowing them to collapse and using our energy to create something
better. What's that we say? Better the devil you know than the devil
you don't. Nonsense. If our reality is devils, we will create them, but
we don't have to. We can create paradise without if we can find
paradise within.

So how does all that I have outlined in this chapter affect us now as
we head rapidly into the 21st century?

To complete the immense consciousness shift now upon us, we are
looking for balance. Positive-negative balance, male-female balance,
physical-spiritual balance. Anything that makes us imbalanced we are
being challenged to unload. We are attracting to ourselves experiences
which give us the opportunity to face our imbalances and move
through them to harmony. This will raise our consciousness, increase
it's vibratory rate, and allow us through the "Quantum Gate", the top
of that symbolic bottle. Hello everyone, I'm home! The immense
emotional cleansing that is taking place, indeed has been taking place
throughout the 20th century, is potentially catastrophic for everyday life
in the short term – if we continue to believe this movie is "real". If,
however, we see each other as actors playing parts which help us to face
ourselves and unload emotional baggage, this period of emotional
cleansing and consciousness rebalancing will be far less traumatic,
because we won't take on yet more guilt and resentment with each new
experience. It's up to us. We need to remember that we are not our
emotional crap. That is not "us". We are the eternal vessel that has
become filled with emotional crap. We are emptying the vessel and
giving it a polish. Look at it. It's beautiful.

The incredible population increases since the last century are due to
the incarnation of billions of souls arriving to face the experiences in

---

[2] Jack Watters, *Transformation: The Plan For A Quantum Shift Of Consciousness*. Published as an
information paper in 1996.

the three dimensional world, which they hope will clear their emotional imbalances built up over countless incarnations, and set their consciousness free to fly through the Quantum Gate. To reach the vibrational levels necessary to pass through that "gate", we need to ditch the emotional weights that are vibrationally holding us down. If my own experience and that of so many others is anything to go by, whatever we are attached to emotionally to the point where it becomes a crutch, will be taken away until we let go of that attachment. People with a crutch walk with a limp and we don't have time for that. We need to run. If you have an emotional attachment to money, if it is your sense of security, it is likely you will lose it. If you have an emotional attachment to a person to the extent that you are emotionally dependent on them, it is likely you will lose them. And remember it is higher levels of *ourselves* that are making this happen, because if our lower levels don't shift, the higher levels can't either. You don't have to lose anything or anyone you love so long as you love them unconditionally and without emotional dependency. Be in balance and at peace with yourself. Let go of emotional dependency and you won't need to face the experience of losing something or someone because you will already have learned the lessons such an experience is designed to offer.

The cleansing also includes dealing with each new imbalance as it happens. This is what you might call instant karma. It is no good ditching the imbalances of centuries and then adding new ones today. It would be like one person emptying the bowl while another continues to fill it up. So we will find that what we put out comes back to us very quickly to allow us to constantly face our imbalances and disperse them. One of the interesting aspects of this dense, separated world is that the process of cause and effect often happened quite slowly. The "karma" for an action may not have rebounded on that person until another incarnation. As the frequency quickens, the period between cause and effect is getting shorter, until at some point it will literally be instant. Time itself is getting faster as more people are noticing. If we don't simplify our lives and take periods to rest, we will be in danger of burning out. Time as we know it in this three dimensional world moves at a certain speed. It is an energy like everything. How fast time appears to pass depends on how our vibratory rate relates to the vibratory rate of "time". If you stand still in a 50 mile an hour wind, your hair is blown all over the place. But if you were moving at the same speed as the wind, all around you would be calm. As the vibrations of this dimension quicken, our relationship to "time" is changing and one aspect of this is that time appears to pass quicker. This will become more obvious every year. The changes in our relation to "time" will help us synchronise with its natural flow. For instance, our natural cosmic time keepers are cycles of the Moon, not the human clock. The manipulation and misrepresentation of time has been crucial to the imbalancing of the human psyche and its imprisonment in the third dimensional reality. The cycle of nature and the cosmos relates to the 13 cycles of the Moon, each lasting 28 days. These 13 Moon cycles are the natural year. This is the true flow of time and you can see this in the woman's 28 day menstrual cycle. But then in 1572 came the edict by Pope Gregory which introduced the Gregorian calendar with its illogical year of 12 uneven months based on the Sun (male) and not the Moon (female). This 12 months, 60 minute, 60 second system goes back to the ancient Egyptians and Babylonians and it has become the accepted measurement of "time" throughout the world. The trouble is that it is out of sync with natural time, cosmic time, and because we have tuned our minds to this Gregorian system we are out of sync with the rhythm of nature. This has delinked us from nature and locked us into the manufactured rhythm of materialism. No wonder we treat the environment as we do. We are delinked from it. We urgently need to retune ourselves to the 13 Moon, 28 day cycle, especially men who do not have the menstrual rhythm to help them. As we increase our vibratory speed during the consciousness shift we will eventually pass through time as it is measured in the three dimensional world and enter natural time or a sense of timelessness. This is a state that people access during meditation and other quiet, daydreaming moments when the conscious mind is still.

Another aspect of the quantum jump is that more people are unlocking their psychic senses. For most people these have been closed down by fear and the constant ridicule and condemnation of the centuries by religion and "science" with regard to psychic powers. The last thing the manipulators of the Fourth Dimension have desired is for humanity to be aware, en masse, of our multidimensional potential. Persuading us to switch off our psychic channels was essential to this. Stories of evil spirits, demons and witches were designed to frighten us into denying our ability to communicate with other levels and dimensions. It is true that some very misguided consciousness exists on frequencies close to this one, which is why some "channelled" information by psychics is so low grade or manipulating. Black magic, voodoo, etc, have harnessed these highly imbalanced levels of negatively dominated energies. But those levels are also being cleansed by the quantum shift and if you can raise your consciousness to beyond that frequency, you can begin to access knowledge and information that offers a far greater insight into the nature of life and what is going on here. Dammit, we are supposed to communicate with other levels and dimensions. That is our natural state. It is as natural as the Sun and the stars, the air and sky. It was when we closed off those channels that we entered the vibratory prison cell and the movement of populations into vast cities of electromagnetic technology which pollute the Earth's magnetic energy field has made a connection more difficult. Even then, everyone continues to "channel" information from the Earth matrix without realising it. Where does our inspired knowledge come from that leads us to certain discoveries or inventions? We channel it from higher levels. We don't have to close our eyes and go into "is anybody there?" mode – knock once for yes. We simply access an inspired thought which appears to be our own, but in fact comes from a matrix consciousness or a higher dimension of ourselves. We are psychic channels whether we know it or whether we don't. The only question is: what level of consciousness can our psychic senses access? The more we open our minds and hearts and let go of the emotional backpack, the higher that level will be.

The consciousness shift will communicate itself in all kinds of psychic effects and symbols of change. People will see, hear and sense other levels beyond the physical; we will enjoy vivid dreams from our nightly journeys to other dimensions of consciousness which we will clearly remember and we will sense what is going to happen before it does; we will see ever increasing UFO and extraterrestrial activity and amazing crop formations as our dimension merges with theirs. The vibrational barriers between other dimensions and this one are rapidly dispersing and so much knowledge is pouring into this three dimensional reality through our psychic channels. But, as with everything, it is important not to accept any information, psychic or otherwise, on face value. Does it feel right and make sense to you? No? Then reject it, whatever the source, and that includes what you read in this book.

The re-emergence of the feminine to balance the excesses of the masculine is at the heart of the transformation and the establishment of balance. The suppression of the feminine energy has created a male gender, and many females too, who are left brain dominated. That is the part of the brain that manifests the masculine "rational" aspect of us. It is the part that says: "I'll only believe it when I can see, hear, taste, smell and touch it". In contrast, the right brain manifests our feminine, intuitive, psychic levels. The right brain represents I Am Me, I Am Free, and the left brain is home to Oh My God. The brain is the computer which allows the eternal consciousness to work through a dense physical body and so it reflects the domination of the male over the female within the lower levels of our eternal self. In the same way, we only use a maximum of 20% of our brains because we are only accessing a fraction of the potential of our multidimensional consciousness. As we use more of our consciousness, we will use more of our brains, and as we balance our inner self we will balance the brain between left and right, rational and intuitive. It is the suppression of our female energy which closed off our psychic channels from their true potential and without the balance of the female polarity, the male energy has run amok. The return of the female, the nurturing, intuitive energy, will bring back into harmony and wholeness the separation caused by the extremes of the male. But its replacement with the domination of female over male would be just another disharmony. It is balance that we are searching for, within ourselves and the world in general. The freeing of the female energy will show itself in more women in positions of influence and a very different kind of man. Macho man is going to become a relic of history, a museum piece. He will be put there by the emerging male-female man: whole person man. Without the macho aspect of the male energy (which you also see in many females), the world created by extreme male energy must crumble because its foundations are disappearing. They are going to be balanced out of existence. For a while many men may feel lost and without a sense of identity as macho man departs, but don't worry and stick with it. A much better future awaits you as a whole person. Different, yes, but better.

The divisions in the world may seem to be growing rather than diminishing, but this is the healing crisis – the break down of the old so the new can emerge. The old was created by a thought pattern which conceded its uniqueness to a herd mentality. As we take our power back, the thought form which held the old world together is disappearing and its physical reflection must therefore disappear as well. A new thought pattern is preparing to take over – one that believes in freedom, true freedom, for all and by all. Its physical reflection will be dramatically different to what we observe today. I have heard people say that if we all expressed our uniqueness there would be chaos. I beg one's pardon here. Chaos? Have you seen the news or read the papers or seen the blank eyes and faces in the street? We have chaos now in this programmed dictatorship that we dare to call "life". There may well be chaos, or apparently so, in the transition period as the old falls apart and the new begins to emerge. But this is only the natural consequence of any status quo being replaced very quickly. What will follow in a world of true freedom will be anything but chaos. The world we see today is the creation overwhelmingly of a tiny part of our multidimensional consciousness. We try to overcome the suppression of our psychic and intuitive levels by using phones and filofaxes, and sitting through endless meetings to "organise" things. But this "organisation" is happening on a very shallow level. It relates to the conscious self which is constantly battered by conditioning messages through the eyes and ears. Compared with our multidimensional self, the conscious self isn't terribly bright. Yet this is the consciousness that "organises" our lives and societies today. Explains a lot, eh?

Look at the alternative. When we deprogram ourselves and shatter the eggshell of conditioned thought, perception, and responses, we fly beyond the delusions of the Earth matrix and reconnect with our multidimensional self (Figure 14 overleaf). This gives us access to knowledge and wisdom beyond our imagination and it this multilevel self that will ensure that our lives are not ruled by chaos in the incredible future that awaits us. Already, for those who are open to greater possibilities, these levels speak powerfully to us through our intuition. The intuition comes to us from levels of consciousness outside the limitations of Oh My God. When we flow with our intuition, we move beyond thought and into feeling. We go beyond what we know as mind – we get out of our heads and into our hearts. Unlike our thoughts, we can often find it impossible to describe what we feel in mere words. It is a knowingness, a sensitivity from outside the realms of human language. It is said that as a rule women are more intuitive than men. This is because women are working with the female energy, the intuitive energy, but as men balance themselves and connect with their feminine they, too, have an equal potential for intuition. It is not the shape of the body, it is the nature of the energy which decides how intuitive we are. This intuition speaks to us in a sort of "knowingness". It shows itself when we say: "I don't know why I have to be in London tomorrow, but I just know I've got to be there". When you arrive in London purely on intuition, something happens, a "coincidence" which makes it clear why your intuition (your higher

Figure 14: As our Eggshells crack and shatter, we open ourselves to multidimensional wholeness

levels) guided you to be there. I lose count how many times this happens to me every week and to all the people I know. Once you open yourself to your higher potential and refuse to be a robot, the most amazing things start to happen to you because you are then connected to the energy stream of guidance from the levels of you that can make those things happen. As long as we follow our intuition and don't succumb to "Oh my God", we are always, and I mean always, in precisely the right place at precisely the right time with precisely the right people. I just follow my intuition and everything happens as it's meant to. You, everyone, can do the same – and more. The future will not be chaos, it will be amazingly ordered, but in an unpredictable way. Life will cease to be an ordeal and start to become a daily adventure.

There was one occasion when I was at home in England watching a video of a stage show called Riverdance which was performing at the time in Dublin, Ireland. My intuition, that knowingness, was urging me to go and see it live. I checked my schedule of talks and workshops and it allowed me only one free day to see the show. A friend in Dublin bought the tickets and I arrived in the theatre a few minutes before the start to find my friend looking very bemused and worried. She said she had overheard a security guard say that the "security seats" were in row S, numbers 25, 26, 27, and 28. Now I knew why she was bemused because she knew that I had row S, numbers 25 and 26. Security seats? For me? No-one knew that I even had those seats, so why the "security". Somewhat bemused myself by now, I went to the seats with another friend and sat down. Although the rest of the theatre was packed and the show was about to begin, row S was virtually empty. What was going on? At this point, heads were turning to the back of the theatre and I saw someone walk in surrounded by a ring of security "heavies". A few seconds later I looked down the row to see Jimmy Carter, the first Trilateral Commission President of the United States, walking towards me with his wife. They sat next to me in the other two "security" seats! I couldn't stop laughing. I had written about Jimmy Carter in The Robots' Rebellion in the course of highlighting how US presidents are merely puppets of the Global Elite. At that time I had just finished …and the truth shall set you free in which Mr Carter featured once again. And here I was sitting next to him and his wife in "security" seats, just days after my intuition had said: "Go and see the show in Dublin – now". As a result of that event, I was to learn more about the background to the Elite pyramid of manipulation. Now, imagine this. You are sitting around a boardroom table with your mobile phone and filofax. The question is asked: "Ladies and gentlemen, we have to arrange for this guy to sit next to Jimmy Carter and his wife in special security seats in a Dublin Theatre and it has to be on one particular night. We don't know when Carter will be in Dublin or even if he will ever be there and there's no reason why our man would qualify for security seats anyway. Any suggestions on how we do this?" The room would be full of glazed faces and drooping jaws. Where on Earth would you start? It would be virtually impossible. But follow your intuition and it happens perfectly without any hassle or preparation at all. If we rid ourselves of the conditioned self, the eggshell, and allow our higher levels to connect powerfully with us, the world to come will be the least chaotic in the modern history of this planet. We will always be in the right place, at the right time, with the right people, doing whatever we need to do at that moment. It may not always be what we want to do, but it will always be what we need to do. You could be put on precisely the right spot at precisely the right time in the middle of South America without a map or a compass. I know, I've done it and anyone can do it.

There are some people who I'm sure will say that this book is simplistic, but it isn't. All I am exposing here are the mental and emotional barriers that keep our conscious level from enjoying a natural and powerful connection with its multidimensional, infinite self. Once that connection is made, you no longer need guidance or advice from those in the dense physical world. You get all you need from the higher dimensions of yourself – dimensions that operate well beyond the delusions of the physical. I hear some in the New Age say that you will only find enlightenment if you do this or do that. I don't accept this view for a second. We are all unique, thank goodness. What I need is not necessarily what you need. We are all on our own path and the only person who knows what is right for us is…us, the higher, guiding, levels of us. Access those, follow that intuitive guidance, and away you go. It's simple. If they tell you it's complicated, they've missed the point – in my opinion anyway.

We are in the process of withdrawing from the illusions of that light at the bottom of the bottle and we are turning our eyes to the real light at the top: the one that is leading us out of here and back to the paradise of multidimensional infinity. We are evacuating the Hassle-Free Zones of dogma and imposition as we realise they are not really hassle free at all. We just think they are. Conforming through fear to this imposed thought and behaviour has caused us enormous hassle within our hearts and our psyche as we suffer the emotional pain and mental despair triggered by the daily battle to suppress who and what we really are. Leap over the wall and there you will find a truly Hassle-Free Zone, that glorious, magical place where you run with the flow of intuitive energy, free from the nagging and the fear of Oh My God. Who cares what people may think of you when you first make that transition from robot to rebel? It doesn't matter what they think of you. What matters is what you think of you. Are you going to let your life be ruled by the views of the sheep who merely absorb the programmed opinions of the other sheep and accept them as their own? Or are you going to set yourself free and escape from the herd altogether? That is the choice which infinity is challenging you to make. For me, the way to achieve this is staring us in the face:

Let us respect our own right to be unique and to express that uniqueness; let us respect the right of others to express their uniqueness, free from ridicule or condemnation; and let us never seek to impose what we believe on anyone else. That simple philosophy will transform your life and life on this planet.

It will bring an end to the mass schizophrenia that underpins the Hassle-Free Zones. If we respect our own right to be unique we cease to be a slave to imposed thought and behaviour. If we respect everyone's right to that same freedom, we cease to be the police force of the other slaves. With that, the herd and the manipulation of the herd is no more. It is time to remember who we are and where we come from. You are not your job and you are not your race. You are not a road sweeper, an airline pilot or a "housewife". You are not an Arab or a Gentile or a Jew. You are not English or German or Asian. You are not your religion or your political "ism". You are not your gender or your sexual preference. You are not even your thoughts. You are the silence between them, the silence from which your thoughts are created. You are a unique aspect of evolving consciousness on the threshold of a dream, a dream you have worked to achieve for so long. Pack your bag, open your heart, and let's get out of here.

Come on gang. We're going home.

Oh yes, one final thought. What do you really want
to do with your life? OK, what are you waiting for…

Just
do

Other books, videos and cassettes by David Icke

The Truth Vibrations Gateway

The remarkable story of his spiritual awakening and the psychic
communications he was given about events over the next ten years
and beyond, many of which are already proving to be accurate.

Days of Decision Jon Carpenter Publishing

A read-it-in-two-hours summary of the themes behind
David Icke's view of life and the present transformation of Planet Earth.

Days of Decision: The Speech • An audio cassette Gateway

Heal the World Gateway

A what-we-can-do guide to personal and planetary transformation.
Heal ourselves and we heal the world.

The Robots' Rebellion Gateway

The fast-selling and acclaimed exposé of who controls the world and
why the spiritual knowledge is suppressed. A devastating dismantling
of the claims and myths of religion and science. A guide to this time
of awakening as the robots rebel. Sold its first print run in weeks and
went through two more reprints in its first year.

...And The Truth Shall Set You Free Bridge of Love

The most explosive book of the 20th century – the names, dates,
places of the global manipulation and how we can bring it to an end.

The Turning Of The Tide • A 2-hour video Bridge of Love

A celebration of life recorded at the Mwldyn Theatre, Cardigan,
Wales. It details the manipulation, naming many names
and offers the spiritual solutions that will set us free.

The Turning Of The Tide • A double audio cassette Bridge of Love

The audio version of the above.

All are available from:
Bridge of Love Publications, Papworth Press, Ermine Street South, Papworth Everard,
Cambridge CB3 8RG, England OR Truth Seeker Co., Inc., P.O. Box 28550, San Diego,
CA 92198, USA. Tel: (800) 551 5328

For details of postage costs and David's talks and workshops, please send a stamped, addressed
envelope to one of the addresses above.

Useful contacts...

Exposure magazine
Head office: PO Box 118, Noosa Heads, 4567 Queensland, Australia
+61 074 852966
European office: PO Box 129, 8600 AC Sneck, The Netherlands
+310 5154 21473

Perceptions magazine
c/o 10736 Jefferson Blvd., Suite 502, Culver City, California 90230,
USA
+310 313 5185

Nexus magazine
Head Office: PO Box 30, Mapleton, Qld 4560, Australia.
USA Office: PO Box 177, Kempton, IL 60946-0177, USA.
UK Office: 55 Queens Road, East Grinstead, West Sussex, RH19 1BG.
Europe Office: PO Box 372, 8250 AJ Dronten, The Netherlands.

Contact magazine
PO Box 27800, Las Vegas, Nevada 89126, USA